Dr. Bryant Stamford's

EXERCISE WITHOUT AGONY

*A Common Sense, Lifestyle Plan for Maximum
Health with Moderate, Comfortable Effort*

Dr. Bryant Stamford's

EXERCISE WITHOUT AGONY

---

*A Common Sense, Lifestyle Plan for
Maximum Health with Moderate,
Comfortable Effort*

M

Minerva Books

Published in the USA by
Minerva Books, LLC
P.O. Box 7311
Louisville, KY 40207
502-852-2688

ISBN 0-9723992-0-8

Printed in Canada

Aknowledgements

CONTENTS

PREFACE

I am an exercise physiologist. I am also a maverick, a renegade, and a contrarian who refuses to bow to the dogma of my profession. Translated, this means that although this is a book on exercise, I promise not to bombard you with umpteen reasons why you need to lace up your high-tech jogging shoes and pound the pavement, huffing and puffing and sweating bullets, driving yourself to the brink of exhaustion, all in the name of promoting health and well being. Not that doing so is a bad thing to do. Not at all, but it's not right for everyone.

For some, like the Big Bad Wolf, huffing and puffing is an excellent choice and it brings great rewards. While such an approach is fine for Mr. B.B. Wolf, it's clearly not a benefit for the three little pigs. The point is, what's pleasurable and productive for one is poison for another. Recognizing this fact and respecting individual differences and the uniqueness of natural tendencies could solve many of the problems we face in the world today, including the problem of constructing a viable exercise program that works and is sustainable for the masses.

I am an advocate of exercise, but I promise I won't harass you with exercise shoulds and exercise musts, badgering you to exercise in a certain way, and threatening you with dire consequences if you don't. There's no guilt in my message, and no "or elses." I used to play that game, but I have learned finally that all my expended energy was misplaced and utterly wasted. Indeed, over far too many years, few succumbed to my pressure, and of those who did, most abandoned their exercise efforts in short order. Clearly, my old message was flawed. It worked for the few, but miserably failed the many.

I finally discovered two things that anyone with even a modicum of common sense knows very well. One, it's human nature to reject what seems unnatural, no matter how forceful the argument is to the contrary. If, for example, jogging feels unnatural to you, you ultimately will reject it regardless of how good it may be for you. And, two, one size does not fit all. There is more than "one right way" to exercise.

For the past fifteen years, I have been trying to undo the public's distaste for exercise caused in large part by the prevailing and deeply rooted fitness dogma that I used to preach ad nauseum. Now I preach a softer and more gentle sermon that addresses natural tendencies and proclaims that individuals are best suited to chose what's best for them.

Along the way, I have learned that empowering individuals is threatening to experts who thrive on telling others what to do, and I have endured my share of hard knocks. There are those who see my stance as New Age mumbo jumbo, arising from planetary alignment and based upon some fuzzy "if it feels good do it" philosophy. Not so. I wouldn't risk my professional reputation as an exercise physiologist if I weren't certain of my stance, and if I felt that my position didn't have a sound scientific base.

Indeed, my new message is backed by plenty of science. In fact, the lion's share of all the medical evidence we have accrued to date supports my new message. Let me add quickly that science also supports the old message. How is that possible? I'll tell you later and give you lots of detail. But for now, in a nutshell, science supports the fact that vigorous exercise promotes health, and the same is true for moderate exercise. In essence, science supports the fact that exercise, regardless of the type, format, or rules applied, is good for you.

This book sets the record straight. It also offers hope and it provides a blueprint for getting the masses moving. If you already are moving, regardless of how fast and how far you go each day, keep right on going. It's doing you a world of good. But please accept that your approach is only one of many.

INTRODUCTION

The latest figures show that, at most, only about 10 to 15 percent of Americans engage regularly in vigorous physical activities, the kind that produces fitness. This, in spite of more than 35 years of beating the fitness drum in a desperate attempt to rally the masses to pull on their Nike's and take off down the road. Why has this prolonged campaign been such a dismal failure?

Lots of reasons and some very practical obstacles. Americans are extremely busy, and exercise demands too much time to fit in with our current lifestyle. Americans demand instant gratification and quick fixes, and exercise is a lifelong commitment. Americans are stressed to the max, and to take the edge off we need something that is relaxing and fun to fill the few free hours we have. Gut busting exercise is perceived to be anything but relaxing, and it's certainly not fun. What's more, the last thing we need is one more onerous obligation that adds to our long list of daily "to-do's."

Ask the average person to describe the essential ingredients of an exercise program and he will respond with the well-established fitness formula. It goes like this: When you exercise you must push hard, driving your heart rate to a high level, keeping it there for at least 20 minutes with rhythmic and repetitively boring movements like jogging, cycling, rowing and the like. You must, in other words, push yourself hard in order to derive any benefits from exercise.

The vast majority of Americans have heard the rules of fitness training and have quickly responded with a strong, "No, thank you!" The no-thank-you crowd, in fact, outnumbers the exercise crowd six to one, and no amount of pleading, cajoling, nagging or threatening has been able to budge this ratio over the past three decades.

Because exercise is perceived as being (by necessity) demanding and punishing, there are those who don't exercise because they believe they can't. But the closer look I provide in Part I reveals that my new exercise formula can be done by anyone and under a wide variety of circumstances. This includes those who loath vigorous exercise and those who believe they are too busy. It also includes victims of special circumstances, such as the bed bound and individuals confined to a wheelchair.

But what if you have kids tugging on you all day long? It's challenging, but there are many exercise options that involve taking them along. What about very young youngsters? Use a baby carrier and off you go. What if you are very old? There are things you can do, too, and need to do. The need, in fact, gets progressively greater the older you get, and daily exercise may be the most important thing you do to ensure that you can remain independent and a fully functioning member of society. As you will see in the coming chapters, for every excuse there's an answer. Everyone needs some form of daily exercise.

It may seem trite, but when it comes to exercise, the old saying applies very well — "Where there's a will, there's a way." Unfortunately, at present, Americans seem to be weak willed when it comes to exercise.

The Solution

It's time for a new concept of exercise and fitness, one that has the potential to break down the massive walls of resistance that have been erected over the past 35 years. It's time to get the word out that exercise can be less physically and athletically demanding, even to the point of being downright comfortable and enjoyable, and still do you some good.

Isn't this blasphemy? Some think it is, but medical science supports the notion that moderate exercise is an excellent choice. Unfortunately, many hard liners have a difficult time accepting the fact that while fitness-producing exercise like jogging is a good thing to do, it's only one of many roads to success — if success is defined as being healthy, managing your weight, looking good and feeling good. Alternative roads include moderate exercise that can be fun and can fit easily into everyday life.

At times I have encountered hostility from fitness buffs who perceive that my new message bashes vigorous exercise. Not so. Fitness-producing exercise, the kind that makes severe demands on your body's physiology, is a wonderful thing to do and the rewards are great. My purpose in promoting a new message that touts softer and gentler exercise is not to say that those who engage in vigorous exercise should stop and switch. On the contrary, if you jog, swim laps, row on a machine, or whatever, keep plugging away. Your vigorous exercise is an extremely valuable endeavor, and I would never want to dissuade anyone from pounding the pavement, if they enjoy it.

It's the 85-90% of the population that does not engage in such activities that I am trying to reach and convince that they don't have to produce fitness in order to get involved. So let me be clear. If you jog or engage in other forms of vigorous exercise, you are at the top of the exercise heap. If you choose to get involved at a lower level of effort, the benefits you derive will be nearly as great, but not quite. Thus — and here's the essential point — you should base your exercise choices on what you would like to do, rather than on what you think you must.

It is my hope that this new message about exercise will do what 35-years of the past message has failed to do. It's time to get the masses moving, and knowing that exercise can be easy and fun and can fit into your busy day just might work.

In this book I'll examine the ins and outs of exercise, and the information I present will benefit everyone, whether you are a die-hard couch potato or a seasoned fitness buff. I'll cover a variety of topics, including how to get started, how to progress, and how to stay motivated; pitfalls to avoid; how to make a comeback; how to tweak your training to be more beneficial; how to warm-up and cool-down; the list goes on. I'll cover all different types of exercise, including those designed to strengthen your heart, lungs and cardiovascular system, and those that add strength and muscle mass.

After reading this book, hopefully, if you are not already exercising on a regular basis, you will pledge to yourself to do something. Anything. As the preacher says on Sunday morning, whatever you can manage to give is acceptable... just give. All it takes is the decision to get involved and the commitment to stay with it. And in so doing, a major blow will be struck in the war against obesity and the chronic diseases which plague our country in epidemic proportions.

And if you already are physically active, congratulations. I trust you will encounter enlightening information to aid your efforts, no matter how advanced you are on the fitness continuum.

PLEASE NOTE: For the past 25 years I have written a newspaper column, The Body Shop, which covers a variety of topics, especially exercise. Readers are encouraged to write and ask questions via e-mail. It's time consuming, but I try to answer everyone who writes, and some inspire a full blown column. In this book I have included some of these questions and my answers. I have deleted the names of those who wrote, protecting their privacy, and often I have combined questions from more than one reader into one larger conceptual question that addresses pertinent issues.

PART I

FACT VERSUS FICTION

1. THERE'S MORE THAN ONE "RIGHT" WAY TO EXERCISE

To most of us, the thought of exercise conjures visions of racing your pulse in a painful frenzy, breathing hard, pushing to the limits. For the vast majority, anticipating an exhausting workout after a long day at work is about as appealing as looking forward to a root canal.

We have this vision of exercise, because it's the vision crafted for us by fitness gurus, myself included, who have told us that in order to achieve good health you must drive yourself to a high level of fitness. Is it any wonder that despite billions of dollars spent promoting and marketing the concept that fitness is healthy, only a small fraction of the American public participates?

Ironically, the push for more fitness has created a bumper crop of couch potatoes, because if punishing yourself physically and emotionally is the only way to exercise, why bother doing anything at all? No sense walking to the store if the walk does you no good. Jump in the car and get it over with quickly so you can get back to the TV. Why bother cutting the grass when the kid down the street can use a few extra bucks. Gardening, playing badminton, or washing the car? These things don't build fitness, and since they don't, they're useless.

That's the message we've heard, but are such activities really useless when it comes to promoting health? Not at all.

Setting the Record Straight

After years of beating the fitness drum and trying to push everyone I could get my hands on into fitness producing exercise, I stepped back and reexamined the issues and was amazed at what I found. Yes, in order to be healthy it's necessary to be physically active on a daily basis. But no, the intensity of physical activity does not have to be exhausting.

16

When I released a summary of my findings, my colleagues accused me of blasphemy, but research backs me up. Many medical studies show quite clearly that moderate exercise is nearly, but not quite, as effective as vigorous exercise when it comes to improving health. Moreover, it's common sense. For years, we've known that people who are moderately active and who follow a nutritious low-fat, low-sugar diet are every bit as healthy as high mileage joggers. And they're likely to be much healthier than marathon runners who regularly consume double-bacon cheeseburgers.

This is a welcomed message, a breath of fresh air to those who are willing to be active, but are not willing to train in pain like an athlete. It's a message that is more appealing to the masses and may result in a resurgence of physical activity in this country that, ironically, has been dormant since the onset of the fitness era.

I provide the scientific evidence that backs up my stance in Chapter 2. But for now, please accept the exciting news that you no longer are bound to the few fitness-producing exercises deemed acceptable in the past. On the contrary, if you choose to be active, there's a whole smorgasbord of activities from which to choose. To help get you thinking in the right direction, please consider the 4-C's approach.

The 4-C's

The 4-C's exercise approach slants toward health promotion and away from performance, because improved physical performance is not what most Americans want or need. The 4-C's approach emphasizes Consistency, Convenience, Comfort, and Cost.

Let's first consider the importance of consistency. The overview of research findings presented in the next chapter shows clearly that, when it comes to exercise, the key to health is the "process" of being physically active, rather than the end product — the production of fitness. Once you have achieved at least a modest level of fitness, in fact, further pursuit of fitness does little for your health. The effectiveness of the "process" to promote health depends largely on how consistently you exercise.

Not so fast, you say. Aren't many highly fit people also very healthy? Indeed they are, but are they healthy because they are highly fit? Probably not. As I've said, any improved health status due to exercise is due to the "process" of performing exercise. In this case, the exercise of choice happens to be fitness producing exercise, but it doesn't have to be.

A walker or gardener who exercises as much as a fast paced jogger may achieve similar health benefits from exercise, if all three are similarly consistent in their exercise habit. The point is, there is no need to perform vigorous fitness-producing exercise in order to fulfill the requirements of the first C (consistency). You can engage in virtually any type of exercise you prefer, as long as you do it regularly, and every day, if possible.

Research also demonstrates that convenience is the key factor underlying consistency. If you purchase a membership to a commercial gym, for example, the major factor governing use of that membership is convenience. Convenience overrides the amenities of the physical structure, the quality of the staff, price, etc. You are much more likely to zip down the road a piece to your local gym, even if it's not much to boast about, than you are to drive across town to an opulent facility that combines the best of what Las Vegas and Disney World have to offer.

The same is true for home exercise equipment. The more accessible it is, the more likely you are to use it. Ironically, most of us are unwilling to trudge up a flight of stairs to the attic or down a flight to the basement in order to get on a treadmill or stationary bike. The thought of "traveling" to the equipment may be just enough to discourage us. If, on the other hand, the equipment is right in front of us, practically forcing us to climb over it, we are more likely to climb on, even for just a little while, and exercising for just "a little while" can be beneficial.

What If I'm Still Too Busy?

Just because exercise is convenient, doesn't necessarily mean it will fit into a busy schedule. That's true, and to accommodate a truly busy individual, it's nice to know you can perform physical activity in bits and pieces, squeezing it into any nook or cranny that appears in your schedule. Climbing a few flights of stairs, walking further from your parking place to the store or your office, and making extra trips from the car while bringing in the groceries, all count as exercise. The same is true for mini-bouts of exercise on your home exercise equipment.

Doubtful? Don't be. It's the sum of the calories you burn

throughout the day that counts, not the number you burn in a compressed time frame. Burning a hundred calories in four separate stints counts just as much as burning them all at once. You can tally your calories throughout the day, easily meshing physical activity into your lifestyle, the way the Europeans do.

I know what you may be thinking. (Firmly established thought patterns die hard.) Won't expending the calories all at once, in a compressed time frame, produce more fitness? Yes. But since fitness is not the prime factor we once thought it was, we can set it aside and take advantage of more convenient approaches — approaches that can more easily be included in busy lifestyles and that will reduce the number of excuses we have traditionally relied upon to keep us from getting involved.

Comfort also is a key. But by comfort I don't mean sitting comfortably in your recliner chair. You have to move your body, and there's no getting around that. You simply have to find ways of moving your body that are comfortable for you.

Unless you are a former athlete who is used to punishing your body with the no pain-no gain approach to exercise, you likely are turned off by things that are uncomfortable to do. Isn't it nice to know that taking a comfortable walk is healthy? That working in the garden burns calories and helps you lose body fat? That taking your sweetie out for an evening of ballroom dancing pays your exercise dues for the day?

Since walking, gardening, dancing and light sporting activities are now valued as health-promoting, all you need to do is follow a program which, at minimum, expends at least 150 calories a day, and ideally about twice that much. (Please note: I use the familiar lay term "calories" throughout this book, even though the technically correct term is "kilocalories.") To give you an idea of what this means, consider that the average-sized man will expend about 100 calories per mile of brisk walking (3.5 mph or faster). Women are smaller and will expend about 20 percent fewer calories doing the same things as men. As a rule of thumb, about 30 to 45 minutes of moderate daily physical activity (performed consecutively or in small doses) will do the job.

As I have already stated, this message often is misinterpreted as demeaning vigorous exercises like jogging or swimming laps as unproductive and unattractive. That's not the intent. Instead, the purpose is to provide an appealing alternative to vigorous exercise for those who have never exercised a day in their life and are not likely to engage in jogging or other demanding forms of exercise.

The fourth C is cost. The high cost of a gym membership, home exercise equipment, or high-tech footwear and garb can discourage those on a tight budget from exercising. Such items are necessary to effectively navigate the world of high fitness, but they no longer are compulsory if enhanced health is your aim, along with losing a few pounds, looking good and feeling good. Since almost anything that moves your body counts as exercise, many of the options available come at relatively little cost, and some, of course, cost you nothing.

If, for example, you enjoy working in the garden, expand your garden plot and plan to spend more time working on it in order to flesh out your exercise program. Cost? There is no cost over and above the investment you have already made initially to get your garden started. If you like to dance, you would no doubt already have a pair of dancing shoes, and therefore you can dance the night away for no additional cost. I think you get the idea.

A Calorie is a Calorie is a Calorie!

What about weight management? Don't you have to work hard to burn off calories? Not necessarily. When the legions of overweight individuals contemplate losing weight they mistakenly believe that exhausting exercise is the key. Not so! Forget past perceptions and embrace a new philosophy. A calorie expended running laps on a track or grinding away on a rowing machine is the same as a calorie expended walking through a park. Running will expend more calories per minute of effort, but you can easily compensate by walking longer. The choice is yours. If you enjoy running, rowing or swimming, go for it. If not, it's comforting to know you can accomplish just as much with a pleasant walk.

You can maximize the number of calories you expend by walking (or participating in other moderate physical activities) after meals. Being active after eating increases caloric expenditure by 15 percent. Walking a mile on an empty stomach may burn 100 calories, but walking the same distance at the same speed will burn 115 calories after a meal. You also get the benefit of using the fat you are digesting as fuel, rather than allowing it to be stored. Moderate exercise also aids digestion, making it more efficient.

It is important to emphasize that you cannot exercise vigorously after a meal. What mom always told you is true — you can't go swimming after eating. Demanding exercise interferes with the digestive process and can be dangerous, possibly causing discomfort in the gastrointestinal tract, and even in extreme cases, cramping. But moderate exercise, like walking, aids digestion. I'll discuss this in greater detail later.

Getting Started

To help get you started into a more active lifestyle, here are some examples of the kinds of things you can do and the number of calories you will burn per hour. The two columns are arranged for an average size male and an average size female. Caloric expenditure is related to body size, and therefore, if you are a large person you will expend more calories than indicated, and the opposite is true if you are smaller. But don't make this more complicated than it has to be. Merely use these values as gross guidelines to get you moving. And remember, anything that requires you to move your body counts, so use your imagination. Once you have established the habit, regardless of what activities you choose to get you moving, just continue in course and know that your efforts will reward you in many ways.

Activity	calories per hour 180-lb male	calories per hour 130-lb female
Walking (2-2.5 mph)	288	208
Walking (3.5 mph)	432	312
Jogging (6 mph)	756	546
Cycling (10 mph)	486	351
Swimming (slow crawl)	630	455
Weight Training	342	247
Dancing (ballroom)	288	208
Hiking (hilly)	648	468
Horseback ride (trot)	504	364
Racquetball	738	533
Table tennis	342	247

Activity	calories per hour 180-lb male	calories per hour 130-lb female
Tennis (singles)	522	377
Tennis (doubles)	324	234
Digging ditches	701	507
Gardening (dig, hoe)	575	416
House cleaning	288	208
Mowing lawn	486	351
Painting (outside)	378	273
Raking	270	195
Snow shoveling	702	507
Wash/polish car	270	195
Weeding	360	260
Stair climb (per 12 stair flight)	4.5	3.3

NOTE: The actual number of calories you may expend in any of the above activities can vary greatly depending not only on the size of your body, but also the intensity of the effort you put forth, the environmental circumstances (heat, humidity, altitude, etc.), and the consistency of movement.

The Bottom Line

The bottom line is, when asked what they would like to accomplish from an exercise program, most will respond that they would like to feel good, look good, and be healthy. You can do this with moderate physical activity. Simply select things you enjoy doing and do them every day. For those who also would like to have a high level of physical fitness (because they enjoy mountain hiking or other physically demanding recreational activities) the old rules (provided in Chapter 7) still apply. Drive up your heart rate and keep it there for a prolonged period. The important thing is to know the difference and not feel obligated to only one approach.

A Reader Writes:

"I disagree with your advice on exercise. I am 68 years old and I do a vigorous program of weight training and aerobics, and in my judgement your advice advocating mild exercise is setting people up for failure. They should be alerted that an effective program is working out several days a week, at least three, and the workouts should be demanding. If you don't take the body "to the woodshed," nothing is accomplished. The pay off is better health, a stronger body and higher quality of life. If a person wants to play, play with children at the playground."

My Response

Thank you for your letter. You make an important point. That is, for those who enjoy training like an athlete, my advice may be too simplistic and unappealing. In your case, you engage in tough workouts and you get a great deal of benefit from them. Keep up the good work. You set an excellent example for all of us, and especially for those who are getting up there in years.

But is it likely that your approach will appeal to the masses? Unfortunately, the answer is a resounding "No!" We need to get the couch potatoes off the couch, but to do that, we must coax them and bribe them with comfortable, convenient and fun activities. Thirty-five years of the fitness movement has taught us that the average American will not do what you have done. Only a small portion of Americans, in fact, exercise the way you do, and a pitifully small percentage of persons over sixty years of age follow your example.

Should we keep beating a dead horse, preaching the same message — that Americans need to sweat buckets in the gym or on the asphalt — knowing that the vast majority have heard this message time and again and have chosen to ignore it? Logic says, no. It's time for a new message.

To be sure, you are achieving great health benefits from your workouts. But you need to know that pushing yourself in the gym is only one way to succeed. A much softer approach to exercise, especially when combined with eating right, will achieve much of what you have achieved. It won't produce as much fitness or strength, but it will help you look better, feel better and be healthier and lose weight, and that's what more than nine out of ten Americans want to achieve. Moreover, it's more appealing to most Americans.

It would appear you are assuming that a high level of fitness is a prerequisite for health. You also may be assuming that high fitness is protective against heart disease and other chronic illnesses. If this were true, we wouldn't see heart attacks among marathon runners and body builders who ignore the importance of diet and other healthful practices.

In my workshops and talks I often encounter anger from those who are doing mega-doses of exercise. They demand that everyone else do the same. I have come to learn that such people really don't like to exercise and they view their workouts as a chore. What's more, if they have to do it, by golly, everyone else does, too. It's unfair, in other words, if someone else achieves nearly the same health benefits by doing something enjoyable like walking in the park. On the other hand, those who really enjoy their workouts take a "live and let live" attitude — logging time in the gym or jogging the streets because they like it, not because they believe they have to. (See Chapter 8, which addresses the question: What kind of exerciser are you?)

If your workouts are a chore, chances are your exercise habit won't last through the years ahead. For now, your willpower is winning, but it can't win forever. I suggest you take a look at what you are doing and evaluate it honestly. If your exercise routine is a chore which can only be tolerated because there is a rewarding sauna at the end, why not soften your approach and have more fun along the way? You may sacrifice some fitness and some strength, but all in all you'll be doing just fine.

A Reader Writes:

"I have an unusual question for you. I have a player piano that requires a lot of strength to play. If I play 3 or 4 piano rolls at night, would this be good exercise? If I play a lot, I do perspire. I like to walk, but won't get out and walk when it is cold. Would this be a good substitute? I think it gets my heart rate up."

My Response

I love your letter. Thanks for sending it. You make the point I have been emphasizing for years. That is, find a physical activity you truly enjoy doing and do it as often as possible. Because using your player piano makes you work a little and you enjoy it so much, it is a splendid alternative to walking outside on cold days. But don't abandon your walking. When you are able and the weather cooperates, get back out there and do your thing.

2. FITNESS AND HEALTH

Exercise is good for you, everyone knows that, and there is a long list of benefits. Many of the health enhancing qualities of exercise are probably familiar to you, and some may be surprising.

The Health Benefits of Exercise

Exercise reduces the risk of heart disease and stroke in many ways. It controls blood pressure, increases HDL cholesterol (the good kind of cholesterol); controls blood sugar through increased insulin sensitivity, and contributes to effective weight management. Exercise builds stronger bones by preventing loss of bone mineral density (calcium), particularly in women. Exercise adds years to life and life to years. Older men who exercise live longer, and exercise improves the quality of life in both men and women by increasing stability, helping to prevent falls, and resistance exercise decreases muscle weakness and muscle wasting.

The list goes on. Exercise relieves stress and eases signs of anxiety. It contributes to better sleep habits, and promotes a generalized feeling of well being. Exercise benefits moms to be by contributing to on-time delivery, and helping keep weight gain in check. Exercise benefits kids, too, helping children grow to be healthier and more fit adults, and preventing childhood obesity, which often contributes to adult obesity — the plague of modern man.

Exercise may be effective in helping to combat the damage done by naturally-occuring free radicals. There may be a greater production of the body's own antioxidants, soldiers that take on free radicals and neutralize them. If this is true, it has great implications for combating heart disease, cancer and many of the deleterious effects of aging.

Exercise bolsters the immune system, increasing its power to combat infection, and is especially effective in reducing the risk of upper respiratory infections in the elderly. A more efficient immune system may reduce the risk of certain types of cancer.

A Hidden Benefit

One way exercise enhances bodily functions, and the immune system in particular, is through its impact on the lymphatic system and the flow of lymphatic fluid. Enhancing lymphatic flow is at the core of many ancient far eastern therapies and exercise programs, but in the U.S this effect has been largely ignored — until recently. One reason we are not tuned in to what's going on in our lymphatic system is that most of us know very little about it, other than awareness of swollen lymph nodes in the neck when infection occurs, or the frightening involvement of the lymph nodes as cancer spreads throughout the body. Let's take a closer look.

The lymphatic system is your "other" circulatory system. It's a maze of lymph ducts snaking throughout the body that can be compared with a vast underground river, flowing and moving great quantities of fluid without notice.

The lymphatic system serves an important function in support of your cardiovascular system. You constantly circulate blood through major arteries which split into progressively smaller arteries, then finally the blood flows through the microscopic capillaries. In the capillaries, nutrients are pushed out and toward the tissues that need them to survive. Some fluid is also pushed out of the capillaries, leaving the blood stream.

Approximately 90 percent of the fluid that leaves the capillaries returns to the capillaries, which then flow into the veins, and back to the heart to be recirculated. The 10 percent of the fluid that cannot be returned to the capillaries ultimately moves into the lymphatic system. Thus, the lymphatic system serves as a drainage device. Eventually, lymphatic fluid reenters the blood stream on the venous side in the upper chest cavity. If it weren't for the lymphatic system, fluid would collect throughout the body causing edema (severe swelling).

The lymphatic system also serves as a filtering device. Throughout the lymph ducts are nodes that trap unwanted invaders and destroys them with killer immune cells.

In a healthy body, the drainage and filtering functions of the lymphatic system work well. There can be problems, however, caused by sluggish flow, which can allow the build-up of fluid and toxic materials. If flow is strong, lymph fluid shoots through the ducts and nodes and reenters the blood stream, headed toward the major filtration systems of the body in the liver and kidneys.

Unlike the cardiovascular system with the heart acting as a powerful pump that propels blood through the vessels, the lymphatic system has no pump. Thus, overcoming the effects of gravity is a challenge. Fluids moves through the lymph ducts with the help of muscular movements which squeeze the ducts. One-way valves ensure that when the ducts are squeezed the fluid will move in the right direction, toward the heart. With this in mind, almost any form of physical activity that involves the major muscle groups will have beneficial effects that promote the health of the body.

Process or Product

No one doubts that exercise promotes health. The problem is, it is generally perceived that it is the fitness produced by exercise that is health promoting, rather than participation in exercise itself. Not true. As I stated earlier, it is the process of being physically active that is critical, while the fitness accrued is less important.

I realize that this concept is hard to accept after so many years of hearing the traditional fitness message. To help you accept the truth of this concept, here's some scientific proof. If you already accept the notion that moderate physical activity is beneficial, you can skip to the next chapter. I have gone to some lengths to make certain that skeptical readers are aware of the abundant data base supporting my position, and reading this stuff can be a bit tedious and boring if you don't need convincing.

The Proof is in the Pudding

The following is by no means an exhaustive account of all the proof that exists. Rather, it is a sampling, but that's all that is needed, because the conclusion of study after study supports the benefits of moderate exercise. The findings are remarkably consistent, in other words, even if they don't appear to be at first blush.

Over the years, there have been several epidemiological studies (the study of populations and their traits) which demonstrate conclusively that moderate exercise that does not produce a high level of fitness can promote health and well being. Several of these studies were conducted at the Institute for Aerobics Research in Dallas, Texas, founded by Dr. Kenneth Cooper, the father of vigorous aerobic exercise.

In 1989 more than 13,000 men and women were studied at the Institute for Aerobics Research and it was found that — (1) a low level of fitness increases the risk of many diseases and dying young; (2) such risk can be greatly reduced by regular moderate exercise; and (3) a high fitness level does not decrease risk significantly further than the level achieved from a moderate level of fitness. The meaning of these findings was summarized by the principle investigator of this study, Dr. Steven Blair, who remarked, "It doesn't take an enormous amount of exercise to obtain considerable health benefits."

In 1987 results of the MRFIT (Multiple Risk Factor Intervention Trial) were published in the Journal of the American Medical Association. This was a multi-year study involving several cites around the U.S. The purpose was to examine the impact of exercise (and lack of exercise) on heart disease risk factors (high blood pressure, high cholesterol, etc.) in men. The study was coordinated by Arthur Leon, M.D. and colleagues from the University of Minnesota School of Public Health.

Here's what was found. "Men at high risk for coronary heart disease (CHD) who self-selected moderate amounts of predominately light and moderate nonwork physical activity had lower rates of CHD mortality, sudden death, and overall mortality than more sedentary men." Doing a little is a whole lot better than doing nothing, in other words. But here's the punchline of the study. Men who engaged in at least 30-minutes daily of "moderate leisure time physical activity" achieved the same level of protection from fatal heart attacks as men whose exercise levels were three times that much.

At Stanford University, a 1978 study conducted by Dr. Ralph Paffenbarger investigated the exercise habits of 17,000 Harvard alumni. It was found that an exercise level that equates to expending 2,000 calories a week afforded substantial protection from heart disease. I remember when I first read this study, or should I say, "misread" it. I quickly assumed that the 2,000 calories were expended during jogging and other vigorous exercises. But when I went back years later and examined the details I found that most of the 17,000 participants who expended 2,000 calories per week were doing so by walking, stair climbing (and getting their exercise in bits and pieces), gardening, light sports, etc. Few of them were engaged regularly in fitness producing exercise.

In the Harvard alumni study, couch potatoes (expending 500 or fewer calories per week in exercise) were at high risk for heart disease. As the caloric expenditure climbed from 500 to 2,000 the risk decreased progressively. Interestingly, increasing the expenditure further, from 2,000 calories per week to 3,500, afforded no additional decrease in risk. This underscores the fact that performing mega-doses of exercise may greatly increase fitness, but it does not necessarily translate into better health.

From these studies and others, Dr. William Haskell of Stanford University offered guidelines for exercise participation. At a minimum, you should seek to expend at least 150 calories per day (1050 per week), to an optimum level of 285 per day (2,000 per week). In the previous chapter, guidelines were presented to show you how easy it is to expend 150 calories per day. A brisk walk of 1.5 to 2 miles will suffice, for example, as will 30-minutes of cutting the grass.

I'll cite one more study to make my point. In 1966 a study published in the Journal of the American Medical Association on 110,000 men went largely unnoticed. I found it when digging deeply into the medical literature while investigating these issues. Participants in the study (nonsmoking men) were divided into three groups according to their level of daily physical activity — least active, intermediate, and most active. The study examined protection from heart disease and found that the most active group received the highest level of protection — an expected finding.

What was unexpected was the fact that the intermediate group enjoyed almost as much protection as the most active group. Lots of extra exercise added only a modest increase in protection, in other words. And when comparing all three groups, there was a sharp break between the upper two groups and the least active group. The authors of this study suggested that "a substantial reduction in mortality might be achieved through a relatively small increase in habitual physical activities of the most inactive men in a given population."

Many other studies over the past two decades have reported

identical results. Even so, the public perception persists that it takes gut busting exercise to promote health. Oftentimes, this misperception has been promulgated by exercise scientists who fail to acknowledge the value of moderate exercise and who, without realizing their bias, misinterpret what the data are really telling them. I have to admit I did this for years without realizing it.

Readers of my column, The Body Shop, have seen a major transition in my stance on exercise. Years ago I was totally committed to vigorous exercise and the need to achieve a high level of fitness in order to be healthy. Then I had a road to Damascus experience and my eyes were opened to the truth, which greatly softened my message. (I'll discuss my transition in detail in the next chapter.) This transition and my softening on the issues antagonizes many fitness buffs who like to challenge my "fluffy" view and my belief that it is the process of being physically active on a daily basis that is important in promoting health, and that producing a high level of fitness is of secondary importance.

Die Hard Fitness Buffs Keep Pushing

Fitness advocates like to tell me how ill-informed I am and that it's time I woke up and smelled the coffee. To support their case, they often send me scientific research articles from prestigious medical journals which conclude in no uncertain terms that fitness is important. Here's an example.

A recent article that reported the health status, death rate, and fitness of 20,000 men was published in the American Journal of Clinical Nutrition. The sender was a friend of mine who is a physician. He attached a brief note which read: "People need to get FIT!" He added a few good natured jabs, just to make certain I got the point that I should be emphasizing fitness in my column.

I read the article, paying particular attention to all the sections highlighted for my benefit. The repeated message was, the men in the research study who were fit were healthier than those who were unfit. This was true even if both groups had the same level of body fatness. The conclusion was, if you want to live longer and avoid many of the chronic diseases which plague our society, exercise vigorously and produce a high level of fitness.

How could I possibly disagree with these sophisticated up-to-date scientific findings? The answer is, I don't. It's not surprising that the fit men were healthier than the unfit. But I disagree with the notion that everyone needs to strive to be highly fit in order to be healthy. Ironically, a careful look at this study (and others of a similar nature) reveals that the data agree with my stance. Let me explain.

How Fit is Fit?

Many studies which proclaim that a high level of fitness is necessary for good health are guilty of confusing results that are "relative" with results that are "absolute." For example, who is stronger, a man who can lift 200 pounds or a man who can lift 400 pounds? The answer seems obvious. But let's add more information to the mix. The man who can lift 200 pounds weighs only 100 pounds. And the man who can lift 400 pounds weighs 500 pounds. This information shows that the smaller man is much stronger in relative terms (according to size), while the larger man is much stronger in absolute terms. When examining scientific findings, it's critical that you understand the interpretation of the author of the study and how the data are being presented.

Here's another example. If someone had 20% body fat and went on a diet and reduced their body fat to 19%, how much of a change would this represent? If you said 1% you'd be correct. If you said 5%, you also be correct. The reduction equals 1% when expressed in absolute terms of body fat (presented as a percentage), but 5% when expressed relative to the starting point (a decrease of 1, from 20 to 19 represents a 5% reduction). You can see how complicated this is for the layperson. You also can see how easy it would be to make any case you choose simply by reporting the results in a fashion that supports your argument.

Now back to the study that my friend the doctor sent me.

When I examined the data from this study, I asked myself — how fit were the 20,000 adult American men who participated? Because they are adult American men, how fit could they be? The answer is, not very. Only about 10 percent of adult American men are fit in the way that fitness advocates define it, and thus, only about 2,000 of the total of 20,000 participants were likely to qualify as fit. In addition, it's likely that of the 2,000 fit participants, only a small proportion could be categorized as highly fit. Moreover the ages of men in the study ranged from 30 to beyond 80 years. It is important to note the deep decline in fitness that occurs beyond age 50, which means the amount of overall fitness in this massive group of 20,000 men may have been even smaller than I am suggesting.

The authors of the research study ranked the 20,000 participants according to fitness from top to bottom, then the group was split in half, taking the top half and labeling them as "fit" and the bottom half and labeling them "unfit." The health status (blood pressure, serum cholesterol, body fatness, etc.) and death rate of each group was determined. From this, it was found to no surprise that the "fit" group was better than the "unfit" group.

Now for the key ingredient necessary for accurate interpretation of findings. Do we really have a "fit" group? No, we don't. We have one group that is more fit "relative" to the other, but the more fit group in no way qualifies as being fit (in absolute terms) according to well established fitness standards. The vast majority of these 10,000 so called "fit" men couldn't run even one mile, cycle very far, or swim laps without stopping. On the contrary, they are labeled as "fit" only because they are more fit than the couch potatoes who compose the "unfit" group.

An old saying emphasizes my point. "A one-eyed man is king in the kingdom of the blind." A person who can walk up a flight of stairs without passing out is more fit than a person who must stop halfway up the flight, because of exhaustion. One is more fit than the other (in relative terms), but neither qualifies as fit (in absolute terms).

A better interpretation of the data from the study of 20,000 men would be that those who are sedentary and very unfit run a high health risk. Moreover, those who strive for at least an average level of fitness have a lower health risk. This is consistent with the studies I mentioned earlier and many that I didn't include for fear of boring my readers to tears.

Although the "fit" group members are not truly fit, it's likely they are more physically active as compared with the "unfit" group. This means, it would be reasonable (and more accurate) to label the groups as "active" versus "sedentary," which would remove fitness as a consideration, and would emphasize more appropriately, in my opinion, the association between being physically active and being healthy — the point I have been making for years.

I realize that this sounds like a bunch of technical mumbo-jumbo, but I assure you it's not. In fact, because this stuff is technical and not easily understood, it is the source of much needless confusion and disagreement about the issues. In this case, one side is saying, based on scientific research studies, you have to be "fit" — you have to push yourself hard and build a high level of fitness — in order to be healthy. Ironically, I'm using the exact same research studies to support my claim that simply being physically active on a daily basis, and not worrying about seeking a high fitness level, is an important means to improving health.

I must add that a moderately fit man (or woman) who follows a healthy diet will be much healthier than a highly fit person who eats like a typical American. In fact, as is often the case, highly fit individuals tend to be a bit snobbish about their daily mega-doses of exercise and foolishly believe they can eat whatever they want, because they will burn it off. If this were so, we wouldn't have marathon runners dropping over dead of heart attacks.

What's critical to recognize, and the thing I have emphasized repeatedly in my writings, is that highly fit and moderately fit people are pretty similar in health status, but they are much healthier than those who are sedentary and totally unfit.

All in all, isn't it nice to know you can achieve a basket full of health benefits by either jogging miles a day, or participating regularly in activities you enjoy — activities that don't force you to push yourself long and hard in pursuit of a high level of fitness? The answer is obvious.

The Bottom Line

The bottom line is, when it comes to exercise, be consistent, and do something that moves your body every day, if possible. Convenience and comfort will be factors that influence consistency, so choose physical activities that are easily accessible and that you enjoy, regardless of whether or not they promote fitness. Such activities will provide you a modest level of fitness, and that is sufficient when it comes to promoting health, because increasing your fitness level further adds little health benefit. In fact, if you truly want to improve your health, overhaul your diet. That's where you'll get the biggest bang for the buck.

3. THE ROAD TO DAMASCUS

How does one transcend a marine boot camp mentality about fitness and exercise and evolve to one that is best described as the Mary Poppins approach? Here's my story.

My Battle

Thinking back, there were a number of factors which shaped my attitude. The first was my own struggle with weight and body image. Mine was not a monumental struggle, but it was up-close and personal, and it left a strong impression. I remember being eleven years old and on the verge of puberty. Many of the guys I hung out with in the neighborhood had already zipped into the pimple-popping gauntlet and their bodies began taking on the muscular proportions of a man. But I lagged behind and I was fleshy and soft. Fortunately, I looked okay in my clothes, and I wasn't the butt of fat jokes. These were reserved for a friend we called, "Pig."

I never took my shirt off in public. On hot summer days, during marathon baseball games on dusty ballfields, Pig and I had our shirts on. I was too ashamed of my pot belly to take it off. Everyone teased Pig about keeping his shirt on. No one said anything to me. I guess they thought I had a different reason for not exposing my flesh.

I remember my first pair of Boy Scout shorts. I didn't want to wear shorts (back then, none of the guys wore shorts in public), but I had to have them for summer scout camp. They were size 36. Not massive, but pretty darned big around the waist for an eleven year old boy weighing about 145 pounds. If I had those shorts today, they'd be loose on me, and I'm more than 60 pounds heavier than I was then.

I didn't like my body at the time, but I accepted my status. I was destined to have an inferior body and there was nothing I could do about it. Then, one fateful day, I dropped by to visit a friend who was lifting a long heavy steel bar over his head. He pressed it upward time and again like a barbell. Immediately, I was attracted to the notion of getting stronger and possibly changing my body and I jumped in and took my turn pressing the bar. We worked to exhaustion, and when we couldn't do any more, we made a pact to come together every day and exercise. The pact lasted a few days, until the bar disappeared.

Determined to continue exercising, I borrowed a set of resistance springs — the kind you pull apart across your chest. I used the springs every day, and I did push-ups, sit-ups, pull-ups and anything else I could think of. My body began to change. I dropped inches from my waist, I could pump out forty push-ups without stopping, and you could see a bulge in my biceps when I made a muscle.

Having overcome my modest body image problem at a young age, I couldn't resist being full of myself. My confidence gradually turned to arrogance. And why not? Without help from anyone, I sought out a cure and pounced on it. I had the will power and motivation to grab my problem by the throat and squeeze it until it died. When it would have been easier to just loaf with the guys, I worked out instead, pushing myself to the limit, determined to remake my body. My success convinced me that with enough effort, anyone who wanted to be different could be.

The depth of my zeal was increased by my choice of professions. I am an exercise physiologist and health professional who believes that health is largely determined by the kind of lifestyle you choose to lead. To be sure, heredity plays a role, but most of us can overcome a bad heredity if we want to. And on the other side of the coin, slothful living can wrinkle even the best set of God-given genes.

Early in my career I preached mega-doses of exercise as the cure for all that ails us — especially a poochie belly or flabby thighs. Much to their detriment, the unhealthy and the obese failed to grasp my wisdom, and they balked at my message. They weren't about to buy a pair of Reeboks and start jogging, no matter how much preaching I did. Was I deterred? Not initially. Like a true professional, I tried harder, convinced that if I put forth more effort I could get through. But I couldn't, and the harder I tried the more frustrated I became.

Was I to blame for their failure? Surely not. The fault must lie with those who need to improve their health and lose weight, but are unwilling to try. Eventually, in self defense, I found myself condemning them, berating and dismissing them as unworthy of my talents and effort.

The Transformation

So, with all this baggage, how did I manage to make a complete turnaround? What inspired me to preach a softer message, to be more understanding and compassionate, and to finally realize that you capture more flies with honey than with vinegar? Several factors contributed to my transformation.

As stated above, my philosophy of exercise was "the more the better" and the harder you push the better. I also applied this philosophy in my personal and professional life. The result? I became not only a fervent exercise addict, but also a hopeless workaholic in the process. To be sure, there were many external rewards, and I was successful in many ways, but at a terrible price.

I was so totally addicted to exercise that I couldn't see the forest for the trees. I knew I had to exercise every day, and exercise hard, no matter what. In the dead of winter, I remember arising well before dawn, the temperature less than 20 degrees F, the wind howling and the wind chill a bone frosting minus 10. Regardless, I pulled on my exercise gear and hit the streets for a punishing three to five mile run.

I had to run early, because my day was so full, especially considering the hour and a half I needed for pumping iron in the weight room each afternoon. And if I couldn't get my morning run in for some reason, I had to do it when I could, even if it meant jogging the streets after midnight. Weather didn't matter. Snow and ice were obstacles to be overcome. In deference, I jogged more slowly, but jogged nonetheless.

I was hooked and never thought about changing. I exercised the way I lived the rest of my life — at full throttle. I didn't feel the need to change, or want to change, because I didn't know any other way to live. Besides, working hard pays big dividends. I short circuited the promotion process at the University of Louisville, gaining tenure and promotion from assistant professor to associate professor in only two years. Then, I was promoted to full professor after only seven years total.

I had cut the process in half time-wise, but never slowed down despite my success. I was working harder than ever, setting lofty goals, pursuing them, attaining them, then setting new and loftier goals. It was a vicious cycle that was killing my soul, but I didn't know it.

Fortunately, a life changing event stopped me in my tracks. Thankfully, it wasn't some horrible injury or a dreaded illness. I agreed to get involved on a volunteer basis with mentally challenged individuals in the greater Louisville region through the Council for Retarded Citizens. This was to please my new wife at the time, because she was a pioneer in championing the rights of the mentally retarded. I saw myself as a philanthropist, a good samaritan, who was going to bring some sunshine into the lives of these unfortunate individuals. Boy, was I wrong! It didn't take long for me to realize that there was something very special about these individuals, and it wasn't their lack of mental acuity.

The people I met were special, because they intuitively knew what was important in life. Love! They had an incredible capacity to love and accept others for who they are, regardless of their success in life, their socioeconomic standing, their family tree. As I observed I began to realize that I had been brought to this situation, not as a philanthropist or good deed-doer, but as a pupil who needed schooling about life's important messages.

As I began to "get-it" I started a long period of self examination, and I didn't like what I saw. I saw a self absorbed, ego driven, anal retentive, compulsive neurotic, Type A workaholic whose only real joy in life was setting goals and achieving them. I had bought into our nation's productivity ethic hook, line and sinker. And I realized regretfully that I valued only those who produced in abundance, while demeaning those who could not produce, condemning them as dead wood.

The mentally challenged are essentially non-producers and that's why they are at the bottom of the totem pole in our society. But I saw that their ability to live mindfully, in the present moment, rather than in the past or future, was a great gift and an example to all of us on how to live most effectively in order to maximize the days we have on this earth. Finally, it dawned on me that I had been an utter fool in my approach to life and I desperately wanted to change. And change I did. I changed everything in an effort to put my life on a meaningful track.

It was then that I had to confront my extreme exercise habit. How could I become the person I wanted to be while still adhering to an addicted, punishing, goal oriented approach to exercise? Obviously, I couldn't. For the first time I stared my exercise habit in the face and saw it for what it was.

Exercise was supposed to be an antidote for stress. I preached this in my writings and taught this in my classes. Indeed, by exhausting my body through exercise I bought myself a few moments of release. But, overall, I had to admit that my exercise routine was an enormous source of stress, because of the rigidity I applied to it and the amount of time it robbed from my already hopelessly overcrowded daily schedule. Exercise was supposed to be an energizer. I preached that, too. But for me, it was a drain. My workouts were so demanding they left me feeling numb. In order for a weight training session to be a truly bona fide workout, I had to crawl out of the weight room without one ounce of energy left to call upon. The same was true for my runs. Every run had to be pushed to the max—longer, faster, more intense.

To add to the insanity, I had a load of chronic orthopedic injuries that contributed a generous dose of pain and discomfort to the mix. My knee throbbed when I ran and would swell and need icing when I finished to bring it back down to near normal size. I took aspirin before I ran and ibuprofen afterwards. In the weight room, my elbows felt like someone was jabbing at them with an ice pick. My shoulders ached constantly, and especially while I was working out. My left wrist was so badly damaged that I had to wrap it tightly with layers of bandages so that it wouldn't bend while lifting heavy weights.

I was a prisoner to exercise. I was a cripple, mentally, emotionally and physically. I knew what I had to do. Did I have the guts? Yes. I quit exercising cold turkey. Like a cigarette addict who quits, I laid my exercise habit down and refused to pick it up. Believe me, this was a tough time for me. Every fiber of my being craved a workout. Withdrawal was murder, but I persisted. Eventually, it got easier and to my surprise I began to feel an incredible sense of liberation. All of a sudden it was as if my days had expanded from 24 hours to 30 hours of more. I could get things done without rushing, without charging ahead like a wildman. What's more, I had energy to burn. I felt like a new man!

I knew that at some point I had to get back into some form of exercise, but I was afraid that I'd relapse. This was a risk I had to take. I started with walks in the neighborhood. Nothing too demanding. No set distance. No set time. This worked well. I kept up my walking, looking for pretty places to walk so that I could appreciate the scenery and if I felt like it, stop and smell the roses. I especially enjoyed long hikes in the woods. Eventually, I ventured back into the weight room and started lifting light dumbbells in high repetitions.

My Physique and Health Profile

When I quit my heavy exercise regimen, I was terrified that my health would plummet, because I had erroneously equated my high level of fitness with a high level of health. Not only did I not possess a high level of health, my health profile was anything but outstanding. As a heavy exerciser I needed lots of calories to keep me going, and it was not unusual to consume 5000 to 6000 calories per day. The problem is, my diet was full of red meat and dairy products. I was bombarding my body with a ton of saturated fat on a daily basis, but I had assumed that my exercise was burning it off. Wrong! My serum cholesterol was well over 200 mg/dl and my HDL was a miserable 34 mg/dl. My all important cholesterol/HDL ratio was 6.2:1, a level which indicated that I was at high risk of atherosclerosis (clogging of the arteries) — the underlying cause of 95% of all heart attacks.

When I learned this, I radically changed my diet, ultimately becoming a vegetarian. It took about a year, but I cut my cholesterol in half and my health profile improved dramatically.

What happened to my physique? Surprisingly, I still looked pretty good. I wasn't as large, with bulging muscles, but I was becoming more muscularly defined. My body fat declined and the love handles I had been sporting for decades began to fade. This, in spite of not blistering my body with daily gut busting exercise. The ultimate irony was that I was better off in many ways without the heavy exercise.

As I went along, I began to experiment with all forms of "exercise" options. I learned to appreciate the value of doing chores and counting them as exercise. I paid my exercise dues by cutting the grass, hauling mulch, digging in the garden, washing my car, the list goes on. I also enjoyed the feeling that comes from a job well done. It's a pleasure looking out the window at my landscaping, knowing that not only did I create a beautiful yard, I got some valuable exercise in the process.

My personal transformation inspired me to reexamine the role of exercise in health promotion from a professional's point of view, but this time I did it with an objective eye. This led to the more reasonable interpretations of the data outlined in the last chapter. The combination of my personal experiences plus an objective evaluation of what the scientific literature is really saying about exercise has led me to my present stance.

It is my wish that you will benefit from my growth and development and the philosophy I've developed. If you are a non-exerciser, perhaps you will be inspired to give exercise a shot. Who knows, you just might enjoy it. And if you are a chronic exerciser, perhaps you will come away with new insights to apply that will make your habit more satisfying.

The Present Day

My approach to exercise today combines all aspects of the message I am preaching. For several years I did not run and I did not lift heavy weights. At times, however, I wondered if I could again do demanding exercise without getting hooked. Like an alcoholic or reformed drug addict, however, I was afraid to indulge myself for fear of getting caught again. Eventually, I have found that I can enjoy a brisk bout of exercise, but without the baggage.

I now go to the gym and enjoy a demanding weight training workout approximately once a week. And if I am in the mood, I may take off and run a few miles, pushing myself up the hills. I must admit that the feeling of pushing myself is still exhilarating in the same way it was more than a decade ago. But there is an important distinction. I have no sense of obligation to engage in such exercise any more often than I like. And when I am in the midst of a workout, I can quit any time I like.

In the gym, I don't count repetitions, or set goals for how much weight I need to lift. Indeed, my weekly workouts vary considerably and do no follow any particular pattern. I do only what I feel like doing. Often, I may go to the gym with the intent of pushing myself, and end up walking on the treadmill. My exercise options have expanded. I may perform Tai Chi, yoga or a stretching routine. If I cut the grass, that's my exercise for the day. In the past I'd hurry through my grass cutting chores so that I could get out and run, or get to the gym to pump iron. My new approach allows me to relax and actually enjoy the hum of the mower and the almost meditative state of mind that ensues as I pace back and forth across the yard. It's liberating to know that my vigorous exercise choices do not produce any greater health promoting effects than my more moderate choices. The bottom line is, I'm free and I don't feel obligated to follow any set rules. It's a wonderful feeling that greatly contributes to my overall quality of life.

4. EXERCISE FOR WEIGHT LOSS

The Surgeon General recently declared war on obesity, and for good reason. Americans are fat and getting fatter decade by decade. What's more, we are getting fatter faster! The latest findings suggest an alarming trend among youngsters. Type II diabetes, the kind that comes on later in life, usually in middle age, is proliferating among kids as young as 10 years old! The main cause is too much body fat. Amazing, isn't it, that in just 10 years our children are accumulating sufficient body fat to bring on a disease that typically would not be manifested for several more decades.

Exercise is a key preventative, but few of us regularly engage in doing much of anything that entails moving the body. The couch potato segment of our society, in particular, is growing by leaps and bounds along with the incidence of obesity, and tens of millions of Americans get no exercise at all, avoiding it, in fact, at all costs.

The Role of Exercise

It's not unusual that humans tend to shy away from exercise. It's a natural response, in fact, because the body is programmed to equate survival with having enough energy, and storing energy as body fat is exactly what the body likes to do. Burning off valuable energy through exercise, on the other hand, is viewed by the body as life threatening. At least that's the way things used to be thousands of years ago when eating was less predictable and disruptions in the food chain necessitated going without eating for prolonged periods of time.

Today, with fast food restaurants on every corner, our survival is no longer dependent upon carrying around a storehouse of energy. On the contrary, our well developed genetic ability to store body fat is no longer a plus, it's a liability. We are destroying our bodies with the very energy that used to save us in times of need. With this in mind, it's obvious that the human species is undergoing a great transition, from valuing slothful living and the storage of energy, to recognizing that such traits bring on a host of chronic diseases (heart disease, cancer, diabetes, etc.) that were unheard of eons ago. It's time for a more active lifestyle.

Body fat results from a positive caloric balance in which you consume more energy than you expend. To reverse this, you must create a negative caloric balance in which you expend more than you consume. To get this done, you can consume less energy (eat less), burn more (through exercise), or both. Research shows clearly that doing both is the way to go. There are many reasons for this, but mainly, it's easier and more effective to take a moderate approach to both diet and exercise, rather than an extreme approach to one or the other.

With this said, I want to especially emphasize the importance of diet, because dietary indiscretion can exert an incredibly powerful effect with minimal effort. Wolfing down a large piece of cheesecake, for example, can provide more than 30 grams of fat and 400 calories. In order to undo the damage done by a piece of cheesecake — damage that can be imposed in just a few minutes — it would be necessary to walk briskly for an hour. It's not fair, but that's the way it is.

(I go into great detail about these issues in my book The WEIGHT LOSS READER (Biosynergic Health Press, 2001), and I refer you there for more information, because the more you know the better equipped you are to cope successfully. I also refer you to my Jack Sprat Low-fat Diet (University Press of Kentucky, 1995) for a complete dietary plan that will take you by the hand and lead you safely through the gauntlet of weight loss challenges.)

Although I emphasize the importance of making good dietary decisions, you won't be successful in managing your weight over the long haul without a program of daily exercise. Yes, you can dump weight quickly on a crash diet and without exercise. But the weight you lose is a combination of glucose (sugar), water and muscle, with rather little fat. This is the reason why 99% of all crash diets fail to keep weight off. Your goal should be to lose body fat, not body weight. This is a theme I pound away at in my weight loss books.

The First Law of Thermodynamics

To lose body fat, your approach must honor the First Law of Thermodynamics — energy can be neither created nor destroyed, it can only be transformed from one form to another. This means that when you attempt to lose body fat, you must account for all the energy that is stored there. One pound of body fat contains a whopping 3500 calories. That's a whole lot! To give you an idea of just how much energy this is, a marathon runner who completes an entire marathon of 26 miles will expend less energy than is contained in one pound of body fat.

On a typical crash diet, it's easy to lose several pounds of weight in just one week. If, for example, you lost 5 pounds in one week, and if the weight you lost was fat, you would have to account for 17,500 calories (5 pounds x 3500 cals/pound = 17,500). This would require incredible effort, equivalent to running more than five full marathons in one week. No one does this, of course, which means the loss of 5 pounds was not 5 pounds of body fat. What was it?

Almost all of the weight that was lost was muscle. Muscle affords only a measly 700 calories per pound — one/fifth as much as body fat. Five pounds of muscle would equate to only 3500 total calories for the week (5 pounds x 700 cals/pound), or the amount in only one pound of fat. Accounting for this vastly reduced amount of energy according to the First Law of Thermodynamics is easy, and it explains how rapid weight loss can occur.

But what if you decide to exercise while you are on a crash diet? Won't it help you hold onto the muscle and lose fat? Unfortunately, if you are not taking in enough calories to satisfy essential daily nutrient needs — the definition of a crash diet — exercise will actually cause you to lose more muscle and less fat. The reason is, it will thrust you into an even greater nutrient deficit (because exercise will increase the body's demand for nutrients) and it will create an even greater negative caloric balance. There's no two ways about it, when you attempt to lose body fat, you must first be certain you are covering the body's daily requirements, which means you must consume a substantial number of calories, and all of those calories must be nutrient rich. (For guidance on the number of calories you require for varying bodyweights, please consult my book, the WEIGHT LOSS READER.)

Because you are a sane and thinking individual, it's obvious that you don't want to lose muscle. But you will if you reduce your caloric intake too drastically, because you won't have enough carbohydrates to feed your brain and spinal column — the central nervous system (CNS). Carbs are the only fuel the CNS can use, and not having enough carbs coming in sends the body into a panic. In response the body goes after your muscle mass, tearing it down, dismantling the proteins into amino acids, and sending the amino acids to the liver to be converted to carbohydrates (glucose) that are then dumped into the blood stream to raise your blood sugar level — the fuel that feeds your brain. The result is very rapid weight loss due to cannibalization of your muscles.

The appropriate approach to losing body fat is to make certain you are consuming enough nutrients, particularly carbohydrates, to keep your body from shifting into the panic mode. Combine this with an increased level of physical activity, and when you do, it will be possible to burn off about one pound of fat per week. This seems slow, I know, but it's the only way to lose fat and keep it off. If you greatly increase your daily exercise it's possible to burn off as much as 2 pounds of fat per week. But that would require at least an hour of highly vigorous effort daily, or two hours of moderate physical activity.

The More the Merrier

Previously, I told you that in order to be healthy, your daily exercise program should expend at least 150 calories, up to an optimal level of 285. If losing body fat is your goal, however, don't feel bound by this range. If you choose to go well beyond 285 calories per day, go for it. My point in the previous chapter was that performing mega-doses of exercise does not enhance health to a greater extent. That's a different issue from losing body fat, and I want to make that point quite clear.

You now know you have a number of options that can help you expend calories through exercise. Virtually anything that requires you to move your body qualifies as bona fide fat busting exercise. The key, again, is consistency. And consistency largely depends on convenience and comfort.

At this point it's a good idea to start plotting how you will increase your daily exercise level, if you are not currently physically active.

Use your creativity and don't restrict yourself with dogma and old rules. They no longer apply.

Take your time and solidify your new exercise approach firmly into your lifestyle. To initiate a new habit requires about 30 days, and an additional 30 days helps fix the habit. After you have adopted a number of exercise options and have increased your daily caloric expenditure, I urge you to consider taking on some resistance training with weights (see the next chapter).

A Reader Writes:

"I read your column about the benefits of mild exercise on weight loss. Your argument sounds good and for some people it's probably all they can do. But I think you are doing a disservice to true exercise. By that I mean the kind that makes the old ticker pound with a fury, the body's blast furnace metabolism stoked to the max. You seem to have overlooked the fact that intense exercise burns calories not only while you do it, but also for hours afterwards. This is a huge benefit and should not be overlooked by those who seek to lose weight through exercise."

My Response

This is a good point. When exercise is intense and prolonged, it takes quite a while to bring things back to normal and the body's metabolism remains elevated even though exercise stops. The same is true for your car after driving it some distance. The hood will stay warm for a long time after you park it, because the engine remains hot even though the car is no longer moving.

The sustained elevation in metabolism is called the "afterburn" and this adds to the total caloric expenditure of a bout of exercise. But the number of calories you burn is not as great as was once thought. Research studies conducted years ago reported that the body's metabolism was elevated above typical resting levels for 24 hours or more after exercise. While it's true that running a marathon would require lots of time for the body to readjust back to a normal state, it's unlikely that most things exercisers would choose to do would cause more than a few hours of elevated metabolism after the exercise is over.

That's not to say the afterburn is not important. It is, because anything that adds to caloric expenditure is valuable. But I don't think it's a compelling reason to go back to the notion that intense exercise is the best, or only, way to lose body fat. On the contrary, there are trade-offs that compromise intense exercise in favor of moderate exercise.

When you compare the afterburn from vigorous and prolonged exercise with the metabolic bonus boost you get from moderate exercise after a meal that was discussed earlier, the results are likely to be pretty similar in most circumstances. Keep in mind that post-meal exercise cannot be vigorous, because vigorous exercise sets up a competition between the working muscles and the gastrointestinal (GI) tract for blood flow. The muscles will always win this battle, and the result can be GI discomfort, and even cramping and nausea.

As you can see, my argument in favor of allowing a choice between vigorous and moderate exercise still holds. You can get considerable calorie burning and fat reducing benefit from demanding exercise on an empty stomach, and part of that benefit will be due to the afterburn. You also, however, can get similar calorie burning benefit from moderate exercise after a meal. Isn't it nice to know you have a choice?

5. FAT BURNING EXERCISE

Over the years I have encountered many individuals who pass themselves off as professional exercise physiologists, even though they lack even an elementary academic preparation. Some may not have had even one college level class on the subject, and still they go about the business of advising the public on what to do when it comes to exercise. Unfortunately, there is at present no national certification procedure for becoming a licensed exercise physiologist, but that likely will change in the future.

Most of these unqualified individuals are harmless enough, if they know their limitations and stick to what they've learned from experience. And, in fairness, some can be quite competent from being self taught. But the ones who can't resist exerting themselves and offering advice on issues that are over their head are the ones who scare me. Usually, their advice is so off target that it would be comical if it weren't for the fact that an unsuspecting public believes it, and that it contributes to confusion and the mountains of misinformation that pummel our society at every turn.

Arm Yourself

How can you protect yourself from taking advice on exercise from someone who knows very little about the topic? Learn a few basic principles and ask for an opinion about them. If the response you get is reasonable, be encouraged. If, on the other hand, you get a load of hocus pocus, run fast in the opposite direction.

A perfect example is so called fat burning exercise. I have had "exercise experts" who don't know me and are not familiar with what I do in my day job, tell me with a perfectly straight and sincere face that if you want to remove body fat, you must perform "fat burning exercise in

48

the fat burning zone." They explain this as exercise at a low intensity that is at minimum 20-minutes in duration, because (according to them) "it takes 20-minutes of exercise before you begin burning fat as fuel" (before you enter the so called "fat burning zone"). For the first 20-minutes of exercise, you are supposedly, in other words, burning something other than fat. But after 20-minutes, bingo! The fat switch is turned on and you are burning entirely fat as fuel.

This whole explanation is amazingly absurd, and here's why. (Please note: It's perfectly fine to exercise for 20-minutes at a low intensity — a brisk 20-minute walk, for example. No problem. But thinking that by doing so you are doing something that shifts you into becoming a purely fat burning machine is nothing but a bunch of foolishness.)

When you are at rest, your fuel mix is composed of fat and carbohydrate, with fat accounting for the lion's share — as much as 60-70 percent of the total. Obviously, you don't have to exercise for 20-minutes before you enter the fat burning zone. That's bunk, because you are there right now, sitting in your recliner chair! In fact, when you are at rest, you are at your fat burning best! But stay with me, there's more to the story.

When you exercise the fuel mixture changes, progressively favoring carbohydrates as the work gets harder. During a brisk walk the mix shifts to about 50-50, equal portions of fat and carbs. During a slow jog, carbs begin to take over and account for about 60-70 percent of the mix. As the intensity of effort increases, the contribution of fat in the fuel mix decreases further, and when you work at the limits of your capacity, you will be burning purely carbohydrates as fuel.

Setting Tthe Record Straight

If a fuel mix that favors fat is as important as some so-called experts would have us believe, then your best bet would be to stay on the couch. And when it comes to exercise, the less you do the better, because the more you do, the more you depend on carbs as the fuel source. This suggests that exercising vigorously, or even moderately, would be a waste of time when it come to losing body fat. This, of course, flies in the face of common sense.

What's the answer? Fuel mix is essentially an irrelevant consideration. The key to losing body fat is the total number of calories you burn, and for lots of reasons it doesn't matter whether those calories come from fat or carbs. For example, at rest with a fuel mix that heavily favors the burning of fat, you will burn 60-75 calories per hour (the bigger and more muscular you are, the more calories it takes to keep you alive). Compare that with the 600-900 or more calories you will burn from an hour of exercise in which carbohydrate is the major fuel component. No contest!

To place this in another perspective, assume that the exercise you are doing burns a fuel mix of 45 percent fat and expends 300 calories per session. You would burn 135 calories of fat (300 x 45 percent) per session. But, if you shift to a "fat burning" workout at a much lower intensity (which hypes the fat portion of the fuel mix to 55 percent — proportional fat usage gets higher the closer you get to resting metabolism), you would expend only 220 calories in the same time period.

This means, despite the higher percentage of fat in the fuel mix, the overall number of fat calories you burn is now reduced to (220 x 55 percent) 121 calories. You actually burn less fat even though the fuel mix is more favorable. And more important, you burn substantially fewer calories overall with fat burning exercise. As you can see, when placed in an appropriate perspective, there's not much substance to the "fat burning" exercise approach.

This gets me back to my basic exercise advice. Do something you enjoy and do it every day. The more you do the more calories you will burn and the more fat you will lose. It's as simple as that.

Shifting from Carbs to Fat

Another issue that galls me is so-called "professionals" who give advice on how to shift the fuel mix away from carbs and toward fat by exercising first thing in the morning on an empty stomach when the blood sugar level is low. Although this seems perfectly logical, your body doesn't think so. In a nutshell, when you are low on carbs (a typical situation when on a crash diet) your body goes into a panic, because your central nervous system (brain and spinal column) can use only sugar (glucose) as fuel. Thus, when you are low on carbs your body finds itself in a desperate situation, because obviously you must continue to fuel the brain.

Let me repeat something I've said before, and will say again, because it's critical to understanding how to lose body fat and avoid losing muscle. When carbs are low, the body knows that it can break down the proteins that are in muscle and take the amino acids that make up the proteins to the liver where they can be converted to glucose. As such, when carbs are low in the body, the body does not shift to fat as fuel, it shifts to protein and begins breaking down muscle. Low carbs brings about cannibalization of the body, in other words, and this, of course, is best avoided. For more detailed information on this and related issues, please consult my book THE WEIGHT LOSS READER.

6. THE MAGIC BULLET?

As a typical American, you probably have been disappointed by a number of so called magic bullet weight loss schemes in the past. I don't have a magic bullet for you, but if you take a long range approach, I have something that's pretty close. It's pumping iron.

How can that be? Pumping iron (also called resistance training, or lifting weights) burns only a handful of calories per hour, hardly enough to make a dent in the 3500 calories of energy stored in just one pound of fat. In contrast, walking briskly at 4 mph burns about 400 calories per hour, and jogging comfortably at 6 mph burns about 725 calories per hour. Rowing, cycling, cross-country skiing and other well established aerobic exercises burn lots of calories, too, and generally these are the exercises of choice for those who are trying to trim down. And indeed they should be the core of an effective weight loss program (along with other moderate forms of aerobic exercise), because there are many benefits to be derived from a daily schedule of such rhythmic caloric burning exercise choices.

But if you don't include resistance training in your program, you are missing out on an important weight management tool. Resistance training builds muscle. This is important because muscle represents 40 percent or more of your total body weight, and it largely determines your metabolic rate. As we age we lose muscle mass, and as we do our metabolism declines. Conversely, increase your muscle mass and you will increase your metabolism.

The Numbers Game

The implications of increasing your metabolism are quite substantial in the long run. Consider, for example that a typical resting metabolic rate is about 1 calorie (kcal) per minute. For men it will be higher (1.0 - 1.4 calorie/minute) because men are larger, and the opposite is true for women (.75 - 1.0 calorie/min). At 1 calorie per minute, you would expend approximately 1440 calories per day. This is the core of your metabolism. Add to this the energy required to digest food, and the energy you expend moving around and exercising, and you can increase your daily caloric expenditure by hundreds of calories.

Bolster the muscle mass on your body and you can increase your resting metabolism. For example, let's assume you work out vigorously for one year and add several pounds of muscle to your frame. In so doing, you might increase your metabolic rate from 1 calorie per minute to 1.03 calories per minute. Big deal, you say. All that work for a lousy .03 calorie/minute boost. Hardly worth the effort, is it? I think it is. Let's take a look.

You will be burning that extra .03 calories per minute every minute you are alive. It's programmed into your system, in other words, and there's nothing you have to do to get the benefit. Given a long range view, you could expend an extra 15,768 calories per year (.03 x 60 minutes x 24 hours x 365 days). Each pound of fat contains 3500 calories, and this means you could lose 4.5 pounds of body fat simply by boosting your metabolism. It is assumed, of course, that you don't increase your caloric intake by the same amount. But if you did, it's nice to know that you could be eating lots more without gaining weight. You would be providing yourself a nice cushion, and an increased margin of error that could prevent future weight gain.

Aerobics

Aerobic exercise also contributes some nice numbers. Walk daily for 30 minutes and expend 200 calories per session, or 1,400 calories per week, and 73,000 calories for one year. That adds up to 20.8 pounds of body fat.

But what happens if you can't walk daily, because you get too busy? You lose the aerobic component entirely and probably will gain weight unless you restrict your caloric intake. In contrast, if you work out one day per week you probably will sustain your newly formed muscles quite well. This is the advantage of weight training. It exerts a chronic effect, helping you 24 hours a day. Aerobic exercise exerts an acute effect, boosting your metabolism only while you participate (and for a while afterwards as you recover).

Obviously, there are advantages to both aerobic exercise and resistance training, and therefore it's smart to do both. An ideal approach would be to engage in weight training 2 or 3 days a week, and do aerobic exercise on the alternate days.

Women and Dumbbells

The concept of combining women and dumbbells is as old as time. Ask most women and they'll tell you they've lived much of their lives with dumbbells, dating them and even marrying them. Women know the ins and outs of dumbbells, in other words. But when it comes to the other kind of dumbbell, the solid iron kind, women are less familiar, and probably a little intimidated. They view weight training as a male thing, a foreign concept that if pursued will rob them of their femininity.

This is not true, but it's easy to see how this misperception came about. All you have to do is look at competitors in female bodybuilding contests. Many are as muscular as men, some even more so. But these few examples are extreme, and they are the product of years of intense training, and, often at the elite level, the use of masculinizing drugs (anabolic steroids).

Most female bodybuilders, however, go about their training without drugs, and their bodies respond beautifully. The prime example is Linda Hamilton, the actress who starred in the movie, *Terminator*. She was lean, pleasingly muscular, but clearly feminine. This is the goal of most female bodybuilders — very few aspire to outdo the men in muscularity. I must add, however, that in order to become as lean as Hamilton you would have to combine a very strict diet with the weight training.

When women lift weights, they get stronger and they develop increased muscle mass. (See Part IV for more detail.) But because they have a limited supply of testosterone in their system (thank goodness), their bodies do not respond to weight training in the same way as the male body. Results are limited, but that's good, because the feminine physique is sustained while muscle is being added. You won't, in other words, wake up one morning after a tough workout and see Arnold Schwarzenneger's body in the mirror. You couldn't accomplish this even if it were your goal, so you can relax. Also, because women tend to store much of their fat just below the skin (subcutaneous fat), even with added muscle mass there still will be a desirable level of softness in the physique.

It's Hard Work

I am a strong proponent of moderate exercise, and I encourage finding an exercise that is fun and comfortable and doing it every day. Since this is my philosophy, am I not being inconsistent by encouraging people to train with weights, a very demanding form of exercise. I must admit that if you want to add muscle, it takes a lot of hard work. You can't go to the gym and merely go through the motions. You must challenge your muscles, overloading them, forcing them to do more than they want to. This is because your muscles will resist your efforts to make them grow. They are programmed that way. Here's why.

Ironically, your body hates muscle because it is high maintenance tissue that gobbles up a lot of energy. Since your body's goal is survival (and survival is dependent upon having enough energy available), the last thing your body wants is a bunch of hungry muscle sitting around devouring your energy supplies. This, of course, is a holdover from our earlier evolution as a species when food was scarce and our survival depended on the judicious use of energy. Today, consuming enough energy on a regular basis is hardly a concern for most of us. Still, the body is programmed to think in the old way. Maybe thousands of years from now this may change, but for now we are stuck with this age-old perspective.

Although building new muscle takes considerable effort, holding on to what you have doesn't. And this may be enough for you if you are satisfied with where you are right now. You would be using weight training as a preventive measure, in other words, anticipating the loss of muscle with age if you don't take steps to avoid it. In this case, a gentle workout, going through the motions without pushing the muscles too hard, will accomplish your goal.

In this way, my argument in favor of moderate exercise holds up. Again, you have a choice. You can perform the intensive workouts in the gym required to build muscle. Or, you can work out in a more comfortable fashion knowing that you are benefiting your body by preserving the muscle mass you currently have.

Getting Started

Weight training isn't rocket science, but there's a lot to consider. (That's why I've included a separate and comprehensive section on strength and muscle building issues.) With this in mind, the best way to get started is with the guidance of a personal trainer (PT). A PT will demonstrate the variety of exercises needed for a comprehensive program and how to perform them properly. You also will learn how much weight to use in each exercise, how to breath when lifting, how long to rest between exercises, how many repetitions ("reps) to perform and how many sets of reps are best, how to progress, etc.

The best place to find a PT is at your local commercial gym or YMCA. If you need motivation, you may want a PT to guide you through every workout. Or, if you are self motivated, three or four sessions with a PT may be enough. PT's generally change from $30 to $50 per hour. You can be trained at the gym, or in your home if you have adequate equipment.

Where's the best place to train? That depends on you. Home training offers convenience and privacy. But you have to invest in the equipment and have the space. Training at the gym is nice, because there's lots of others there doing the same thing, and this is stimulating. You also have a wide array of exercise equipment to use which adds variety to your program. But the gym may offer restricted hours, and there is travel time to consider. (See chapter 14 for more detail.)

In my case, I try to get to the gym at least once a week. I thoroughly enjoy the mix of clients working out there. I see elderly women heaving 8 pound dumbbells, working out side by side with bruisers pumping out reps with 250 pounds in the bench press. Everyone is polite and accommodating, and it's clear that everyone feels welcome. But when I can't get to the gym, I have enough home equipment to do most exercises. It's nice having both options.

Regardless of where you train, pumping iron is a wonderful activity that will help you manage your weight, and will help you cope with the natural physical deterioration brought on by aging. If you haven't discovered the benefits of weight training, now's the time to explore. You're never too old, but if you are over age 35, check first with your doctor to make certain there are no underlying health problems.

Spot Reduction Gadgets — The Billion Dollar Fraud

When I log on to my computer to check my e-mail, or tear into a new batch of letters from readers, one thing is certain. I will be asked my opinion of the latest exercise gadget. Throughout the day infomercials on TV tout the extraordinary benefits of the Flab Fighter, the Stomach Stomper, or the Pooch Puncher. Viewers are told how it takes only five minutes a day to remove inches of unwanted flab from the waistline, the hips or the thighs — all in just one month. Success cases are interviewed. They, of course, have a body like Cindy Crawford and claim that just a short while ago they were fat and sloppy and afraid to appear in public wearing anything that was the least bit revealing. For the guys, there's Rock Biceps who displays his cut-to-ribbons abdominal muscles and swears he never sweats when he exercises on his Tummy Trouncer.

Such ads suggest a magic bullet, an elixir, a quick fix for the layers of flab that depress us when we look in the mirror. A little voice deep inside tells us such ads are too good to be true. But we want them to be true, and as we watch the ads we see that hundreds of gadgets are being sold right before our very eyes. Quickly, we get the feeling we are the only ones on earth who are not jumping on board. Desperate we pick up the phone and commit to four painless monthly payments of $39.95 each.

Six weeks later the exercise gadget we ordered arrives. Somehow it doesn't look like it did on TV. Indeed, it's nothing but a few pieces of metal piping plugged together, padded, and painted black. It doesn't feel like you thought it would it either. It's flimsy and stiff and doesn't move the way the Cindy Crawford look alike made it move on TV. You lie down on the floor and crawl into it and try to make it do something. You tug and pull and finally get it moving, rocking precariously back and forth. You go through the motions for a minute or two, feeling nothing.

You come back later for another workout. Maybe the lack of

effect is due to your lack of experience and knowledge. You rock and roll again, this time for five minutes. No effect. The next day you try again. Still nothing. How, you ask yourself, can they justify charging this much for this useless piece of junk?

The answer is air time. Infomercials cost a fortune to produce and air on TV. Precious little money goes into product development, while the lion's share goes into marketing. You have been had.

An Honest Effort

Disillusioned, you wish you had your money back. But you are understandably reluctant to take action and go through all the frustration of cashing in on the money back guarantee, because you've been here before. A number of times, in fact, with crash diets, bogus weight loss supplements and the like. But you've had enough and this time you intend to see it through and get your money back.

After 17 phone calls you finally get through to a real live person. You explain your dilemma. They listen attentively and say they understand completely. They apologize and then confess a bit of confusion on their part, because you are the first person to complain out of the thousands of satisfied customers. Then, they ask you. Did you put forth an honest effort? Did you follow the instructions to the letter and do your workouts daily for one month? They already know the answer. No. Of course you didn't. This is followed by a pep talk.

Feeling a bit guilty you hang up with the promise that you will fulfill your obligation and use the machine faithfully everyday for one month. You also are bolstered from the pep talk and feel confident that when the month is up you will look like Cindy Crawford. A week later you find an excuse for not exercising. In two weeks your list of excuses has grown. After three weeks you quit and take the machine to the attic and toss it on the pile with all the other pieces of exercise equipment you've purchased over the years. Someday soon, you vow, you will have a big yard sale and recoup some of your losses.

What If?

But what if you had iron-clad will power, relentless drive and unwavering determination, and you faithfully used your Tushy Toner every day for five years? Would you look like Cindy Crawford? Sorry. If you made no other changes in your life (switching to a healthy low-fat and low-sugar diet, for example, and including legitimate forms of exercise in your lifestyle), you would still look virtually the same. Here's why.

In order to lose body fat you have to put your body into a negative caloric balance. You must burn off more calories than you take in. When using one of these exercise gadgets for a few minutes daily, you burn very few calories — perhaps as many as 10-20 in five minutes. Such a ridiculously small caloric expenditure can easily be overwhelmed by a piece of chewing gum, or a few extra bites at the dinner table. What's more, in order to lose only one pound of body fat, you must create a deficit of 3500 calories!

And even if you were able to burn more total calories while using one of these machines, you'd never accomplish your goal. This is the crux of the matter. Exercising your abdominal muscles may strengthen those muscles, but it does absolutely nothing to remove the layer of fat which covers the area. The abdominal muscles, in other words, cannot reach out and grab the fat which covers them and use it as fuel. On the contrary, body fat is mobilized (set free) symmetrically from all over the body during exercise. You may, for example, during sit-ups and crunches (partial sit-ups which exercise the abdominal muscles more effectively) be using fat which has been mobilized from the arms, the back or the face.

This is a well established principle in exercise physiology. Put another way, there is no such thing as spot reduction. You cannot pinpoint an area of your anatomy and decide you will selectively lose fat from that area. No amount of sit-ups and crunches will reduce fat from your waistline. No amount of leg extensions will reduce fat from your thighs.

The Only Bona Fide Approach

If your goal is a smaller waist, you must create a negative caloric balance. The best way to do this is with a combination of restricted caloric intake, increased caloric output through exercise, and as stated above, maintaining and possibly increasing your muscle mass.

When selecting exercises to perform, it's smart to go with those that burn the most calories per minute. These typically are so called locomotor exercises which move the entire body — walking, jogging, swimming, etc. As you create a negative caloric balance, fat will be lost from the entire body, and, of course, eventually fat will be lost from the areas you desire. The exception to this rule is the stubbornness of lower body fat in females, which lags way behind fat loss from other areas of the body.

Research studies have compared the effects of hundreds of sit-ups per day with a walking/jogging program. The results showed essentially no change in abdominal obesity from the sit-ups over many weeks, compared with a reduction in abdominal obesity associated with walking and jogging. Why? The sit-ups burned only a handful of calories per day. This is because the abdominal muscles used in sit-ups are quite small and cannot burn many calories no matter how hard they are worked. In contrast, when using the large muscles of the legs, trunk, hips and buttocks during walking and jogging, the number of calories expended is many times greater.

When doing all those sit-ups, it's possible to mold your abdominal muscles into a rock hard mass. But no one will be able to tell, because the layer of fat overlying the muscles will be intact and will hide the hardness of the muscles underneath.

Too Many Calories to be True

While it's true that aerobic exercise can burn lots of calories in a workout, beware of outrageous claims that are intended to lure you into buying a piece of exercise equipment.

A Body Shop reader sent me an ad which claimed you could burn over 1000 calories per hour while pedalling a stationary cycle. Is this possible? The answer is yes. Under some circumstances, it may be "possible." Is it likely that the everyday person who buys this equipment will burn this many calories, or anything close to it? The answer is no. Let's look at the facts.

A highly trained cyclist would probably have a maximal energy capacity of approximately 20-25 calories per minute on the bicycle. But it is possible to tap only a portion of that capacity over a prolonged period of time, and over an hour, a trained cyclist can probably tap about

80 percent. This would result in an energy expenditure of 960-1200 calories over one hour.

This demonstrates that the ad possesses a thread of truth, at least for a trained cyclist.

The story is strikingly different for the average person. First, the maximal energy capacity will be about 15 calories per minute — for young men, and a little lower (about 12) for young women. For older persons, the maximal capacity would be substantially less than 12-15 calories per minute.

Second, the average person probably won't have the stamina or tenacity to continue pedalling for a whole hour. But if they could go for an hour, it would be difficult for them to sustain an intensity of more than about 60 percent of maximal. This means that over one hour the average young male would expend 60% x 15 calories = 9 calories x 60min = 540 calories. An average young woman would expend less, and older persons would expend quite a bit less.

The ad also says: "Just 12 minutes, 3 times a week is all it takes to improve your cardiovascular fitness on the..." This limited approach is probably a more realistic to exercise for the average American than a whole hour, but each 12 minute session would result in the burning of only about 108 calories for the average young male. That's equivalent to the number of calories in a banana.

The ad obviously is intended to appeal to the desire of most Americans to lose body fat, and lose it easily. First, there is emphasis on burning off 1000 calories per hour. Then, the emphasis shifts to the need for only three 12 minutes sessions per week. Unfortunately, such sessions, burning at the rate of 108 calories per workout, three days per week, would take nearly 11 weeks to burn off one pound of body fat (3500 calories). This assumes, of course that you don't wipe out your efforts with a slight dietary indiscretion, like eating an extra piece of bread each day, or an apple. I don't think I need to tell you what effect eating a chocolate candy bar would have. Clearly, this is not what buyers have in mind.

With all this said, I don't mean to discourage you from purchasing a piece of home exercise equipment. But before you do, please consider that the vast majority of home exercise equipment goes unused. There are many reason for this, but a major one is that buyers have unreasonable expectations of what they are going to get out of it.

The Latest Scam

Scenes from commercial gyms back in the 1950's showed clients with a wide leather belt around their waist that was attached to a machine. When the machine was turned on, the belt vibrated and shook the client. Supposedly, the vibrating belt caused body fat to miraculously disappear. Did it? Of course not, and eventually the vibrating belt went the way of the Edsel.

This doesn't mean that Americans have wised up. Far from it. Americans have simply shifted their attention from one foolish scheme to the next, hoping for the elusive magic bullet that will remove excess body fat without effort. As long as this desire exists, there will be a robust market for bogus cures.

In addition to the vibrating belt, there are wraps that tightly encircle the body from neck to toe. The pressure of the wrap is supposed to melt inches of fat away in just a matter of hours. There are creams that promise to remove fat and cellulite when rubbed into the skin. There are herbal concoctions that are supposed to burn fat while you sleep. The list goes on.

The above items are passive interventions and require no effort on the part of the user. Without effort, there can be no effect, and, thus, they can best be characterized as "too good to be true."

The Electric Belt

When it comes to downright foolishness, I never would have believed that anything could trump the vibrating belt. Well, there is something, and it's sweeping the nation. It's the electric belt. Manufacturers claim: Wrap it around your waist and "presto!" — low level electric currents penetrate into your muscles, causing them to burn fat. All you have to do is sit on the couch while the fat disappears.

Recently, I examined one of these belts. I unpacked it, put it on a willing volunteer and cranked up the current. The volunteer reported an irritating tingling sensation, but nothing more. There was absolutely no effect that could impact body fat to any greater degree than a vibrating belt, the body wrap, or cellulite creams.

The premise behind the belt is that muscles respond to electric currents and they contract. This is true, but as far as the electric belt is concerned that's as far as the truth goes. The current that is applied from the belt to the underlying muscles is so low that it doesn't cause any movement. A few muscle fibers may contract, but not enough to amount to anything greater than the effect you might produce by blinking your eyes.

If the current were stronger it would produce jerky movements that would be very uncomfortable and the muscles would fatigue quickly and potentially be thrust into a cramp. Introducing a stronger electrical current into the body also could be dangerous. Highly trained physical therapists may use electric currents to stimulate muscles to reduce atrophy when the nerves have been damaged. But this takes skill and professional experience and the purpose is not to burn calories. If it were, there would still be only a very tiny expenditure of energy, even though the current would be magnitudes stronger than the electric belt.

The most compelling evidence that the belt is bogus was packed in the box with the belt. There was a plastic bottle that contained a supplement that hypes the metabolism. (Such supplements do more harm than good and are best avoided.) There also was a pamphlet that told users to cut calories. A reasonable interpretation could be that if you take the supplement and slash your caloric intake, you may accomplish something in spite of wasting your time using the electric belt.

How Do They Get Away With It?

Unfortunately, many Americans believe that if something is advertised to the public it must be true. Otherwise, the government would put a stop to it. Wrong! In general, the only way an advertiser of weight loss schemes or exercise equipment is going to get into trouble with governing bodies is if they make medical claims. Otherwise, there is a hand's-off approach and advertisers can say almost anything and get away with it.

And even when the government decides to crack down, it takes so long to investigate claims and bring a bogus company to justice, the owner would have plenty of time to sell tens of thousands of units and then simply go out of business. Later, they are likely to pop up again somewhere else with a new product backed by incredible claims that cannot be supported by scientific facts.

One of the great benefits of being an American is that our government allows us to choose what we believe is best for us, even if that choice is absurd—choosing to smoke cigarettes, for example, or purchasing an electric belt for the purpose of losing body fat. Regarding the latter choice, it is testimony to the accuracy of the old saying "a fool and his money are soon separated." It's a jungle out there. Buyer beware!

PART II

EXERCISE BASICS

7. THE ABC's OF FITNESS

To this point, I have emphasized the value of moderate exercise and the fact that it promotes health nearly as well as vigorous running, rowing or cycling. The key word here is "nearly." Moderate exercise is nearly as healthful as fitness producing exercise, but not quite. Thus, if you want to go for the whole enchilada and adopt a fitness-producing program, here are some basics upon which to build.

The Americanization of Fitness

Fitness has been on our minds ever since President John F. Kennedy gasped at the implications of a research report which showed American children to be less fit and more fat than European kids. To set things right, he established the President's Council on Physical Fitness. (Later, in the Nixon administration, it was changed to the President's Council on Physical Fitness and Sports.)

The result? Forty years later, the gap between American kids and European kids is laughable. We are so much fatter and less fit, it would take a miracle to bridge the gap.

Ironically, Americans know more about fitness than Europeans, and we have many more fitness opportunities. We are bursting at the seams with books, TV shows, infomercials, gyms, sporting goods stores, high-tech home exercise equipment, personal trainers, and a legion of fitness gurus. Europeans as a rule don't have all this stuff. Instead, as the Nike slogan says, they "Just do it!"

They incorporate physical activity into their daily lives, squeezing it into every nook and cranny, maximizing stolen minutes for exercise. Not for exercise's sake, of course. Rather, walking to the store for a purpose, or enjoying a stroll around the local lake or along the river, rather than stretching-out in front of the TV. Europeans don't seek fitness, in other words, any more than a fish seeks water. It's simply there, as part of their lives.

In fairness to us, we have a larger number of highly fit citizens than other countries. We have our die hards who train like athletes, running road races, climbing mountains and the like. But we also have a huge portion of the population at the lower end of the couch potato scale — far more than the Europeans. We are a nation of fitness extremists, while the Europeans are content to reside mostly in the middle.

Fitness Defined

A wonderful thing about the human body is that it has the capacity to adjust to the stresses placed upon it. If you run long distances every day, you get better at it and each run becomes less stressful. You improve your fitness, which means you improve your capacity to perform physically. This, unfortunately, works in the opposite direction as well. If you are in a hospital bed for a prolonged period of time, without any physical stresses, your body will lose its capacity to perform. You gain or lose fitness, then, depending upon the demands you place on your body.

Technically, fitness entails a number of capacities. There is muscular endurance — the capacity of a muscle or group of muscles to continually contract before fatigue sets in. An example is doing 50 push-ups. Strength is a component, as is flexibility. But the aspect which captures the most attention is aerobic fitness. This was thrust into the forefront when Dr. Kenneth Cooper published his book, *Aerobics* (which means "with oxygen"), back in the late 1960's, touting the health benefits of aerobic fitness, and how best to achieve it.

Physiology of Aerobic Fitness 101

Increasing aerobic fitness requires a complex interplay of many physiologic systems of the body for the purpose of helping the muscles use as much oxygen as possible to produce energy during exercise. The more energy your muscles have available, the greater your endurance and the more exercise you can do.

To acquire aerobic fitness, you must enhance the capacity of two major components. The "central" component controls the ability of the body to deliver oxygen to the working muscles. Oxygen delivery is determined by the capacity of the heart to pump blood, and the capacity of the blood to carry oxygen.

The second component is the "peripheral" component. Just because you can deliver a large amount of oxygen in the blood doesn't necessarily mean it will get into the muscles and be used by the muscles to produce energy. In order to move oxygen from the blood into the working muscles, the blood must get close to the muscles through tiny vessels called capillaries. Once inside the muscle cell, the oxygen is used to produce energy by special metabolic machinery (called the mitochondria). Without an adequate peripheral component (well developed capillaries and an adequate number of mitochondria), the oxygen in the blood can go largely unused by the muscles — even though the muscles are crying out in need of more oxygen.

The Stimulus Variables

In an aerobically fit individual, both the central and peripheral components are well developed. In order to develop both components and produce fitness, you must successfully manipulate the stimulus variables, which include intensity (how hard you work), frequency (how often), duration (how long) and mode (type of exercise). Each variable must meet a minimal standardized expectation if you are going to be successful.

Research performed in the 1950's demonstrated that a threshold exits for intensity, below which no fitness gains occur. That threshold is in the neighborhood of 70% of the maximal heart rate. This means a younger person (20 years of age) with a maximal heart rate of approximately 200 beats per minute (bpm) (estimated from 220 - age) would have to exercise at a heart rate of <u>at least</u> 140 bpm. The exercise heart rate determined with consideration of age, exercise history, goals, etc., is called the "target" heart rate. Further research has demonstrated that the harder you work the more fitness you produce, and thus intensity (governed by the magnitude of the target heart rate) is considered to be the key stimulus variable.

That's not to say the other stimulus variables are not important. They are. You must exercise at least three days a week, and preferably more. The minimal exercise session should be 20 minutes in length, and preferably more. And the type of exercise you choose (the mode) must involve major muscle groups of the body, and must be rhythmic in nature. Jogging, of course, fits the bill perfectly and is the kind of exercise that comes to mind when most of us think of aerobic fitness.

As your fitness improves, you will have to push harder in order to drive your heart rate up into the target zone. Pushing harder guarantees continued progress. If, on the other hand, you are content with your level of fitness, a maintenance program can be adopted in which you work less hard simply to stabilize your gains.

All this seems like pretty straight-forward stuff, and it is. So straight-forward, in fact, that it forms the backbone of the well established fitness dogma which dictates how we think about exercise. If I want to start a successful exercise/fitness program, I must adhere to these guidelines. If I don't, I won't increase my fitness.

Fitness is Task Specific

The peripheral factors operate within specific muscles. When you cycle, for example, you develop the peripheral factors located in the quadriceps (thigh) muscles. When you swim, the upper body muscles are employed to do the work and the peripheral factors are developed in the arms and shoulders. For this reason, if you should decide to switch to swimming after a year of cycling (or jogging, or any exercise which emphasizes the legs), you would encounter a difficult transition, because the peripheral factors established in the legs from cycling or jogging would not be present in the arms and shoulders.

Thus, although you would be able to pump large amounts of blood from the heart, and transport large amounts of oxygen in the blood, getting the oxygen directly to the working muscles would be a problem because of a lack of capillaries. Also, even if you could get the oxygen into the muscle cells, because there are not sufficient mitochondria present, the oxygen would go unused. You would be unfit for swimming, in other words, even though you are highly fit for cycling or jogging.

Aerobic Fitness Versus Endurance

When it comes to building aerobic fitness, intensity is the key ingredient. Running two miles as hard as you can will build more fitness than jogging slowly for six miles. But when it comes to endurance, the situation flip-flops. Long slow training is better.

Endurance means stamina, the ability to keep going at a brisk pace. In technical terms, endurance is defined as the ability to exercise at a high percentage of your maximal capacity (your fitness) for a prolonged period of time. For example, John may be able to work at 85 percent of his capacity for more than two hours. He has high endurance. Bill, on the other hand, can work at 85 percent for only thirty minutes. If Bill runs for two hours, he will have to lower his pace to only 70 percent of his capacity. Bill has lower endurance. What's more, Bill may not be able to run for the full two hours, regardless of how slowly he runs, because his training does not favor the enhanced endurance required for prolonged exercise. The key here is that fitness and endurance are not necessarily the same things, and therefore the training requirements differ. This is yet another example of the importance of specificity of training.

In order to ready yourself for a prolonged endurance event, you must gradually increase the amount of exercise you impose on your body. Recent research supports duration (how long you exercise) as more important than frequency (how often). Two 60-minute workouts per week were found to improve endurance to a greater degree than three 40-minute workouts. This occurred even though the total exercise time per week was the same 120 minutes and total distance covered was the same.

You may be wondering, why not simply run long distances every day and get the best of both (frequency and duration) worlds? The answer is, such an approach would soon cause overtraining. You would suffer from chronic fatigue and may injure yourself. In addition, you want to include fitness producing exercise to promote your overall capacity, because an improved performance will be a combination of a high aerobic capacity, plus the ability to exercise at a high percentage of your capacity.

The bottom line when it comes to training is, you must overload the body. When it comes to endurance, longer but less frequent workouts overload the body's endurance more than more frequent but shorter workouts. When it comes to aerobic capacity (fitness), shorter and more intense workouts will be more effective, and interval training is the way to go.

Interval Training

Interval training was designed to maximize intensity of effort during training sessions. There are many different types of interval training approaches, and there is an entire science that has evolved that deals with the ins and outs. A basic exercise physiology text will be an excellent primer for anyone interested in pursuing this form of training.

In a nutshell, interval training entails demanding bouts of exercise alternated with brief periods of rest. The length and intensity of the exercise bouts will dictate what energetic system of the body is impacted. To improve aerobic fitness, half-mile intervals are a good way to go.

As a reference point, take your best one-mile run time and divide it in half. If you can run one mile in six minutes, your first interval half-mile would require 3 minutes to complete. This would not be an exhausting bout, but would impose an intensity of approximately 90% of full capacity. The rest interval is the same length as the half-mile run, or 3 minutes, during which you walk to recover. You, of course, would not fully recover in 3 minutes and would carry over some of the fatigue of the first bout into the second, thus increasing the intensity of the second bout to nearly 100%. All remaining bouts would be performed at 100%. The limited rest periods increase intensity without altering the 3 minute time frame for the running and rest intervals.

Gradually build up until you can perform six interval half-mile bouts. This is highly demanding training and cannot be performed more than about once a week. Engaging in interval training too often can lead to overtraining (See Chapter 34).

The Exercise Prescription

The core component of cardiac rehabilitation is promoting aerobic fitness, because the heart patient must increase fitness in order to return to society as a fully functioning member. Fitness improves the capacity of the heart to perform, and with heart disease that capacity may be compromised. During a heart attack, for example, part of the heart muscle may have died which means the remaining portions of the heart must be strengthened to compensate, and the strengthening process entails aerobic fitness exercise.

Be careful not to misinterpret what I'm saying. Strengthening the heart pays dividends to a heart patient whose heart has been compromised due to illness. But strengthening the heart does not necessarily make the heart healthier. The health of the heart is dictated in large measure by the health of the vessels that feed it, which in turn is dictated mainly by the diet. A diet high in saturated fat leads to an increase in serum cholesterol which clogs the arteries and restricts blood flow.

I point this out because many fitness buffs like to argue that vigorous exercise makes the heart larger and stronger, and therefore you must exercise vigorously if you are going to have a healthy heart. In response, I argue back that your heart can be as large as a volleyball with walls several inches thick, but if your arteries are compromised you cannot furnish sufficient oxygen and nutrients to nourish hungry heart tissue. You can, in other words, have a huge and powerful army, but if you don't feed it, it soon will be impotent.

Heart patients need exercise, but because they are at high risk of dying from a heart attack, prescribing an effective exercise routine is a bit tricky. This is where target heart rate takes center stage. Careful evaluation of the patient (usually through a diagnostic treadmill stress test) is required to establish a target heart rate that will provide a sufficient stimulus for improving fitness, but without unnecessarily placing the patient at risk. A high-wire balance act is required, in other words, and the science had better be pretty darned good. The same is true for pulmonary rehabilitation programs, and working with diabetics, etc. All in all, the science of exercise makes a great contribution to promoting health and it accomplishes a great deal.

Use Heart Rate to Compare Modes Of Exercise

An often-asked question is, what's better, cycling or running? Cycling and running are two vastly different exercises that are difficult to equate (How many miles of cycling equals one mile of running, for example?). They can be roughly equated, however, and the best way is to match the heart rates and the amount of time you exercise (the duration). If your three mile runs require 30 minutes and your heart rate is 150 bpm during running, do the same while cycling — pedal at a heart rate of 150 bpm for 30 minutes. This can be a little tricky, because when cycling your heart rate will be lower when coasting down hills, but may be higher when pumping uphill. But in general, if your heart rate is in the same ball park for approximately the same period of time, the fitness benefits you seek will be about the same. This also is true for other fitness activities, like swimming, rowing, stair-stepping, etc.

A Walk/Jog Program for Beginners

It's important to ease into a fitness-producing exercise program, especially one that involves jogging, because jogging is so demanding on the body in many ways. A good approach is the walk/jog in which you alternate back and forth between walking and jogging. Begin with a short overall distance of, say, one-half mile. Start with walking 100 paces, then jogging about 25, then walking 100 paces again. Continue until you have covered your pre-set distance. Gradually, add approximately one-quarter mile per week, until you reach a total of 2 miles. Next, gradually increase your jogging interval, adding 25 paces per week, until you are alternating 100 walking paces and 100 jogging. After a few weeks, begin reducing the walking interval by 25 paces per week, until you are jogging 2 miles without walking.

This approach is a bit of overkill, I admit. But since you are going to be exercising the rest of your life, it won't hurt to be conservative on the way in and be certain to avoid orthopedic problems that are so common among joggers. If, eventually, jogging two miles at a time doesn't satisfy you, add distance at a rate of no more than one-quarter mile per month. You also can play with the speed if you like, jogging faster at some points, then slowing to a crawl at others.

Over the years, I have used many approaches to jogging. The older I get, the more I like the walk/jog approach, because it is more user-friendly on the joints of my legs and hips. A walk/jog approach is not just for beginners, in other words. Jogging up hills is not as demanding on joints as jogging on the level or downhill. So, I look for hills to jog, then walk down, splitting the level parts between walking and jogging. My goal is to simply maintain a reasonable level of fitness, and to control my weight. The beauty of a walk/jog approach is I can work hard if I want to by pushing myself up the hills. Or I can be more relaxed. I allow how I feel to dictate the pace of my workout.

The Bottom Line

If you want to produce aerobic fitness, there is an established process to follow, and it involves the stimulus variables of intensity, duration, frequency and mode. Drive your heart rate up into the target zone and keep it there for at least 20 minutes. Do this a minimum of three times per week, using large muscle activities, like jogging, cycling, swimming, etc. As your fitness improves, you must push harder to raise your heart rate into the target zone. As a rule of thumb, the harder you work, the more aerobic fitness you will produce.

8. WHAT KIND OF EXERCISER ARE YOU?

Over the years I have observed lots of folks exercising, and I've categorized those who exercise vigorously for the purpose of promoting increased fitness into various types. There is overlap among types, and rarely are individuals purely one type. In addition, your type can change as you enter different phases of life. Mine certainly has.

If you are a regular exerciser, I thought it might be fun to examine the following categories and see which ones fit your approach. Hopefully, if you see yourself, perhaps what I've written will provide food for thought. If you are not an exerciser, see if you can identify the traits of friends who pound the pavement and try to convince you to come along.

The "Love-Its"

The love-its truly enjoy their exercise — moving their body, sweating, and challenging themselves. And while they appreciate the effects of exercise — looking and feeling better, being healthy, the sense of accomplishment, etc., this is not their primary motivation.

Love-its work hard, but they are not compulsive about it. No pulse-taking, no stopwatches, no logging distances, no hysterics associated with having to miss a workout, etc. They make time in their schedule for exercise, but it's not like paying dues. Rather, it's more of a reward and something they look forward to.

I recently watched a large group of women in a jazzercise class, and I think many of them were love-its. There was upbeat music, an obviously well qualified instructor, all sorts of exercise equipment (mats, dumbbells, large balls, elastic bands, etc.), and great camaraderie among participants. Their facial expressions showed effort, but there also were lots of smiles and giggles along the way.

Love-its often participate in vigorous physical activity, but they don't consider it as exercise *per se*. Those who regularly play full court basketball, for example, play because they love to play. Running up and down the court, jumping, pivoting, and playing defense demands tremendous effort, expends lots of energy and promotes aerobic fitness. The love of the game keeps them coming back, not the need to exercise. The same is true for cyclists, serious rollerbladers, singles tennis players, etc.

When I lived in Borden, Indiana, and there were hiking trails literally right across the road from my home, hiking was my exercise of choice. During those years, I so loved taking off with my dog, I'd be gone for hours exploring the area, trudging up and down the knobs of southern Indiana. I never bothered to question whether my hiking was as productive as the jogging I had given up. It didn't matter. Even if it weren't, the fun factor more than made up the difference.

If you are among the "love-its" you have it all. I don't have to encourage you to keep up the good work because, as you know, there is no work involved.

The "Got-tos"

Got-tos have a neutral attitude about exercise. They take steps to "sugar-coat" it to make it palatable, preferring user-friendly exercises and group classes, trying to mimic the love-its. When they are actually involved in exercise they don't mind it, but they don't necessarily look forward to it either. It's an intelligent commitment that pays dividends in the form of improved health, looking better and feeling better, and this is the key motivation. Got-tos respond well to motivational schemes (make a pact with a partner, accumulate reward points for exercising, then treat yourself, etc.).

The "Begrudgers"

Begrudgers dislike exercise, but do it anyway for the benefits. To them it's a required inconvenience. They like the way exercise makes them feel, and they usually feel best when the workout is over and they have paid their dues for the day. Begrudgers are highly disciplined, highly motivated, likely to be Type A personalities, and they possess considerable willpower. They're serious about exercise and rarely miss a workout.

Begrudgers tend to choose traditional fitness activities, like jogging, swimming laps, rowing, stationary cycling, etc., which maximize the benefits per minute invested. They closely adhere to the rules of fitness training (drive the heart rate up into the fitness-producing zone and keep it there for at least 20-minutes without stopping) and do not consider non-fitness-producing activities as bona fide exercise.

Some individuals criss-cross back and forth between being a love-it, a got-to, and a begrudger. They pay their dues by performing "real" exercise like jogging three or four days a week, then play and have fun by rollerblading or gardening on their "off" days. They earn the right to play by doing what they are supposed to do during their real workouts.

The "Strivers"

Strivers set goals and train like athletes. Often they are former competitive athletes who don't know any other way to exercise. Every workout is a challenge to push harder, longer, and faster. They plan their workouts in detail and keep an eye on the stop watch. There is ample interval work, sprint training, grueling long distances, punishing hill climbing and the like.

Strivers tend to take for granted the health benefits of exercise and seek something more. Their reward is an improved performance, and they demand to always do better. They probably never stop to think about whether they love exercise or hate it, because it's part of them. I suspect that sometimes they love it — when things are going well and fitness is increasing and goals are being met. At such times, training is close to blissful. At other times when injury strikes and training is difficult, if not painful, hatred sets in, but they keep on keeping on.

Most of the pack at the Kentucky Derby mini-marathon held in Louisville and other sponsored road races are strivers out to improve their personal best performance. All are aware that they have little or no chance of winning. There can be only one winner, and the winner is likely to be a current young competitive athlete at the top of his or her game who turns in a performance that is clearly out of reach. Even so, road races are thrilling — the crowds, competing with yourself and thousands of others, the potential for a personal record.

The "Compulsives"

Compulsives have lost control of their exercise habit. It controls them and they are addicted. Exercise takes on a religious quality that must be satisfied. If not, there is a hefty dose of guilt often accompanied by depression. I have seen compulsives train with severe injuries, their faces contorted in pain, limping over long distances. I have done this.

As I have already mentioned, I was addicted to exercise and was at the extreme end of the "compulsive" continuum. Years ago I was so addicted to exercise that I had to exercise every day or else. Since I feared confronting the "or else," I exercised without fail.

I needed a constant update on my progress, and for years I entered every road race that came along, and I was bitterly disappointed if my performance wasn't up to the standard I set for myself. Missing a goal was a tragedy which forced me to train harder and longer. And when I hit that goal I didn't enjoy it, but instead immediately set another goal that was more ambitious and demanded even more training. I injured myself frequently from overtraining, but still I persisted. It was insane and at some deep level I knew it. But I couldn't stop.

It's not easy to spot a compulsive exerciser. For one thing, they seem perfectly well adjusted and are likely to be professionally successful and highly productive members of society. Such individuals are driven, and they possess great discipline and willpower—traits valued by our society. Thus, being a compulsive exerciser is not viewed as a negative. On the contrary, most psychologists would categorize exercise addiction as a positive addiction. It's an addiction, but the outcomes are largely positive (improved health, weight management, an outlet for stress, etc.).

Exercise can become a negative addiction when it gets so far out of whack as to interfere with professional productivity and domestic interactions. I've known only a few individuals who fit this extraordinary pattern. They miss meetings or appointments at work, because they have to exercise, knowing that if they don't, right then and there, they won't be able to fit it in the rest of the day. Or they skip family functions and don't follow through on promises or obligations for the same reason. Such individuals cannot separate job and family obligations from exercise obligations, obviously with disastrous results similar to those associated with negative addictions such as alcohol and drugs. I was extreme, but I knew there were limits.

The "Exorcisers"

There is a small group I call the exorcisers, because they use exercise to compensate for bad habits — to exorcise the negative impact of what they are doing to their bodies. A unique example is a friend of mine who loved to drink copious amounts of wine. He exercised hours a day to exhaustion, then drank wine the rest of the day. In his mind, he was balancing his bad habit with a good one. He wasn't, of course, but at least he was better off being a compulsive exerciser than if he were sedentary.

Another example is cigarette smokers. I was amazed to discover how many heavy exercisers also have heavy smoking habits, believing naively that exercise can exorcise the impact of cigarette smoke. Not a chance. A more common example of failed exorcism is those who choose to eat mega-doses of fatty sludge daily, believing that they are burning it off like a blast furnace. If this were true, we wouldn't have marathon runners collapsing from lethal heart attacks.

My Goal

Since fitness producing exercise has been viewed as the only way to go, it's natural that those who subscribe to it would adapt many coping strategies as outlined above. With the shift, however, to a softer and more gentle approach to exercise it's likely that the Love-it and the Got-to approach will grow and there will be less begrudging and less compulsivity. Ultimately, my goal is to convince everyone to adopt some sort of exercise program as a Love-it. It's possible, but first the message must be spread that exercise can be fun, convenient and comfortable.

9. FINDING TIME FOR EXERCISE

Being physically inactive is as damaging to your health as smoking cigarettes. The vast majority of Americans shun smoking because of the health implications. Why, then, aren't more Americans willing to exercise? A big factor is time. Workouts are time consuming, and it's hard to find time in a busy day to get to a gym, change, work out, shower, change again, and drive home. Unfortunately, for more than 80 percent of Americans, exercise is viewed as an impractical burden that complicates rather than complements the lifestyle.

Since moderate physical activities like brisk walking can promote health nearly as much as vigorous workouts, there are many more options for exercise than we once thought. But softening the rules doesn't mean you can play checkers on your lunch hour to satisfy your body's need for physical activity. On the contrary, you must be vigilant to ensure that you build adequate whole body movements into your lifestyle with a minimum of 30-minutes of moderate physical activity daily. The good news is, as you are now aware, you can accumulate your exercise minutes in bits and pieces, more easily fitting them into a busy day. Here are some tips on how to incorporate an effective exercise program into your life.

A 12-Step Plan

1. Make a commitment. You owe it to yourself and your family to be as healthy as you can be, and committing to 30-minutes of daily physical activity is an important component of a healthy lifestyle.

2. Set short term and long term goals. A short term goal could be starting from scratch and adding a minute a day to your exercise regimen. A long term goal could be losing weight, or improving your health profile by lowering your blood pressure.

3. Set process-oriented goals. Commit to exercise daily for two

months, letting nothing interfere. Do whatever you can to move your body, and count it as exercise. If you can spare only 5 minutes, so be it. Count it. The key is developing the habit. It takes about 30 days to allow a habit to form, and another 30 days for it to set. Obviously, the longer you go the stronger the habit becomes, but the first 60 days are critical to success.

4. Planning is critical. On especially busy days, you may not be able to spontaneously get the minimal amount of daily physical activity you need, and therefore a little planning is called for. Schedule some exercise into your daily routine, pencil in an appointment, and stick to it. I know a number of busy executives who black out time each day on their calendar for exercise and they allow nothing to interfere.

5. Avoid the all-or-none trap. If circumstances prevent you from doing everything you planned for the day, do what you can and don't worry about it. Tomorrow's a new day with new opportunities to exercise.

6. Take a long range view. If you fall off the wagon for a week or two due to injury, illness, or lack of interest, just get back on. Interruptions are part of life and must be expected.

7. Be realistic. Don't try to do things that are unpleasant or uncomfortable. You won't stick to such a program.

8. Be prepared. Spontaneous opportunities for exercise may depend upon having walking shoes available or a quick change of clothes.

9. Have opportunities at your fingertips. Buy a piece of exercise equipment, place it in a convenient location at home and jump on it when you have a few minutes to spare.

10. Recruit a friend to tag along with you. Engaging in physical activities together is a good way to keep a friendship alive.

11. Take advantage of occasions when you have time to spare. On weekends, take a long walk or a hike in the woods.

12. Be creative. The possibilities for physical activity are limited only by your imagination.

Creative Ways to Exercise Throughout the Day
• Use the stairs instead of the elevator or escalator. At home seek opportunities to climb to the second floor as many times as you can throughout the day. For variety, take the stairs two at time, or quicken

your pace. (More on this in Chapter 13.)

• Walk when you can. Park an extra block away from your destination or at the rear of the parking lot. Always look for the longest, rather than the shortest route. (More on this in Chapters 15-18.)

• Get up from your chair (quit using your TV remote) or out of your car more often (avoid drive-through windows).

• When unloading your car after visiting the supermarket, carry one bag at a time into the house.

• Start a hobby like gardening that makes you move.

• View household chores (grass cutting, dusting, vacuuming, etc.) as opportunities for exercise.

• Turn off the TV and play with the children. Spontaneous play with children will tax you as much as you allow.

• Try dancing. There are all types to suit any preference (ballroom, contra, square, country line, etc.)

• Learn new sports. Take golf, tennis, or racquetball lessons.

• Kill two birds with one stone. Emphasize walking while you shop, moving quickly up and down the aisles of the supermarket. You may miss some items and have to return later for them. It's inefficient, in other words, but that's the point.

• Join groups that are active (mall walkers, hikers, cyclists).

For Those Who Enjoy Vigorous Exercise

The challenge is somewhat different for the person who enjoys vigorous workouts but can't seem to find the time on a regular basis. The answer is the abbreviated workout. Have one in your hip pocket you can call upon when time gets tight. The key is increasing the intensity of effort to compensate for the reduction in duration. Run faster (increased intensity) over a shorter distance (reduced duration). Running as little as one mile three times a week at a fast pace can sustain a reasonably high level of fitness. But be careful. High intensity exercise can be hard on joints and may require an extended warm-up. An alternative may be a vigorous activity that is not so punishing as jogging, such as swimming.

Another option is splitting your exercise time in half, doing some running in the morning before work, then more later in the day. Research suggests that the fitness benefits of segmented runs may be as great as one longer effort.

Even resistance exercise can be adapted to a stingy schedule. Take an unloaded barbell and perform as many repetitions as possible of an exercise (barbell curls, for example) in 30-seconds. Shoot for 30 reps, or one per second and maintain strict form throughout. Rest only 30-seconds then shift immediately to the next exercise and again perform as many reps as possible in 30-seconds. Continue this work/rest pace through eight or ten exercises which challenge the major muscle groups of the body and you will have completed a thorough workout in minutes. A word of caution. Although you will be using a barbell that is much lighter than you normally would use, this mini-workout is tough. If you have little or no training experience with weights, rest longer between sets. This will lengthen the time of your workout, but will reduce the intensity substantially. If you are more experienced, add a little weight to the bar and do not rest between exercises.

10. THE BEST TIME TO EXERCISE

What's the best time of day to exercise? I'm frequently asked this question, especially by those who are just starting out. My answer is, there's no one best time. Moreover, there are a number of things to consider when making the decision. For example, what's the most convenient and comfortable time for you that will help you be more consistent? What kind of exercise are you intending to do? Do you want to maximize benefits while minimizing involvement? And, are there any health or safety concerns you need to keep in mind? After pondering these considerations, you'll be able to determine the best time for you.

Convenience

The most critical element of an exercise program is consistency. Doing a little each and every day is much better than knocking yourself out periodically. And when it comes to consistency, by far the most important factor is convenience. Only a small portion of the American public exercises regularly, and most of those who do are not zealous advocates. On the contrary, most are exercising because they know it's good for them, and they feel guilty and out of sorts when they don't. This creates a fragile framework for including exercise in your life that is easily disrupted, and inconvenience is generally the culprit.

The concept of convenience encompasses many components, including time of day. Choose a time that's most convenient for you. Convenience means it not only fits your schedule, but it also fits your lifestyle. Mornings may fit your schedule if you are an early riser. If so, go for it. But if you're not a "morning person," and you try to make it work, forget it. Your good intentions won't take you very far.

Convenience also encompasses common sense. Night owls may be motivated to exercise at midnight, but this may not be a good choice,

84

even though it fits their lifestyle. Exercise tends to arouse you, hyping you with energy for a few hours after you finish, keeping you awake. If you have to get up early the next morning, exercising late may be a bad idea.

When choosing a time, don't feel locked in. Exercise at the regularly scheduled hour when it's convenient to do so, but diverge from the schedule if things get tight. It makes no sense, stressing yourself while trying to keep an exercise appointment. That's self defeating. Be flexible, knowing that sometimes you'll have to catch a bout of exercise when you can. And when you do, lower your expectations of what you intend to accomplish. The most important thing is, you are doing something.

Maximizing Exercise Time

Vigorous exercise tends to be viewed as an event that requires a warm-up which physically prepares your body for battle; the workout itself; a cool-down phase; and a substantial portion of time for cleaning yourself up. All of this takes a hefty chunk of time that is not easily fit into a busy schedule, which means you may not always be able to exercise when it's convenient and desirable.

Less severe exercise, on the other hand, can be spontaneous, not requiring a warm-up, cool down, or clean up. Taking a walk at lunch time is an example. Going out of your way several times a day to climb three or four flights of stairs is another. Workout time can be used for cutting the grass and other chores which count as good exercise. This eases a busy schedule and can be more conveniently included because you are killing two birds with one stone.

Maximizing Benefits

Mild or moderate exercise is easier to include in your schedule, because it can be performed right after meals. Vigorous exercise like jogging or weight lifting requires an empty stomach. I have already discussed post-meal exercise as a good option, but there's more to the story.

Post-meal exercise is not only convenient and can burn more calories than exercise on an empty stomach, it also can help prevent a serious health danger called the "Last Supper Syndrome." Many heart attacks occur in the hours after a heavy meal as the individual watches TV or snoozes. Here's why.

When fat enters the circulation after a meal it triggers the release of blood clotting substances. The greater the amount of fat entering the circulation the greater the triggering effect and the greater the likelihood that clots will form in the bloodstream. This is a potentially lethal situation, because small blood clots can lodge in areas of an artery which have been narrowed due to atherosclerosis (clogging of the arteries). If a clot lodges in an artery feeding the heart, it stops the flow of blood. Blood carries oxygen, and without oxygen the heart muscle will die. This is called a myocardial infarction, or heart attack. If the same thing happens in the brain, it is called a stroke.

A 15 minute walk can easily be inserted after lunch, and after dinner. You might even be able to plug in a 15 minute walk after breakfast if you are not too rushed. If so, you can log 45 minutes of total exercise for the day without squeezing your schedule too tightly.

All in all, with regard to choosing the best time of day, exercising moderately after meals is an excellent choice.

Mornings Can be a Problem for Some

It has been known for some time that heart attacks and strokes (caused by blood clots) occur more often in the first hours of the morning compared with other times of the day. Several factors may contribute.

Upon first awakening, there is a tendency for the arteries to be slightly narrower than they will be later in the day. For the average person, this is not a big deal. But for the individual who has a substantial amount of cholesterol clogging the arteries — narrowing them in certain areas, further narrowing could be catastrophic. In addition, the blood is more likely to form clots, because in the early hours the platelets (blood cells responsible for initiating clotting) are "stickier" and more prone to congregate.

These two factors combined can add up to a heart attack, and they explain why, for some, leaping out of bed and taking off for a jog can be deadly. The situation is worse in cold weather, because the blood vessels constrict, narrowing them further. They do this to conserve body heat. Constriction of the vessels increases blood pressure, adding a third nasty factor to the mix. As such, the worse case scenario would be getting out of bed and immediately moving outside on a cold day to shovel snow from the walk or driveway. To avoid these problems, it's best for those at risk for heart disease to ease into the day.

If you have any questions regarding your degree of heart disease risk, see your doctor. While there, discuss morning exercise, if mornings seem to fit best for you. Exercise helps reduce heart disease risk, but exercising in the mornings may cancel that benefit and add further risk.

Morning Stiffness

There's another reason why morning exercise can be problematic. You may awaken with stiffness in the lower back. It's tempting to get out of bed and begin doing some stretching exercises to relive the stiffness, but don't. Stretching exercises can make the problem worse. Here's why.

At night when you are lying in bed, the body doesn't have to fight the effects of gravity. This causes the discs between the vertebrae to swell, in turn causing the ligaments which run from one vertebrae to the next adjacent vertebra to stretch. Upon standing and encountering the impact of gravity, the stretched ligaments cause stiffness and discomfort. Attempting to perform stretching exercises aggravates the already stretched ligaments. While you may experience some immediate relief, it is only short lived and later there may be more pain and stiffness.

Jogging and other jarring and intense exercises also can be a problem, because the swollen discs will take more of a pounding than they would if they weren't swollen.

The best approach is to realize that the problem is swollen discs and to take steps to gently relieve the swelling. Taking a comfortable walk is recommended. I like to climb stairs, up and down, and after a while I take them two at a time. I don't hurry when I go up and down, but gradually, I can feel my back relax as the fluid moves out of the discs and the ligaments relax.

The Bottom Line

Exercise is good for you, and every effort should be made to include some form of exercise in your daily routine. It's not as hard to do as you might think. Be flexible in your approach and be honest with yourself. When starting out, don't set your sights too high. It's best to simply develop the habit of exercise, no matter how limited your efforts, and having a convenient, comfortable, and safe time of day is critical to sustaining your efforts and being consistent.

11. WARMING UP AND COOLING-DOWN

Everyone, from the seasoned athlete to the novice jogger, knows that warming up is important. But, ironically, there is little scientific evidence available to support warming up as a means to improve performance and avoid injury. Sure, physiologists can construct a theoretical argument based upon the fact that a warm and pre-stretched muscle cell (fiber) will contract more strongly than a cold one. But actual proof on humans is scarce, because it's difficult and psychologically complicated to do research on warming up with humans.

The need to warm-up is ingrained in our psyches, and therefore it's virtually impossible for researchers to collect unbiased data. To illustrate this point, ask someone to sprint full speed on a cool day without warming up. If you are able to convince them to give it a try, they probably won't give you a maximum effort because they are afraid that without a warm-up they may get injured. On another occasion, give them an adequate warm-up, and they will give you a maximum effort. Thus, performance would be shown to increase after the warm-up, but not because of the warm-up. You see the problem researchers face.

Despite these academic issues, warming up is a good idea. Common sense tells us the body is like a giant taffy bar. When cold it's stiff and resists bending. But if you warm up the taffy it becomes pliable, easily bending and stretching to any shape. The demands of vigorous exercise and especially the demands of intense competition require that the body's muscles and joints be like warm taffy — ready to perform, to bend, to stretch, to do whatever is necessary.

The Heart Needs a Warm-up

There is one aspect of warming up that has been investigated and documented. Warming up has been shown to decrease the stress exercise places on the heart. Researchers found that when healthy firefighters with no history of heart disease sprinted up hill on a treadmill for 15 seconds without a warm-up (simulating jumping off the truck and immediately battling a blaze), most demonstrated abnormalities in their electrocardiograms (EKG). Such EKG abnormalities indicate the heart muscle is not receiving sufficient blood flow and oxygen, and may explain unexpected deaths from heart attack in victims thrust suddenly into strenuous activities like dashing to catch a bus.

With a warm-up of jogging in place prior to the treadmill run, few of the firefighters demonstrated problems in their EKG. The researchers concluded that warming-up reduced stress on the heart by lowering blood pressure and increasing blood flow and oxygen to the heart muscle.

There Are Many Ways to Warm-up

In a passive warm-up, heat is applied to the body—sitting in a sauna is an example. Little is accomplished with a passive warm-up, however, because the heat is not likely to warm deep muscles which will be required to do the work.

In an active (general) warm-up, total body exercises like brisk walking, jogging in place or calisthenics are used to raise body temperature. Active warm-up is better than passive, but using a general approach may not specifically warm-up the muscles and joints used in performance. Thus, although you may have the feel of being warmed up, specific muscles and joints that are going to bear the brunt of the exercise may still be cold.

For sporting activities, an active task specific warm-up often is best. In this type of warm-up, the actual skill employed during competition is used as the warm-up. A relief pitcher throws dozens of warm-up pitches, gradually increasing velocity as he gets warmer. Similarly, joggers begin jogging at a leisurely pace, then gradually increase intensity.

Stretching

Everyone equates warming-up with stretching, but stretching may not be the best way to go. Stretching cold muscles is not an effective way to stretch, because the muscles offer resistance (like the cold taffy described above). You are better off performing a general warm-up first, increasing the temperature of your muscles and connective tissues, then progressing to a regimen of stretching. In fact, stretching may be most effective after exercise, when the body is at its warmest.

A Typical Warm-up

There is no set schedule for warming up which can be applied across the board. As a rule of thumb, however, starting with an easy-paced general active warm-up is a good way to begin. Gradually increase the intensity and continue moving until you experience a light sweat (a sign body temperature is increasing). This should take about five to fifteen minutes, depending upon the intensity of effort. But don't do too much. You don't want to fatigue yourself or reduce stored energy that you will need to call upon later.

Next perform light stretching exercises, progressing from larger muscles to smaller. And finally, (if the exercise or sport demands), begin a task specific warm-up employing the skills that will be used when performing. Again, start slowly, gradually progressing in intensity until you reach a level that is at or near actual performance standards.

The amount of warm-up required will depend on several factors, and like most things, warming-up is highly individualized and some may require more than others. People who are less flexible, for example, or less skilled, may require more warm-up to get ready. When performing an unfamiliar activity, a longer, more extensive warm-up can help prepare you for the unexpected.

Golfers Need a Warm-up Too

Maximum or near maximum exercise makes great demands on the muscles and joints, and common sense says, don't go there without a thorough warm-up. Maximum exercise can take several forms. Driving a golf ball is a type of maximum effort, but many golfers fail to adequately prepare themselves before teeing off. Is it possible the high incidence of lower back problems among golfers may have something to do with jumping into a maximum effort too quickly? There is no proof that an adequate warm-up as described above would help golfers avoid such problems, but common sense suggests it might, especially in cooler weather.

Cooling-Down

While warming up is universally accepted, cooling-down has little respect and is often ignored. Ironically, unlike warming up, there is good scientific evidence that cooling down aids recovery from exercise. Waste products created during vigorous exercise are removed from the muscles more effectively during cool-down exercise than when resting, because exercise promotes increased blood flow through the muscles. The waste products are flushed out, in other words. Removing waste products is especially important to athletes like swimmers or track athletes who may be required to compete in more than one exhausting event with little time between.

Cooling down also is important to everyday exercisers. It helps remove adrenalin produced during vigorous exercise. Allowing adrenalin to continue circulating in the blood stream while sitting at rest can be stressful to the heart. Being inactive after vigorous exercise also can cause blood to pool in the muscles, causing a sudden drop in blood pressure which could cause light headedness and possibly inadequate blood flow to the heart. Cool-down exercise helps circulate blood back toward the heart, because muscles squeeze the veins, pushing the blood forward with greater force.

Cooling-down generally consists of mild exercise similar to the exercise just performed. After running several miles, an effective cool-down would be light jogging followed by a brisk walk. Continue until breathing has returned to normal and your pulse approaches its pre-exercise level (less than 100 beats per minute).

Stretching is an important component of the cool-down. After activities which involve running, the leg and lower back muscles tend to tighten. Ignoring this tightness makes things worse, especially if you go right from exercising to the car or sofa, and the muscles may tighten further, causing stiffness, pain and soreness. Post exercise stretching is effective for promoting flexibility because you may be able to stretch the warm muscles further than usual.

When the weather is cold, it's best to perform your cool-down stretches indoors. Being indoors will prevent losing body heat too rapidly, which can cause a chill. It's also more comfortable to stretch in a warm environment.

The Bottom Line
Warming up and cooling down are important components of any exercise program. Be sure to budget adequate time for both.

12. PURCHASING AND USING HOME EXERCISE EQUIPMENT

Sales of treadmills, stationary bikes, stair climbers, cross-country ski machines and other pieces of aerobic exercise equipment are at an all time high. Does this mean American couch potatoes are finally getting the message about the need to exercise? Unfortunately, no. It's one thing to purchase a piece of exercise equipment, and quite another to use it regularly. Many of the pieces of exercise equipment bought today will end up in the attic or garage tomorrow. There are many reasons for this. The biggest reason is that many will purchase a piece of exercise equipment hoping that it will help to convince them to exercise. They didn't make a commitment before they laid down their cash, in other words, and they certainly hadn't decided that they were going to exercise regularly. On the contrary, they hoped in vain that somehow having spent $500 will stimulate them to get going and keep going. It won't.

That's not to say that purchasing a piece of home exercise equipment is a bad thing. Not at all. Just make certain you are ready to use the equipment. Otherwise, why bother?

Having a piece of home exercise equipment is convenient. There is no lost travel time, the weather is inconsequential, and you can exercise any time of the day or night. But in-the-home exercise can be boring, and 30 minutes on a stationary cycle can feel like an eternity. You also are on your own without professional help to get you started on the right foot and keep you motivated. What's more, too often there is a sense of urgency about shaping up and trimming down. This, combined with unrealistic expectations arising from advertising hype, sows the seeds of failure in any exercise program, but especially one conducted at home on your own.

If you decide you are ready to exercise regularly and you are committed to it, then you are ready to purchase a piece of home exercise equipment if you so choose. There is much to consider. First, the purchase is as involved as any major purchase you will make. And second, because exercising on a machine at home is boring, after the purchase you must be creative in your approach in order to sustain your interest.

Making a Successfuk Purchase

1. Be prepared for "buyer let-down" after the purchase. Let me again emphasize the obvious in order to keep you from possibly wasting your money and cluttering your home. Do you firmly believe you will use the equipment regularly? Most people believe they will before they buy it. Then, after the newness wears off in a few weeks, the equipment is abandoned to the attic or basement, never to be used again.

2. Is the equipment well made? It's hard to tell from just looking, and the best approach is to wear your workout gear to the store, get on the equipment and put it through its paces. If it is well made, it will feel right. The movements will be smooth and easy and the equipment will feel solid and durable. Cheap "look alike" equipment often is jerky and gives you the feeling that after several hours of use it will break down, and usually it does.

3. Is the equipment comfortable to you? Something can be well made and durable, but still feel awkward to you. Taking a workout in the store will tell you all you need to know. Pay close attention to how your lower back feels, and the impact on your joints and muscles. You must stay on the machine for a long time to truly test it. Something that feels comfortable for a minute or two in the store may feel quite different after twenty minutes at home.

4. While trying out the equipment, use a critical eye. Watch for things like stability, the ease with which you can use controls, noise level, and seat padding.

5. What type of exercise equipment is best? Each type of exercise equipment will feel different to you. You have treadmills for walking and running, stationary cycles, cross country skiers, stair steppers, rowers, and all sorts of hybrid machines which combine aspects of traditional machines. Test them all and choose the one that feels best to you. Disregard advertising hype. Each exercise device claims unique properties. Some pieces of equipment, like the cross country skier and stationary cycles with arm pumps, exercise both the upper and lower

body muscles. This is an advantage, but only if the exercise feels right to you. Walking on a treadmill can be just as good if you add a few light dumbbell exercises at the end of your walk.

6. Do you have room for the equipment you want? Is there a place where you can put the equipment and be certain it won't be in the way? If you have to store the equipment away and out of sight, or worse, if you have to disassemble it (even just a little), this will serve as a strong disincentive when it comes to exercising. At the least, it will destroy any spontaneous urges which may arise. Beyond the need for ample floor space, bear in mind that exercise equipment can be noisy and your exercise sessions may bother others if you are too close.

7. How can you get the best equipment at the best price? Expect to spend at least a few hundred dollars. If you spend less, you probably will be disappointed. Spending more — up to many thousands — is possible, but not necessary. You can keep the price down by leaving out the bells and whistles. Some exercise equipment is quite costly because it offers cardiotachometers which monitor your heart rate, and computerized programs for determining calories expended, time elapsed, and so on. While nice to have, you don't need this stuff to get the benefits you seek. And unless you are an athlete, you may not require heavy-duty equipment with capabilities far beyond your needs.

After The Purchase
Making a savvy purchase is only the first step. When you get it home, you must cope with boredom and time constraints. Here are some tips:

- Exercise in front of the TV or a window. Listen to music or books on tape. Some exercises (stationary cycling, for example) allow reading.
- For variety, create a routine with several pieces of equipment. Walk on a treadmill for several minutes, then switch to a cycle, then to a rower, then back to the treadmill. A less expensive version of this routine would be to have one major piece of exercise equipment as the core, then use other less expensive options to complement it. Walk on the treadmill, for example, then get off and immediately begin a step aerobics routine.

Other options include using Heavy Hands, light dumbbell exercises, or calisthenics.

- Consistency is the key to success in any exercise program. Unfortunately, time constraints often won't allow a complete workout. No problem. You can exercise in bits and pieces without always having to keep going for thirty minutes consecutively. Three ten minute mini-workouts can be as effective as one 30 minute workout. And when you are really rushed, do what you can and don't worry about the rules.
- Don't feel confined to an indoor exercise program. For variety, get out of the house and hike on weekends, or when the weather is rough, try mall walking.

How to Use Exercise Equipment — The Nitty Gritty

There are many subtle things to learn about exercise equipment that will help you use it more effectively. If you exercise at a commercial gym, there should be professional guidance available to help you get started on the right foot. At home, however, you are on your own. Study the manual which comes with your equipment to learn the ins and outs of proper technique and upkeep. In addition, pay attention to how the exercise feels. In the long run, the "feel" may be the best indicator that you are exercising correctly. Never exercise with discomfort or pain. If you do, an injury is likely.

Each of the following pieces of exercise equipment will provide an excellent workout either in the gym or at home. To improve aerobic fitness, intensity of effort must be sustained at a high level, which can be hard on exercise equipment. Therefore, regardless of the type of equipment you use, it must be well made, stable, highly durable, mechanically smooth and offer uniform resistance. Depending upon quality and the extras desired, the following machines will range in price from approximately $300 to as much as $3000.

Treadmill:

1. You can walk, jog or run. Walking is the least stressful on the joints and each stride imparts an impact force of less than twice the bodyweight. With jogging, the force climbs to three to four times bodyweight. The running surface of a treadmill can be quite hard, which

means it does not absorb impact forces easily. Some expensive treadmills have more resilient running surfaces, and if you intend to jog or run, the increased investment is worth it.

2. Walking briskly uphill can provide a workout that is as intense as jogging. Going uphill also can make slow jogging as intense as running. Either way, the impact forces on an incline are less when compared with faster speeds on the level. For this reason, a motorized bed incline is an important option.

3. If you are content to walk only, you can get by with a narrower and shorter belt (running surface) which can reduce cost. Jogging or running, on the other hand, require a greater surface area (especially length), which necessitates purchase of a larger treadmill.

4. Holding the handrails while exercising reduces the intensity of effort and the energy cost. Once you have mastered the skill and balance required for treadmill exercise, remove your hands from the rails and keep them off. But even though you don't grip the rails during exercise, be certain the rails are stable and strong enough to support your weight and are placed appropriately to assist you should you lose balance and grab them for safety.

5. When walking or running uphill maintain an upright posture with only a slight bend at the waist. Leaning too far forward, places strain on the lower back.

6. Programmable workouts add convenience, but also hype the price considerably. Speed and degree of incline are automatically manipulated to impose walking on the level, then hill climbing, etc. If the controls are easily accessible and you can instantly regulate speed and incline, a programmable workout may not be worth the added cost. Programmable workouts are available on most types of electric exercise equipment (stationary bikes, rowers, etc.), and the same considerations apply.

7. Self propelled treadmills (non-motorized) are considerably less expensive, but may be uncomfortable and may not provide the kind of workout you seek. Test both types thoroughly before choosing.

8. Some treadmills come equipped with resistance levers for upper body exercise. This allows upper and lower body exercise in one movement, but the movement may feel awkward during a prolonged workout.

Stationary bike:

1. Workload is a product of the resistance times the number of pedal revolutions (which determines theoretical distance covered). Mechanically braked bikes impose resistance with a friction belt or "pinchers" over the front flywheel, or by use of air resistance against flywheel "fans." Either type will offer a smooth ride. For efficient operation, be certain you can easily adjust the level of resistance with a simple twist of a knob. Beware of cheaper bikes that impose resistance on the front flywheel with rubber pinchers which resemble the braking apparatus on racing bikes. Beware of this type because the result often is a jerky ride unless the bike is well made.

2. In mechanically braked bikes, as pedalling rate increases, workload increases. Thus, intensity of effort can be increased by either increasing resistance or rate of pedalling, or both.

3. Electronically braked bikes adjust workload automatically — as pedalling rate increases, resistance decreases (and vice versa), keeping workload constant. Programmable workouts are possible and offer a variety of intensity levels.

4. Newer bike models offer a recumbent design which reduces strain on the lower back.

5. When considering machines with a seat (stationary bikes, rowers, exercise riders) be certain the seat is comfortable for a long exercise session. Comfort includes not only the padding, but the shape overall and the shape of the "horn" in front. Padded biker's pants can help increase comfort of a bike seat, but the choice of seats should not assume that padded pants always will be worn.

6. Some models offer arm cranking which can allow arm exercise only, leg exercise only, and arm plus leg exercise. Arm plus leg exercise is an advantage because the greater the muscle mass employed the greater the energy expenditure. In addition, because the workload is spread over a large muscle mass, there is less fatigue encountered for a given energy cost.

7. Make certain the handlebars are positioned comfortably. Some bikes use racing bars which require that you bend forward excessively at the waist. Most noncompetitive bikers find this position uncomfortable.

8. Seat height should be set so that there is a slight bend in the knee when the leg is extended. A lower seat height will fatigue the thighs

quickly. A higher seat height will cause leaning and over-compensation from side to side with each push on the pedals.

9. Use pedal clips which lock the feet in place to allow the legs to pull the pedals, as well as push. Clips also hold the feet in place when standing and pedaling, to mimic to a degree the act of running without the severe impact forces on the legs.

Stair climbing machine:

1. An intense workout is possible without severe impact forces on the legs. This allows those with injuries to begin training again earlier than would be possible through running.

2. Machines for the home use pistons for resistance which are attached to wide pedals. Some models offer linked pedals (the dependent type) in which the action of one pedal (going down, for example) influences the opposite pedal (forcing it up). Unlinked models offer independent steps which provide a more natural stepping rhythm.

3. Stepping height ranges from about two inches to eighteen inches. For best results keep the pedals in the midrange without topping out or touching the floor.

4. Maintain an erect posture while climbing. Leaning forward stresses the lower back. Keep the knees positioned over the feet when stepping.

5. Keep the feet flat on the pedals to reduce stress on the Achilles tendon.

6. Hold the handrails lightly for balance. Leaning on the rails greatly reduces intensity of effort.

Rowing machine:

1. Although it would appear that rowing is mostly an upper body exercise, if the rowing stroke is performed properly 75 percent of the force of the stroke comes from the legs.

2. There are two basic types of rowers — the hydraulic, and the flywheel which offers a more natural feel of rowing on water.

3. Maintain an erect position when sitting on the seat as bending forward can stress the lower back. Also, don't hyperextend at the finish of each movement.

4. The seat must move back and forth freely and smoothly and the resistance must be uniform.

5. When a bar or pull-handles are involved (as in rowing, skiing machines, or an exercise rider), be certain they are padded and comfortable to grip, even after many minutes of exercise.

6. Keep your elbows close to your body when pulling.

7. Rowing is often perceived as being the most boring of indoor exercises. Perhaps it is because it is the least familiar movement. Or it's because you can't read and it's difficult to watch TV. Whatever the reason, give it some consideration prior to purchasing.

Ski machines:

1. The cross-country skiing action engages the upper and lower body muscles more than any other exercise machine. The caloric cost is quite high, especially when the front of the machine is elevated slightly to mimic skiing uphill.

2. The feet do not leave the ground during skiing, and therefore you get a high intensity workout with essentially no impact forces on the lower legs.

3. It's best to purchase a skier which allows separate adjustments for upper body and lower body resistance.

4. Learning to coordinate the upper and lower body actions on the skier is not easy. It takes time, but everyone should be able to master the movements.

Elliptical trainer:

1. The elliptical trainer is the new kid on the block. A full range of resistance levels can provide a mild workout or an exhausting one.

2. Elliptical exercise requires a combination of gliding and stepping movements that greatly reduces impact forces on the lower legs while requiring forceful muscular contractions.

3. A bonus is being able to use the arms with a pumping action to increase overall muscle mass involvement. Another option is to hold on to stationary handles and challenge the legs more vigorously.

4. Although there is some coordination of movements, it's easy to master the rhythm required for effective exercise on the elliptical trainer, and it's much easier to master than the cross-country ski machines.

5. Elliptical training has become my exercise of choice in recent years. It babies my bum knee and the smooth rhythm puts me in a meditative state that is enjoyable.

13. ALWAYS TAKE THE STAIRS

Technology has brought us many wonderful advancements, easing the physical strain of everyday life. Obvious examples are escalators and elevators, which have made climbing stairs in public buildings all but obsolete. In fact, if you want to avoid automation and climb stairs, chances are you'll have trouble finding them. No problem. The masses don't use stairs anymore — at least that's what architects must assume, and those who do seek to climb stairs are probably up to no good, or are mentally deficient in some way.

I'm teasing, of course, and although often there are stairs adjacent to the elevator, most of us would rather wait a long time for the elevator rather than climb even one flight. It's amusing to hear people complain about a sluggish elevator, while never even considering the stairs as an option. In fact, when I take the stairs in a public building I am greatly surprised when I encounter another human being. (What are they up to? I wonder.)

Lost Opportunities

When you climb a flight of stairs you burn calories and you challenge your leg muscles, helping to keep them strong and fit. Avoid stairs, and the opposite occurs. You conserve energy, promoting fat storage, and your muscles deteriorate. The latter has become a fact of life in a society that is getting fatter year by year, and losing physical capacity at an alarming rate.

When you climb a typical flight of stairs (12 to 16 individual steps) you burn approximately 3 to 4 calories per flight (assumes you walk up and down), depending upon your size. The bigger you are the more energy it takes to move your body and the more calories you will expend when climbing stairs. With this in mind, climbing approximately

25 flights of stairs would be comparable to briskly walking a mile, and 30 flights would compare favorably with the cost of jogging a mile.

That's crazy, you say. What sane person would choose climbing 25 flights of stairs over walking a brisk mile? No one, perhaps, but that's not the choice I have in mind. Indeed, climbing 25 flights of stairs would be a daunting task for even the most highly motivated among us. But, if those 25 flights were split up into many smaller climbs, the task becomes more reasonable.

Assume, for example, that you work on the third floor of a major office building, and that frequently you need to go to the sixth floor. If, throughout the day, you took the stairs instead of the elevator, you easily could accumulate a total of 25 or more flights. The best part is, you would be integrating stair climbing into your everyday life, making it a natural thing to do, and burning calories and getting stronger without going out of your way. And if you don't have to go to another floor, make the decision to periodically get up from your desk and take a mini-walk that includes a flight or two of stairs.

Short Changing the Elderly

As we get older we become less active. This, of course, results in a loss of capacity, which makes everything we do more physically challenging. In turn, we do less, avoiding challenges, getting weaker and weaker. I have written about this vicious downhill spiral many times, and I have confided how it took such an awful toll on my father who made up his mind upon retirement from his job that the only physical activity he was going to pursue was with his thumb (on the TV clicker).

Climbing stairs is the perfect natural exercise to help us stay strong into our elder years. It's an activity we have done all our lives, and therefore it's not new and unique and it doesn't require learning, or any special skills or attributes. And yet, when climbing stairs becomes the least bit challenging for our elder citizens, we insist that they vacate their two story homes in favor of a one story ranch home, or condo. Without realizing it, when such a change is made, and stairs are avoided, the deterioration associated with the aging process is accelerated.

Admittedly, there are instances where it may be dangerous for some elderly persons to climb stairs. Bouts of dizziness or uncertainty can make stairs treacherous. I worry about my mom climbing stairs, but at the same time, I want her to climb as many flights as possible during the day, knowing the effort is good for her. To ease my mind, I often will climb behind her on the way up, or in front of her on the way down, just in case.

Changing Perception

We are an inactive society and anything we do to increase our level of physical activity is helpful. But making the choice to be active (when being sedentary is easier) will require us to change our perception — the way we see the world. That won't be easy.

Just the other day, I received a phone call from a magazine writer in New York City who was assigned to do a piece on moderate exercise and how such exercise could be incorporated into daily life. As we conversed, I interjected some personal experiences and observations, and she responded. She told me how she would soon move into a sixth floor walk-up apartment. This, she explained, was an apartment on the sixth floor of a building without an elevator.

Wow! I thought, I'd hate to be the guys who moved her. Then, I thought, how wonderful — she has the ultimate built-in exercise program. Given the nature of our conversation, I assumed she had planned it that way. Not! She complained that this walk-up apartment was the last choice on a long list of choices and that she hated the thought of living there and having to climb all those stairs several times a day. This, even though we had been chatting for quite some time about how to build exercise into your daily life. When I pointed this out, she said: "Oh, yeah, I didn't look at it that way."

I don't mean to imply that living on the sixth floor without an elevator would be a picnic. Of course not. Even I can see the challenges. But the irony is, this person was writing a story on moderate exercise and building exercise into your life, but failed to identify that her stair climbing up six flights was a perfect example, offering as many advantages as disadvantages.

The Bottom Line

We're all busy and it's too much to ask most of us to take our precious spare time and invest it in something as onerous as exercise. The solution? Climb stairs when possible and do what you can in bits and pieces throughout the day to enhance your level of physical activity. Even a little daily physical activity will help you manage your weight, and it will help prepare you for the challenges of aging.

14. EXERCISING AT HOME VERSUS AT THE GYM

Seasons change, and for those of us who live in areas where the weather can turn on us as we move into the fall months and beyond, we must beware of the deadly trio that beckons. By late October the days become shorter, the weather gets ugly, and the holiday season descends. This trio is responsible for pounds of weight gain each year. To offset this gain, many join their local commercial gym. Others invest in home exercise equipment. Which approach is best?

There are advantages and disadvantages to each option. The key is what works best for you. Here are some things to consider.

In Favor of Home Exercise

Several factors dictate the degree to which participants adhere to an exercise program, but the main factor often is convenience. Exercising at home is the most convenient approach. Your gym is there, down the stairs, calling you. You can exercise at any time of the day or night. Your appearance is of little concern, and you don't have to worry about being "in style" with the latest exercise garb, or fixing your make-up, or trimming your five-o'clock shadow.

There is privacy at home which is important to the novice who often feels weak and undeveloped, especially when encountering the huge muscles displayed by gym veterans and their "gung-ho" attitudes. Working out with members of the opposite sex also can be intimidating, especially to women.

The home gym is free of distractions, such as loud music chosen by someone else, and superfluous chatter. There is less interference as well, from crowds that congregate at the more popular exercise stations, or from loafers who occupy exercise stations for prolonged periods. And you don't have to work out side-by-side with patrons you don't like, or find annoying.

Home exercise offers control over hygiene. You don't have to get on a bench covered with someone else's sweat, or grip a bar that's been held by someone who rarely washes their hands or who has a cold.

When exercising at home, there are no fees to pay. Many commercial gyms require a contract for one year or more which must be paid whether you attend or not. Equipping a home gym can cost relatively little if you are satisfied with just the basics.

The Down Side of Home Exercise

If you want first class equipment, you can spend big bucks. Home exercise can be boring and tedious if you try to go it alone. This effect of home exercise can be offset by working out with a buddy or by hiring a personal trainer who can motivate you and provide professional supervision. However, employing a personal trainer on an ongoing basis gets pretty expensive. A home gym, no matter how modest, may demand more space than is available in an apartment or small home.

In Favor of Exercising at the Gym

Commercial gyms can provide a stimulating environment because there are lots of members engaged in exercise. This can inspire you to work hard on days you would rather loaf through your routine. The social climate of the gym provides an outlet for meeting new friends and establishing camaraderie. Good gyms offer professional supervision for the novice. Many gyms offer the services of a professional trainer for free in the early stages of your training, and for a fee later on.

A well equipped gym offers many exercise options and you can choose to use exercise machines and/or free weights. There also are treadmills, cycles, stair-steppers, rowers, etc. for a good aerobic workout. Membership in a gym that is part of a chain allows participation in all branches, which means you can exercise for free when out of town. This also allows the option of taking a workout in town after work, or going to the gym near home later in the day. Nowadays, some of the better gyms have gone to a month-to-month membership, which doesn't bind you to a lengthy contract.

The Down Side of Exercising at the Gym

In addition to factors cited above (lack of privacy, distractions, interference, etc.), you have to adjust your schedule to agree with the gym's hours. Usually, this is not a major problem, because most gyms open early and close late. There is travel time to the gym, which expands the amount of time you must commit to your exercise program. Travel raises concerns about the weather, driving conditions, and parking problems. If you have young children, getting to the gym means getting a baby sitter. Some gyms provide this service. Some gyms are staffed by salespersons who are interested only in selling membership, and who possess little exercise background. These so called "professionals" can give you really bad advice on training.

The Bottom Line

Overall, there are pros and cons associated with home exercise and exercising at a commercial gym. Ideally, it would be best to have both options. A modestly equipped home gym with a stationary cycle, a set of barbells and dumbbells and a bench may suffice for occasional workouts when it's too inconvenient to get to the gym. If you must choose between exercising at home versus at the gum, look for the "deal-breaker" aspects. Some aspects may be annoying, while others may be prohibitive. Needing a baby sitter each time you go, for example, may be too much, while exercising with a bunch of screaming macho muscle heads may simply be annoying — until you get to know them, and you find that under the surface they're really okay.

Joining a Commercial Gym — Some Things to Consider

When joining a commercial gym, there are several factors to consider. First and foremost is your motivation. How likely are you to go regularly once you join? Studies show that location is important. If the gym is right down the street you are more likely to go than if the gym is farther from home. You also have to have the time. If you are too busy to exercise at home, you will be too busy to get to the gym.

The vast majority of persons who join health clubs attend regularly at first, then after a few months attendance falls off dramatically, and eventually they don't go at all. Even though they quit going, they may still have a contractual agreement with the gym and if so they must continue to pay on their membership. This is why most gyms try to push you into a long term commitment, at least a one year membership. Many gyms, in fact, sell your membership to a collection agency. This allows them to get their cash up front without worrying about your reneging when you quit attending.

You need to be aware that after you commit to a long term membership, it's in the best interests of the gym that you don't return. It's logical, isn't it? If you're not there, you're not imposing any wear and tear on the equipment, you're not using the hot water for a shower, etc. But you still have to pay. Because of these considerations, I suggest that you thoroughly investigate the membership options offered to you. A well run gym is not afraid to give you a monthly or bi-monthly membership. They have trained personnel who will try to keep you motivated and coming back. It's in their best interest to do so.

Keep an eye out for membership drives. Often you can purchase a membership for a fraction of the going rate if you sign up during a drive. There are seasonal differences, too. Summers are generally the best time to join. Attendance is low and few people are joining and special fees are offered to attract more customers during this down time. If you wait until the fall, however, you are signing on at a peak time and you will pay a premium.

Also keep an eye out for short term trial periods in which you can purchase a two or three week membership which gives you an idea of what it's like to belong. This is the best way to tell. But be careful, because your motivation will be the highest during this initial phase.

If you decide to join, I urge you not to push too hard too soon in the interests of shaping up overnight. Most people don't want to perform one or two hours of hard physical labor after an eight hour work day, and you will flame out quickly. Former athletes can train this way, because that's the way they did it when they were competing. Former athletes subscribe to the no pain-no gain philosophy, and they feel cheated if they don't pound themselves into the floor and have to crawl out of the gym. But the average person will wilt under such pressure, because the harder you work, the more your sessions will feel like a job. When this happens, you don't look forward to attending and you will start finding excuses.

My advice is to keep the "work" out of your "workout." That doesn't mean you shouldn't exercise. On the contrary, you need to keep active for the entire time you are at the gym, but don't subscribe to a workout that is etched in stone, that ties you down to a tedious schedule. Be spontaneous and go with the flow. If you feel like jumping on the treadmill for ten minutes, do it. Then shoot over to the dumbbell rack and play there a while, before moving on to the stair climber. The key is to keep going constantly. This approach will help keep you mentally and emotionally fresh. It may not build as much strength or fitness as the commando approach, but then most wanna-be commandos quit going to the gym a long time ago, because it was too much work.

A Reader Writes:

"I am a woman in my forties and I never thought I would feel comfortable in a weight room. But after reading your column on the value of weight training for weight management, I thought I would give it a try. I must admit that at first I thought I would encounter a tribe of loud-mouthed louts who would do their best to scare me and my flabby arms away. But I found the opposite to be true. The muscle guys have been very helpful to me when I have asked, but in general they smile (actually they grimace, but they grimace pleasantly) and go about their business. I am enjoying my workouts a great deal and I encourage others to give it a try."

My Response

I am delighted you have had a good experience in the weight room. In the old days, weight rooms were likely to be found in dark and dank basements, inhabited only by strange creatures called bodybuilders. I know, I was one of these strange creatures. I must admit that today, when I descend into such a musty basement, it brings back fond memories of pumping iron with my buddies. But that environment was not inviting to civilized individuals like yourself, and women especially didn't feel welcomed.

Fortunately, modern day weight rooms are bright and airy co-ed facilities, loaded with the latest high-tech equipment, including a quality sound system that provides upbeat music to keep you motivated. There's also an air of cooperation that's easily extended to newcomers. But a word of caution. You must be on your toes and thoroughly in tune with what's going on around you. You'll wear out your welcome in a hurry if you stumble around and bang into someone who is concentrating on a heavy set of bench presses. You also don't want to sit glassy-eyed, hogging a piece of equipment that others are eager to get at.

The following letter has a few other suggestions regarding weight room etiquette that are worth considering.

A Reader Writes — Commercial Gym Etiquette:

"As a frequent weight room user, I get tired of lifters not having much consideration for other users. Could you publish these simple guidelines? It would be much appreciated.

1. Always use a workout towel. Put it on the bench to lie on to soak up your sweat, then use it after you're done at a station to wipe up any remaining sweat.

2. Always rack your weights after use, unless the person waiting to use the station asks that you leave them on the bar.

3. Always put weights on the bar with the print side in — they're more stable that way. But —

4. Put the weights on the rack with the print side out, not the smooth side out (this is something a lot of lifters don't seem to get!) The weights are much easier to lift from the rack (because of the lip of the plate) when the print side is facing out.

5. Always put bar weights back on the correct spot on the rack. Don't put a 5 pound plate in a 35 pound spot.

6. Always put dumbbells away with the printed weight facing up, so the next user can see what weight they are — if you can work out with the weight, you can turn it so the weight can be read!

7. Always put dumbbells back on the rack in order of the weight — from light to heavy. They're much easier to find that way.

8. Always keep pairs of dumbbells together on the rack! It's maddening to find one 20 pound dumbbell and have to search for the other which has been buried among the 75 pounders.

9. If you're doing an extended workout at one station, plan to take breaks so that other people can work into the station. Get up and step away, inviting others to participate.

10. Please report broken or defective equipment immediately. This can prevent an unsuspecting lifter from being injured. It also can help to keep a small problem from becoming a big one.

My Response

Thanks for your good letter. I'm certain those who have frequented weight rooms will appreciate where you're coming from.

Your first tip is particularly valuable. Nowadays, people like to train in ragged tank tops that expose a lot of skin. This allows you to watch your muscles in the mirror while they contract. But it also results in sweat pouring off onto exercise equipment that others will use. Being exposed to the waste products of other's skin can have potentially harmful effects and is best avoided. If you don't want to carry a towel, please wear a full cotton t-shirt that soaks up your sweat.

15. WALKING — GOOD FOR THE HEART AND THE HEAD

Everyone knows that daily exercise promotes health. We also are now aware that the kind of exercise required is not the kind that pushes you to the brink of exhaustion. Milder, more comfortable exercises like walking have been shown to produce great benefits. Recent research has shown that walking only a mile and a half daily can cut heart disease risk in half. That's quite a bang for the buck, and exciting news, but there's more to the story. A daily walk may improve brain function as well.

Research results are accumulating which suggest that if we don't use our brains, we lose brain power. The sharpness of our thinking often declines after we retire from the work force, because we ask less of our brains, challenging them less often to solve problems and hatch creative schemes. Research now suggests that if we also retire physically to the couch and move less, the decline in our brain power is accelerated. Walking can help turn this around.

Executive Control Processes

Brain function takes many forms. Recent research efforts have focused on the ability to concentrate, and to perform multiphasic activities (two or more things at the same time) with precision. In addition, physical responses that are a direct reflection of brain and nerve power have been assessed. An example is reaction time. Collectively, these types of functions are referred to as executive control processes.

Walking has been compared with other types of exercise, such as stretching and resistance training and has been found to be superior in producing a positive effect on the executive control processes of the brain. What's so special about walking?

Years ago, I ran across a theory about walking and its effects to promote creativity. Everyone has experienced brain-block. It's when you are trying desperately to be creative, but the creative juices refuse to flow. And the more you try to force the issue, the less progress you make. Often, when you quit in disgust, get up from your desk and leave the house, you experience a burst of creativity. Is this because you changed locations, and the change refreshed you and stimulated your brain? Maybe. Is it because you quit and thus reduced the pressure on yourself to create? Possibly. Or, could it have something to do with the act of walking?

The theory about walking and creativity suggests that the bilateral nature of walking (alternating one foot forward, then the other, and coordinating foot movements with the alternating swinging of the arms) acts to reengage the right side of the brain. Let me explain.

The left side of the brain is generally believed to control rational linear thinking. It's the side of the brain we consult when sitting at the computer, solving math problems, or planning a strategy. The right side of the brain, in contrast, is believed to be more involved with creativity and artistic endeavors. When we experience brain-block, perhaps we concentrate so completely that we engage the left side of our brain, while blocking input from the right side. We try so hard, in other words, we cannot see the forest for the trees.

The act of walking may help pull the right brain back into the action quickly — more quickly than simply changing locations and/or reducing the pressure on ourselves to create. Regardless of the mechanisms involved, it's another point in favor of walking every day as a means to improved health.

The Bottom Line

Exercise is good for you, and walking is good exercise. We have known about the physical benefits for decades. Now, we find that it's possible the walking we do for our heart may be highly beneficial to our brain. This finding, if true, strongly supports increased walking as we age, as a means of preserving mental as well as physical abilities.

16. WALKING/RUNNING SHOES — WORTH THE PRICE?

Paying more money for something generally means getting higher quality. While this may be true, the question arises — how much of the additional cost is actually supporting increased quality, and how much goes for promotion and advertising? If a substantial portion goes for the latter, paying less can work in your favor. With that said, be careful when making decisions which involve your feet. An ounce of prevention can save you a ton of cure. Let me explain.

The foot is a remarkable organ. It's a bag of bones skillfully crafted like a suspension bridge to absorb shock, support the body in an upright posture, and adapt to most any terrain. Although the feet take a great deal of punishment in serving us throughout the day, they will be healthier because they are being used. But the feet must be properly cared for, and this entails a wide range of considerations. Poor overall health can negatively affect the feet. Obesity, diabetes, circulatory limitations, arthritis, etc. can create major problems in the feet. In addition, shoes (quality, fit, and selecting the right type for the occasion), socks, walking or running gait, etc. also can cause problems. Because so many factors can operate, it's no wonder so many adults suffer from painful feet.

If you intend to be a serious walker or runner, you probably are better off staying away from bargain basement, brandless, shoes. They often are made of inferior materials which may substantially reduce longevity of the shoe. But more important, inferior materials may not provide sufficient resiliency, or shock absorption, to protect the feet.

Inexpensive shoes also may suffer from poor overall design and construction. A significant portion of the price of brand name shoes is driven by research and development efforts invested to put together a shoe that not only absorbs shock, but also breathes (allows air to circulate through the shoe to keep the feet dry), protects the arch of the foot, braces the heel, offers ample room in the toe box, etc. Cheap shoes may look just as good as their more expensive counterparts, but "under the hood" there is a big difference.

Am I suggesting that you go out and buy the most expensive shoes available? Not at all. When considering high quality shoes, there will be a wide price range. You can buy an excellent shoe that does everything you need for a reasonable cost, providing you avoid the bells and whistles. A stripped down Mercedes without leather interior runs just as well and is as durable as a much more expensive Mercedes loaded with all the gadgets.

Start your selection process at the low end of the well established lines of shoes. Next, go for comfort, and verify the degree of comfort before buying. Take time to walk or jog around the store in them. Don't be in a hurry to get them off your feet.

Buying a good shoe will ensure resiliency and durability, but there is more to consider. Here's a check list to follow.

1. Shop later in the day, because your feet will tend to swell as the day goes on. Shopping earlier in the day may cause you to purchase a shoe that is too narrow.

2. Wear the kinds of socks you intend to wear when exercising.

3. Have both feet measured, and put your weight on the foot that's being measured. If one foot is larger than the other, try the size of the larger foot.

4. Wiggle your toes to test the amount of room in the toebox. Allow about a half inch between the end of your longest toe and the tip of the shoe.

5. Check width at the widest part of the foot, across the metatarsal joints (where the metatarsals meet the base of the toes). Cramped quarters will create problems.

6. Put the shoes to the test. Rise on your toes like a ballerina, checking to see that the shoe bends easily and comfortably with your foot. Place the ball of your foot on a stool and lower your heel so that it is lower than your toes. The heel of the shoe should hug your heel comfortably. Most sporting goods stores will be large enough for you to jog around a bit and really test the comfort and fit of your new shoes. Maximize this opportunity. It's best to uncover a problem in the store, rather than later at home.

7. Don't assume that a shoe that is uncomfortable in the store (even only slightly uncomfortable) will get better with wear. An uncomfortable shoe could cause unwelcome accommodations in your feet, which could spell future problems.

17. WEIGHTED WALKING

Walking is considered by many to be the ideal exercise. I agree. It burns calories, relaxes the mind and promotes health. What's more, it's convenient. All you need is a pair of comfortable shoes and off you go.

Some fitness buffs downplay the value of walking, however, because it is not vigorous enough to build a high level of aerobic fitness. Race walking can get the job done, but who wants to wiggle and jiggle down the street and be jeered and pointed at? And although walking up steep hills can be vigorous, the intensity is not sustained, because you have to come down the other side, and usually there are long stretches of level ground.

Weighted walking adds weights to the body for the purpose of making walking more challenging. It increases the intensity of effort, in other words, and in the process builds aerobic fitness. Even though the intensity of exercise increases, the orthopedic stress on the feet, ankles, knees and hips, although greater than regular (non-weighted) walking, is still substantially less than that incurred during jogging. During walking, one foot is always in contact with the ground, which prevents jarring impacts with each stride.

You can approach weighted walking in a variety of ways. Hand weights received great attention several years ago with the introduction of Heavy Hands. Walkers grip a weighted baton in each hand which can be adjusted from 1 to 5 pounds each. The intensity of walking can be regulated by the degree of movement of the hands. Simply holding the weighted hands next to the thighs does little to increase intensity. As a rule of thumb, the nearer the weight is to the body's center of gravity (the navel), the lesser the impact. In fact, the military discovered that substantial weight can be carried with reduced effort if the weight is distributed close to the body and near the navel.

To get the intensity up, you have to pump the arms. Bend the elbows and pump the arms as you normally would during a fast walk. The weights should move from thigh level to eye level with each stroke. Coordinate hand and foot movements (the right hand comes up as the left foot moves forward). Adding hand weights and walking as described can increase intensity by as much as 40 percent. In terms of caloric expenditure, a comfortably brisk walking pace (3.5-4 mph) will expend about 80-100 kcal/mile (for an average size adult — slightly more for males because they are larger, and slightly less for females). But with 5 pound hand weights, the cost can increase to about 120-140 kcal/mile. That's more than the caloric cost of jogging per mile. What's more, the heart rate in moderately fit individuals during walking with hand weights easily can exceed the fitness threshold (140-150 bpm for young adults). The heart rate of less fit individuals will be higher. Intensity can be increased even more with exaggerated arm movements, but most people find this to be uncomfortable.

A word of caution. Gripping hand weights can be a problem to those suffering from tennis elbow or carpal tunnel syndrome. To alleviate the stress of gripping, donut cuffs were invented which slip over the wrists. The effect is the same. Try both and choose the one that is most comfortable. Also, never swing hand weights. Momentum of any kind stresses the shoulder joints and can result in injury.

Weighted walking also can be achieved by adding weights to the ankles. The increase in intensity is not as great as the increase with hand held weights, but it is significant. Adding 5 pound weights to each ankle can increase the cost of walking (3.5-4 mph) by 20-25 percent, and increase the heart rate to about 135 bpm in moderately fit individuals.

Adding both hand and ankle weights causes an additive effect, increasing the caloric cost of walking a mile to 140-160 kcal. Heart rate will be comparable to a slow jog, or about 160 bpm — more than adequate to produce a high level of aerobic fitness.

Power walking entails the wearing of a weighted vest. Because of the proximity of the vest to the center of gravity, considerable weight must be worn in order to increase intensity of effort. It is common to wear 50 to 75 pounds in a special commercially available vest.

Why does it take a 65 pound vest to match the intensity of 5 pound hand or ankle weights? The answer is leverage. The further you get from the center of gravity, the greater the leverage, and the greater the effort required. To see how this works, grab a broom by the extreme end of the handle with one hand and raise the broom so that it is parallel to the floor. Hold for several seconds. It's heavy and fatiguing, because the length of the broom exaggerates the impact of leverage. The same is true for the length of the arms when it comes to hand weights.

Some people prefer the comfort of the vest to hand or ankle weights. Walking is thought to be more natural with the weighted vest, whereas walking is more contrived with hand or ankle weights. It is not uncommon for gung-ho fitness types to wear a heavy vest and use hand and/or ankle weights. Despite all this weight, the impact on the feet and leg joints would still be less than that of jogging.

The bottom line is, walking can be altered to become a highly productive fitness activity which can burn as many calories as jogging and other high intensity exercises. But don't get the wrong impression that walking has to be intense in order to be healthful. It doesn't. All walking is good for you.

Tips for Safe and Productive Weighted Walking

1. Start with light weights (1 pound hand or ankle weights) and work your way up. Starting with 5 pounds on each hand or ankle may be too much initially and could cause injury.

2. When walking with weights, walk slowly for a while until your body becomes accustomed to carrying the weights and subtle adjustments are made in your walking gait.

3. Gripping hand weights can be a problem for those suffering from tennis elbow or carpal tunnel syndrome. It's also possible that daily use of hand weights and countless repetitions could bring on such problems. To avoid overuse, walk with hand weights one day, ankle weights the next, no weights the next, then hand weights again, etc. To alleviate the stress of gripping, donut cuffs were invented which slip over the wrist. The effect is the same. Try both and choose the one that is most comfortable.

4. Gripping weights can fatigue the hands. Commercially

available Heavy Hands are designed with a loop which fits over the back of the hand, allowing the hand to loosen its grip while still holding the weight securely.

5. Never swing the weights carelessly while walking. Momentum of any kind can stress the shoulder and elbow joints and can result in injury.

6. It's a good idea to take along a strap or extra shoelace for emergencies that could arise some distance from home. Tie one end to each hand weight and slip the lace (yoke-like) around the back of your neck to support the weights while you walk.

7. Ankle weights are available which wrap around the ankle, or that lay over the instep and are held in place by the shoe laces. Instep weights are held in place more firmly which may be more comfortable.

8. Hand, ankle, and weighted vests can be purchased at sporting goods stores. A set of Heavy Hands handles (1 pound each) costs approximately $20. Adding weights requires purchasing separately screw-on weights in sets of four at an additional cost of approximately $30 per set.

Ankle weights can be purchased in a range of from 1 pound (approximately $10 per pair) to 5 pounds (approximately $20 per pair). Weighted vests have lost popularity in recent years but still can be found. The cost ($50-$75) covers the cost of the vest and the leaded weights. You have the option of lessening the load by removing weights from the specially designed pockets.

9. Test hand and ankle weights and the weighted vest in the store before buying. Wear your exercise clothes to the store and actually work out with the weights by walking briskly around the store for several minutes. It's the only way to tell before you buy whether or not you feel comfortable with such an arrangement.

18. TREADMILL WALKING

How does treadmill walking compare with walking outside?

Several factors can make treadmill walking a little easier. If you are relaxed and comfortable during your walks on the treadmill, the treadmill will do some of the work of walking for you. When you move your lead foot forward, for example, after contacting the walking surface the treadmill carries it back for you. Also, the treadmill has a consistent elevation and the terrain is always the same. When you walk outside, going up even slight elevations changes the energy cost of walking considerably. The walking surface also can be an important consideration. Walking in grass, on cinders, or in snow will add to the resistance your feet encounter, which will increase the energy cost of walking. Walking on an uneven surface also can add to your effort.

With that said, the difference in energy cost is not worth worrying about. If you are walking at 4-miles per hour you are doing a good deal of healthful exercise, regardless of whether you are indoors on a machine or outside. At that rate, the average size male will expend about 100 calories per mile. Females are smaller and will expend about 20 percent fewer calories per mile.

Since outside walking may be slightly more demanding, you may build slightly more physical fitness. But fitness is not the most important consideration when it comes to being healthy. The key is consistency and exercising as often as possible.

Burning Calories on the Treadmill

A number of factors must be taken into consideration when determining the caloric cost of treadmill exercise, or any rhythmic ongoing aerobic exercise.

1. **Size:** The larger you are, the greater the amount of energy

required to move your body a given distance. Generally, caloric values are assigned separately for men and women. Gender is not important, other than the fact that men tend to be larger and heavier than women. Caloric values are based on men who weigh in the neighborhood of 180 (+/- 10 percent) pounds, and for women at approximately 130 (+/- 10 percent) pounds. When considering the values provided below, if you weigh substantially more than 200 pounds, add a factor of 20 percent to caloric expenditure.

2. Mode: Jogging will cost approximately 20 to 40 percent more per mile than brisk walking. This is because in jogging the body must exert sufficient energy to propel both feet from the ground at the same time. In walking, one foot is always in contact with the ground.

3. Speed of walking: Strolling (approximately 2 mph) will cost about 60 calories per mile for women, and about 80 calories for men. Normal walking, up to 3.5 mph will increase these values to 70 and 90 calories per mile for women and men, respectively. Brisk walking at speeds greater than 3.5 mph will cost about 80 and 100 calories for women and men, respectively. Although it will be difficult and uncomfortable for most, very fast walking at 5 mph and greater will up the cost an additional 10-20 percent.

4. Speed of jogging: The caloric cost of jogging doesn't vary greatly per mile within a speed range of about 5 to 9 mph. For men, the cost is 120-140 calories per mile, and for women 100-120. The cost per minute varies greatly, of course, and the faster the jogging speed the greater the cost per minute. You will jog for fewer minutes at a faster pace, which explains how the overall cost per mile can be similar.

5. Terrain: You can vary the terrain on a treadmill by increasing the elevation. It is not possible to generalize about the energy cost of varying combinations of speed and elevation (a walk at 3 mph up an 10 percent incline, for example, or a 6 mph jog at 5 percent). You can grossly estimate the cost by using perceived exertion. If walking at 3 mph up a grade of 5 percent feels to your body like walking at 4.5 mph on the level, make the comparison and use the approximate cost of walking at 4.5 mph as your reference point.

While it is interesting to estimate how many calories you are burning during exercise, don't dwell on it. If you do, you find yourself mired in a compulsive need to achieve at least that number of calories expended per workout. This is natural. When you allow numbers (number of calories burned, number of miles run, number of minutes per mile, number of repetitions per set, etc.) to dominate exercise, you start playing mind games with yourself. You push yourself to achieve a predetermined number, and you feel like a failure if you don't make it. No one likes to be forced to do unpleasant things, and no one likes to fail. Finding ourselves between this proverbial rock and hard place is why most of us quit exercising after a while. True, if you are an athlete, you have to pursue the numbers and push through the mind games. But for the average person, it's the kiss of death.

A better approach is to conjure up ways of using your treadmill that will maximize convenience and pleasantness. Watch TV or listen to your favorite music. Don't set the clock or worry about how long you go. Simply go until you decide to stop. It may be two minutes one time, and seventeen minutes the next. Be spontaneous, and jump on when the opportunity presents itself.

A final point to consider is one that I've made before, but that needs to made again and again. The distinction between the calories that go into your body versus the calories that go out is an important one. The ones that go in are oh-so-easy. A small candy bar is 300 calories — tasty and easy, right? But to get rid of those calories requires an entire hour of walking on the treadmill. With this in mind, the number of calories you burn exercising (unless you exercise hard like an athlete for hours every day) is largely irrelevant if there are too many calories coming in. So, if weight management is your goal, concentrate on the calories coming in, and be less compulsive about how many you burn off.

The bottom line is, be spontaneous about your exercise and make it fun. Do as much as you can, but don't make it a job. The more you make it like work, the sooner you'll give it up.

19. STAY FRESH WITH CROSS TRAINING

Exercise can strengthen the heart, the bones, muscles and joints. It can enhance aerobic fitness, increase muscle mass, reduce body fatness, and promote flexibility. Unfortunately, no single exercise can accomplish all of these goals. Jogging, for example, can enhance aerobic fitness, but it contributes little to development of muscle mass, especially in the upper body. Weight training increases muscle mass, but does not promote flexibility.

Cross training is the answer. Cross training encompasses two or more differing approaches to exercise which can be performed in one workout, or alternated in successive workouts. A runner who runs long distances in training, may also lift weights, perform stretching exercises, and participate in high intensity bicycle sprints.

While cross training seems to make perfect sense, there is controversy regarding its benefits. Cross training contradicts the time-honored principle that training should be limited in scope and as closely aligned as possible to the performance you want to improve. This is known as the principle of task specificity, and it means if you want to be a good long distance runner, your training should consist essentially of running long distances. Moreover, nonspecific activities (weight training or swimming laps for runners) are viewed as a waste of time and effort because they do not contribute to the specific goal.

Many sports scientists argue in favor of the benefits of cross training, and some believe it may be the best approach for maximizing the body's ability to perform. Peak performance in any given physical activity usually involves more than one physiologic attribute. The long distance runner may need a strong sprint to the finish line, for example, and thus success in the marathon may require not only high levels of aerobic fitness, but also high levels of anaerobic fitness as well. In addition, weight training to increase muscular strength and muscular endurance may help reduce fatigue in the upper body muscles during long distance running. Because there is often little or no overlap among attributes such as aerobic fitness, anaerobic fitness, and strength, cross training is required.

Cross training offers other advantages as well, which can pay big dividends not only for competitive athletes, but for those who train simply to keep in shape and manage their weight.

- Cross training offers variety which can reduce boredom and keep interest high while training. Nowadays, you can choose not only from traditional training methods such as running, swimming, and cycling, you can exercise on a cross-country ski machine, a stair-stepper, a ladder treadmill, or on in-line skates.
- Cross training aids development of the entire body, rather than limiting development to specific muscle groups, bones or joints, or specific energy systems (aerobic vs anaerobic).
- Cross training distributes the load of training among various parts of the body, reducing the risk of orthopedic overload and injury.
- Cross training allows you to keep training with an injury, because when one body part is injured, you can train using different muscles and joints. This prevents deterioration of fitness, strength and muscle mass.

A cross training program usually entails the combination of separate exercises, each performed for a specific period of time. To improve aerobic fitness, for example, you can cycle, jog, row or swim for 30 minutes. To increase muscular strength, you can lift weights for 30 minutes. You can do one form of exercise each day, or both on the same day. If you perform both exercises on the same day, you have the option of changing the order in which they are performed from one workout to the next.

Cross training exercises also can be performed in formats which combine varying exercises into a single routine designed to enhance aerobic fitness, strength and muscular endurance. In circuit training you perform high repetition, low resistance weight training exercises, and move quickly from one exercise to the next with little rest. In step aerobics using light dumbbells, weight training movements (curls, lateral and forward raises, etc.) are choreographed into a routine which also entails stepping up and down on a bench, lunges, and other aerobic activities.

You can easily tailor cross training to meet your needs. All you have to do is select exercises from each of the following five categories and put together a program. Competitive athletes should seek the aid of an experienced coach when making up a workout schedule.

1. Aerobic fitness exercises: brisk walking, walking with hand weights or leg weights, power walking, race walking, jogging, running, swimming (water walking/running, water exercises), cycling, cross country skiing, rowing, roller skating, in-line skating, ice skating, elliptical training

2. Anaerobic fitness exercises: sprinting in any of the above exercises

3. Muscular strength exercises: weight training, resistance machine training, isometrics

4. Muscular endurance exercises: low resistance/high repetition weight training, push-ups, crunches, pull-ups and other calisthenics

5. Flexibility exercises: stretching, yoga

Here is an example of a cross training program designed to improve aerobic fitness, muscular strength, muscular endurance, and flexibility, and also to assist in weight management through considerable daily caloric expenditure. This program is not designed to improve athletic performance in any specific sport, and should be considered a means to all-around conditioning.

Monday — brisk walking with hand weights (20-30 min); stretching (5-10 min); upper body weight training (30 min)

Tuesday — jogging at a steady pace (20-30 min); stretching (5-10 min); lower body weight training (30 min)

Wednesday — swimming (20-30 min); yoga (20-30 min)

Thursday — cycling or rowing or cross country skiing (20-30 min); stretching (5-10 min)

Friday — brisk walking (20 min); upper and lower body weight training (45 min) or circuit weight training (20-30 min)

Saturday — jogging at a varied pace (30-45 min); stretching (5-10 min)

Sunday — rest, or comfortable walking (30-45 min); yoga (20-30 min)

Maximizing Gains in Aerobic Fitness and Muscle Mass

Let's assume you want to maximize gains in both your aerobic fitness and your muscle mass. Accomplishing this would require intense effort, overloading your body in two entirely different and potentially competing ways, and forcing it to accommodate the total stresses imposed in order to make the necessary physiologic changes. Can you do both in one workout? Probably not. If increasing both is your goal, you are better off performing weight training exercises one day, and aerobics the next.

But, even though you have split your efforts over two or more days, there still may be problems. This is especially true if you are more advanced and are used to really "busting a gut" in training. Intense training "tears down the body," requiring substantial time to recover, and this is especially true when it comes to strength training. Therefore, running with sufficient intensity to promote increased aerobic fitness on the day after a brutal weight training workout may interfere with your recovery, which, in turn, may impede your next weight training workout. You may, in other words, enter your next weight training workout only partially recovered, reducing your ability to push yourself to a level required for stimulating muscular growth. And if you do push yourself, even though your body is giving you feedback that it would rather not, you run the risk of overtraining.

The good news is, young athletes have tons of excess energy and resiliency and can probably balance both types of training, making good gains in each. Indeed, off-season athletes will strive to improve both muscle mass and aerobic fitness, and they usually are successful.

But do they improve each component to the extent possible? Can you, in other words, increase your strength and muscle mass to the same degree whether or not you include aerobic training on your "off" days?

That's an interesting question and one that has been investigated by exercise physiologists. By and large, research suggests that building strength and adding muscle mass may be somewhat compromised by including intense aerobic training on the days off. The reverse is not so much of a problem, however, and improvements in aerobic fitness can accrue even though intense weight training is included on "off" days. The situation changes, however, if you are trying to prepare for a marathon or other prolonged endurance events. If you are, then what you do on your off days becomes more critical, and intense weight training could cause you to overtrain and enter the valley of chronic fatigue.

Attempting to improve both aerobic fitness and muscle mass at the same time also reduces your margin of error in covering all the bases. Your nutrient needs, the total number of calories required, your rest, relaxation and sleep requirements, etc. all will be increased substantially and must be fully met in order to progress.

Increasing Either Aerobic Fitness or Muscle Mass

If your goal is to increase only one component, while maintaining the other, you have more flexibility in structuring your training. If increased strength and muscle mass are of uppermost importance, it would be best to specialize in this type of training, and do a modicum of aerobics on the side, just enough to stay in shape, but not enough to steal energy away from your primary goal. With this scenario, you could jog an easy mile or two after a weight training workout, then take the next day or two off completely. Or, you could do an easy jog the next day. Regardless of your choice, you should not invest too much energy in jogging.

For those training for a sport and engaging in off-season training, there is a decision to make. Because adding muscle mass takes much longer than increasing aerobic fitness, you may want to specialize in one, maximizing potential training effects, then pick up the other later. Specialize in weight training for many weeks, doing only a modest amount of aerobic work on the side, then about three weeks prior to preseason, intensify your aerobic workouts. This may compromise your gains in muscle mass, but you already should have accomplished most of your muscle building goals, and reporting to camp in the kind of shape required for intense and demanding running workouts is the overriding concern.

Which Comes First?

If you are an everyday person, not needing to add pounds of muscle mass, and not aspiring to run a sub 3-hour marathon, you can easily structure your daily training routine to include both aerobics and strength training. Usually, most exercisers prefer doing weight training first. This is probably because weight training challenges not only the body, but also the mind. You must be mentally prepared for each weight training exercise and you must concentrate while doing it. Being fresh helps in this regard. In contrast, when jogging, you tend to enter a mental zone, sustaining a rhythm, relaxing into your stride. This doesn't require the kind of mental energy needed to push a barbell off your chest.

Breathing also is important in weight training and must be controlled and efficient. You are taught to exhale on the concentric portion (overcoming gravity) and to inhale on the eccentric portion (resisting gravity). To do this effectively, it's a good idea to wait until breathing has returned to normal between sets. Having jogged a few miles may take considerable time before breathing is completely returned to normal and before your gut tells you that you are ready to tackle the weights. Even then, the residual effects of jogging may spill over and interfere with your weight training efforts.

On the other hand, some prefer to be really warmed-up before jumping into the barbells. Jogging a light mile or two prior to lifting can be the perfect way to accomplish this. The key here is the word "light" and not pushing the jog too hard so as to increase breathing excessively.

Circuit Training

Another option is circuit training in which you perform both resistance and aerobic training coincidentally. In circuit training you perform high numbers of repetitions with limited resistance in weight training exercises. Each set may last a minute or longer and you move quickly from one exercise to the next, equating to one continual "aerobic-like" workout. You may alternate an upper body exercise with a lower body exercise, for example, allowing one set of muscles to relax while you challenge another. Exercises are performed in a rhythm and breathing is natural (in both the concentric and eccentric phases), as it is when jogging. You never grunt and groan when performing the exercises that make up a circuit.

The advantage of circuit training is that you can engage in both aerobic and strength training exercise in a short period of time. Most circuits are designed to last approximately 20 to 30 minutes. The down side is, you compromise the impact of both types of training and you are not able to build much muscle mass and strength, or much aerobic fitness. Also, where you train must be set up for it, because it takes a coordinated effort to move easily and predictably from one weight training station to the next. It's difficult to do this in the midst of others performing traditional training, because you may have to wait for a piece of equipment to become available, which would ruin the effect you are trying to create.

The Bottom Line

When it comes to strength training versus aerobics, give priority to the type of training that will help you reach your goals by investing the lion's share of your energies there. Splitting aerobic versus strength training on separate days is probably best, but be careful to structure your training so that one type of exercise does not interfere too greatly with recovery from the other type. If your goals are modest, you may choose to perform both strength and aerobic training in the same workout. If you do, your body will probably prefer to go with strength training first, but not always. Do what feels best for you.

20. PREPPING FOR A ROAD RACE

If it's your intention to enter a recreational road race, there is much to consider. The most popular road race is the 10K (10 kilometers, or 6.2 miles), but distances can range between 3 and 13 miles. Longer distances should be reserved for the serious runner. As a recreational runner, your goal should be to have fun and to run the best time you can without placing yourself in harm's way. The key to achieving your goal is adequate preparation. The following information should help.

1. Are you ready?

Running any appreciable distance is quite a feat requiring a combination of aerobic fitness and orthopedic readiness. The two are not the same. Increased fitness can come quickly and with short (2 or 3 miles) and highly intensive runs. Orthopedic readiness, on the other hand, may take longer to achieve. It means your muscles, tendons, ligaments, bones and joints are capable of withstanding the pounding they will take from running a long distance. This can only be achieved over time, gradually increasing running distance. As a rule of thumb, if in your training you regularly can run approximately half the distance of the race (once or twice a week), and periodically can run nearly the full distance (80-90%) for at least three months without a problem, you are probably orthopedically ready.

2. Check your shoes.

A key factor in orthopedic readiness is your shoes. They are the only thing separating you from the pavement, and they better be up to the task. In jogging and running there is an airborne phase in which both feet leave the ground and the weight of the body comes crashing down on the lead foot with a force 2.5 to 4 times the bodyweight. The faster the pace the greater the impact. Running shoes are specially designed to emphasize shock absorption, and millions of dollars have gone into research and development techniques to maximize this aspect of the shoe. With daily usage, however, shock absorption capability is gradually lost, and eventually running shoes are reduced to the status of sneakers. The more you weigh and the faster you run the quicker this happens. In general, you can expect from 600 to 800 miles of quality running from a good pair of shoes. If you are larger or a very experienced runner who runs hard, the life of your shoes will be decreased to 300-500 miles. If you need to shift to a new pair of shoes do so well in advance of the race and break them in gradually.

3. Honor your routine.

Beware of sudden changes in your routine prior to the race. Maintain a consistent diet. Eat the same items and eat at approximately the same time of day in order to establish a consistent gastrointestinal schedule. Going out for a carbohydrate loading dinner the night before the race may not be a good idea if you are not used to eating at night. Besides, carbo loading is not necessary for distances shorter than a marathon (26 miles). At shorter distances you'll easily have enough carbs in storage as glycogen to finish, whether you load up or not. Most runners train after work which means they run in the early evening. If possible, on weekends perform practice runs in the morning at approximately the same time as the race. Doing this once or twice a week will help your body adjust to the challenge of running at an unfamiliar time. It will also help you arrange your eating schedule to accommodate a morning run.

4. Beware of what and when you eat on race day.

Your body loves carbohydrates. They are the preferred fuel of the body. In anticipation of the race, your best choice is to consume carbs, but you don't have to load up. The fuel your body uses for the race will already be in place the day before you run. Eating the day of the race merely adds a finishing touch. Get up early enough to eat a light breakfast that is easily digested. Avoid meat and high protein foods because they are a challenge to the digestive system, especially if you are nervous. Most runners enjoy toast and jam with juice or fruit. But be careful. Such a breakfast may spike your blood sugar which in turn will cause a severe insulin response that could leave you hypoglycemic (low blood sugar) an hour or so later. This is called an insulin rebound effect.

To avoid this, after finishing your breakfast, graze on small quantities of carbs every 20 to 30 minutes prior to the race, and especially within 15 minutes of starting the race. If you are too nervous to eat, use a sports drink with a high glucose content.

5. Maintain your body's water balance.

As the weather warms, you will sweat more in training, causing you to lose a considerable quantity of fluid from your body. Check your water balance by weighing before each run and after. Any weight that is lost is water weight, and one pound equals one pint of lost fluid. Replace all lost fluid prior to your next training run and check to be sure by bringing your weight completely back to normal. Water may be a sufficient rehydration drink. But if water loss is excessive, more than 4 pints, a sports drink (with low glucose content) is a good idea. It is highly dangerous to gradually deplete your body fluids in training, but this can happen easily if you are not careful. The loss of a pound here and a pound there can lead to chronic dehydration, meaning your water reservoir is too low to accommodate your needs for sweat on race day. Drink approximately 8 ounces of water just before the race, and then drink along the way at every opportunity. A conditioned runner can lose as much as 4 pints of sweat each hour during exercise, which means for most runners with a race time approaching two hours, the amount of sweat loss can reach 8 pints (4 quarts).

6. Dress for the run.

Race day may have high or low temperatures, depending on the time of year. Fortunately, in warm weather, most races are conducted in the coolness of the morning, and high temperatures are not likely. Be careful not to overdress in the coolness. As a rule of thumb, you should not be comfortable in what you have on when you are merely standing around. If you are, you will probably be uncomfortable as the race progresses, because during exercise you will produce tremendous amounts of metabolic heat which must be dumped from the body. The less clothing you have on the easier it is for you to dump heat. At the end of the race, if it is cool, bundle up as quickly as you can. Your body will be geared toward dumping large amounts of heat, but since the race is over, you won't be producing heat in large quantities. Under such circumstances you can cool your body too quickly and experience hypothermia.

7. Run a smart race.

With hundreds and potentially thousands of runners surrounding you it's easy to get caught up in the euphoria of the moment and you may start off with a faster than usual pace. That's okay, but be careful. If you push too hard in the early part of the race, you may experience fatigue that could catch up with you later. Along the route you will be given your splits — the amount of time elapsed from the beginning. Set realistic goals in your mind and try to stay on time. Allow a little extra time for the miles that contain hills. Saving yourself at the beginning allows a stronger finish, and you will find it's a lot more fun to have energy left to zip toward the finish line, than it is to push too hard at the beginning and barely survive at the end.

8. Listen to your body.

Over the years I have encountered many runners with injuries that can be traced back to a long road race. They usually recount that during the race they felt a twinge of pain somewhere, but they weren't about to stop. Pushing themselves onward and finishing put them over the edge orthopedically, resulting in a nagging injury that never quite heals. If you feel even the slightest pain, stop. It may be something that can be stretched out, or will subside with a bit of walking. There may be something in your stride that is unfamiliar because you are running a bit faster than usual, and this will take a toll eventually. Stopping for a spell can get you back into your normal rhythm. If, after stopping, you are still bothered with pain, quit and return another day. Risking an injury is a high price to pay for finishing or beating your best personal time. Ultimately, the goal of running the race is to have fun (which includes surviving without injury).

21. EXERCISE WHILE TRAVELING

Regular jaunts out of town can boost business, but they also can wreak havoc on your exercise program. Travel disrupts your daily routine, causing fitful sleep and enticing you to eat the wrong kinds of food while on the run. The result is stress and fatigue and a washed-out feeling that undermines your desire to exercise. And, once you arrive at your destination, lack of facilities and nonstop meetings can rob you of opportunities. Disrupt your routine often enough and before you know it, it's gone. And without an exercise routine your hard-earned fitness and strength gains fly out the window in a matter of weeks, only to be replaced by the gradual accumulation of unwanted pounds of flab.

But a little planning and effort can reward you with an effective exercise routine that can be implemented in almost any travel circumstance. Begin by reducing expectations when away from home. Sure, you have been training hard to improve your 10 K time, or to increase your bench press, and you are eager to keep momentum going in the right direction. But is this reasonable when on the road? If you are well rested and blessed with abundant up-to-date facilities and lots of free time, go for it. But in reality, when traveling you likely will be shortchanged somewhere along the line and it's best to anticipate this by not expecting too much of yourself. Maintaining strength and fitness is much easier than building it, and therefore when you are out of town it makes sense to concentrate on maintaining your gains through modest training, rather than trying to sustain your typical workout schedule.

Attempting to train intensively while on the road can be risky. Unfamiliar or inferior facilities, and pushing your body while fatigued, can lead to sloppy performance and increase the risk of injury. While you may feel the need to push hard in every workout, periodically engaging in modest maintenance workouts can prove fruitful. If you have been involved in a demanding and protracted exercise routine at home, a break in the intensity and length of workouts, or switching to an alternative mode of exercise, can prevent overtraining and may revitalize your body, giving you more energy for training then you had before leaving. What's more, a comfortable, moderate dose of exercise can energize you, making you more productive in your time away.

Here are some on-the-road exercise tips to keep in mind.

1. Commit to doing some form of exercise. When it comes to your health, consistency is a key ingredient in an exercise program, so don't admit defeat and give up on exercise just because you can't get out for your 3-mile run. Take a walk instead.

2. Plan ahead when choosing accommodations. Choose hotels with good fitness facilities. Call before booking to make certain you will have access to what you need. If a gym is not available at the hotel, inquire as to the nearest facilities.

3. Set the tone for your trip by exercising as soon as you can after arriving. It affirms your commitment, helps relieve the stress and fatigue of traveling, aids in adjusting to traversing time zones, and it prevents you from being sidetracked later by unexpected events that often occur when you are stripped of your daily routine.

4. If you can't get a bout of exercise in immediately, schedule workout time by blocking out an hour in your daily planner.

5. If you are strapped for time, seek exercise opportunities in bits and pieces. Avoid escalators and climb the stairs. Fast walk in the hotel hallways, or if you are within walking distance of an appointment, forget the cab. When confronted with a layover, use the time walking instead of sitting.

6. Build some fun into your exercise routine. Ask the hotel concierge to help you map out a scenic walking tour that includes sights worth seeing. Walking through a city can give you an up-close and personal experience that can't be matched on a tour bus. But make certain you know where you are going and avoid areas where being a pedestrian could make you a target.

7. Be careful when jogging. If you must jog on sidewalks know

that cement is hard on tender hip and leg joints. Reduce the speed and distance of your run.

8. Pack gear that will prepare you for a variety of exercise opportunities. Appropriate shoes (jogging or walking) are a must. Take exercise clothes suitable for indoor and outdoor (cold weather) conditions, and pack a swim suit.

9. Don't underestimate the value of exercise in your room. Old standards such as push-ups, lunges, crunches, and the like require only your bodyweight and a small space. Plan ahead by designing a 15-20 minute routine that keeps you moving.

10. Bring your own mini-gym. You can get a good workout with rubber exercise tubing, hand grips, plastic dumbbells you can fill with water, a jump rope, or audiocassettes with fitness, yoga, or stretching routines. And don't forget sports equipment — tennis or racquetball racket, golf clubs, etc.

11. Check the TV for exercise programs that encourage you to follow along and that don't require special equipment.

12. Dancing is not only fun, it's tremendous exercise. Learn how to do it well and practice your steps so you feel comfortable in unfamiliar surroundings.

Despite the best intentions and a pocket full of strategies, travel can still disrupt your exercise program. The best back-up is a healthy low-fat, low-sugar diet. Exercise can partially counteract a bad diet, but not entirely. Large doses of exercise can sustain effective weight management, but other unhealthful aspects can creep in, and the unexpected heart attack deaths of marathon runners underscores this point. Unfortunately, eating well on the road can be as challenging as maintaining an exercise program, and it also requires some forethought and effort.

Restaurants are making it easier to eat well with vegetarian dishes, and broiled and grilled entrees of poultry and fish. You can request special preparations without butter and oils, and low-fat desserts such as sherbets. On the plane you can ask ahead for the vegetarian or low-fat meal. Avoid the peanuts — the tiny bag contains a whopping dose of fat. Carrying some food with you in your briefcase or a small cooler ensures healthful choices and helps you resist skipping meals and later gorging on fatty sweets because you are starving.

The bottom line is, traveling does not have to blow a big hole in your exercise plan or disrupt your attempts at leading a healthy lifestyle. But in order to tilt the odds in your favor, plan ahead. The old saying "an ounce of prevention is worth a pound of cure," is especially applicable to time spent on the road.

22. EXERCISE AND SMOKING — WHY DO I GET WINDED?

Surprisingly, lots of people who exercise regularly also smoke cigarettes. Many believe their exercise program will cancel the bad effects of their smoking habit (see the "Exorciser," Chapter 8.) Is this true? No. But being an exerciser and a smoker is better than just being a smoker.

A frequent question that arises from smokers and former smokers who begin an exercise program is: Why do I get winded so easily? Is it because of my smoking? Maybe. Let me explain.

When you first begin a jogging program, your body is not used to exercise and is not prepared to respond adequately to the physical stress imposed. It may overreact in many ways, including heavy breathing (getting "winded") and even nausea. The physical stress is unpleasant and your body will do everything it can to get you to stop. But if you persist over several weeks, things will get better, because your body will begrudgingly make necessary changes which allow you to cope more effectively with the demands. As these changes occur, your breathing lessens and is more easily controlled.

Ironically, being "winded" is not caused by limitations imposed by the lungs, and a healthy set of lungs in an unfit person can easily handle the most demanding exercise. The reason for the labored breathing in beginning joggers is because the heart is having difficulty pumping enough blood to the muscles to meet the demand for oxygen during exercise. Because the muscles are starved for oxygen they send signals to the brain to stimulate greater breathing (erroneously thinking that this will solve the problem). So you breathe harder and harder, but still cannot deliver enough oxygen because of limitations imposed by the heart. As the heart is strengthened and gets in better shape and is able to pump more blood, the signals from the muscles for more oxygen abate and, in turn, your breathing lessens.

That's the scenario for healthy lungs. Smoker's lungs may be a different story entirely, and they may impose limits on your ability to exercise. The only way to tell is to keep plugging away, and if you see improvement in your breathing during exercise you know your lungs are not limiting you. If, however, you keep pushing yourself, but your breathing continues to be "out of whack" you will know that smoking has already taken a big toll.

Here is a rundown of the kinds of things that may be going on in a smoker's lungs which could impede progress as a jogger. It is common for chronic smokers to have some symptoms of chronic bronchitis and emphysema, and either or both will compromise lung function. In chronic bronchitis the pathways to the lungs inflame and thicken, creating resistance to air flow. There also is increased resistance from excess mucus production, and jogging may break some of this loose, aggravating the situation.

Over many years of abuse from smoking, emphysema is possible. In emphysema the site of damage is deep in the lungs, in the tiny air sacs where oxygen is exchanged for carbon dioxide. With emphysema you usually can inhale normally, but you have trouble exhaling. And because you have to force the air out, you may wheeze and labor excessively while breathing.

If you determine that your labored breathing during exercise is due to lung damage, you obviously should pause and consider the long range implications. Things will only get worse with continued smoking. If you could find a way to stop smoking, you may be able to reduce the impact of chronic bronchitis relatively quickly. The damage from emphysema, on the other hand, is not reversible. Even so, stopping the damage at its present level by stopping smoking may leave you with sufficient lung function in the future to live a reasonably normal life.

23. FIGHT PMS WITH EXERCISE AND A HEALTHY LIFESTYLE

Premenstrual syndrome, or PMS, has become a scapegoat among comedians for the difficulties commonly found in male/female relationships. But premenstrual complications are not amusing to women who experience one or more unpleasant symptoms prior to their monthly periods. Symptoms, including breast tenderness, bloating, headache, and backache often are accompanied by irritability, depression, food cravings and other behavioral changes. Women prone to migraine headaches may experience them more often just prior to their period. Usually, premenstrual symptoms increase in intensity as the cycle date approaches, followed by relief when the period begins. But relief is short lived in many who experience menstrual cramping and pain.

While 90 percent of women experience one or more symptoms prior to their menstrual period, only about one in ten women actually are diagnosed as having PMS. According to experts, sufferers of PMS experience symptoms that are so severe they interfere with lifestyle and relationships on the job or at home. In PMS, symptoms generally rage in two out of three menstrual cycles, ceasing abruptly when the period begins. But whether you have diagnosable PMS, or suffer from any of the many premenstrual symptoms, relief is welcomed. Fortunately, many of the strategies to reduce PMS also will help relieve menstrual cramping and pain.

Regular exercise is the cornerstone of a PMS prevention program. Moderate exercise such as walking can help alleviate premenstrual symptoms by relieving stress and contributing to weight management. More demanding exercise such as brisk walking on hilly terrain and light jogging may increase the release of endorphins in the brain. Endorphins are natural pain killers which bolster feelings of well being, which in turn combat depression. Jogging has been shown to reduce fluid retention and bloating, breast tenderness and overall premenstrual symptom intensity.

Unfortunately, the vast majority of American women (and men) rarely exercise. Lack of time is most often cited as the excuse, and for good reason. Women who attempt to cope with the responsibilities of home management, child rearing, and a full time job outside the home are pinched for time. What's more, taking valuable time to exercise is viewed as a luxury, and even selfish, by women who typically are better at taking care of others than they are of taking care of themselves. Changing such beliefs is difficult at best, but steps must be taken to convince women that they are responsible for their health and that a regular exercise program is a practical approach to a very real and disturbing problem.

Although a full blown exercise program, 6 days a week and at least 20-30 minutes a day is optimal, this is probably out of reach for the masses. A gradual indoctrination beginning with only one or two days of exercise per week, perhaps on the weekend when time is more available, is reasonable. Gradually, as the habit of exercising takes hold, more frequent bouts can be added. Walking is a good choice because it is familiar to those who have never participated in a regular exercise program. Walking also can easily include other family members and can be construed as a social outing, as well as beneficial exercise. And it's probably the most time efficient mode of exercise, because it doesn't require a change of clothes and you can do it anywhere on the spur of the moment. The only requirement is comfortable shoes designed for walking that absorb shock.

For those who are more ambitious, walking can progress gradually into a jogging program by including alternating periods of walking and jogging. Walk 200 paces, for example, then jog 50, walk again, etc. Each time you exercise, add a little to the jogging phase until your intervals of walking and jogging are equal. Then, begin reducing the walking phase. Swimming, cycling, rowing, cross country skiing and other activities that involve the major muscle groups of the body, are rhythmic in nature, and elevate the heart rate and keep it at a higher level throughout the exercise, are good choices, too.

In addition to aerobic exercises such as walking and jogging, stretching exercises as applied in yoga may help relieve menstrual symptoms. An example of a yoga exercise is the so called "child" pose. Start on the floor, kneeling, sitting back on your heels in an upright position. Bend forward slowly, placing your forehead on the floor, your hands extending to the rear. Breathe deeply, inhaling through your nose then exhaling. Pause momentarily, then inhale again. Begin with a brief comfortable pose, then gradually lengthen the time to several minutes.

Diet is a critical component of a comprehensive premenstrual symptom prevention program, and a healthy low-fat diet that is loaded with complex carbohydrates is best. Complex carbohydrates may possibly stimulate production of serotonin — a neurotransmitter in the brain which helps control mood, appetite and sleep patterns. The best sources for complex carbohydrates are vegetables, legumes (peas and beans), and whole grains. Calcium intake is important for many reasons, and in women should be at least 1000 mg daily. Calcium may help reduce water retention and help stabilize mood.

Avoiding certain food is important, too. Stay away from caffeine (found in the 3-C's — coffee, colas and chocolate) because it stimulates the nervous system, and during the premenstrual phase, being calm rather than hyped is the way to go. Avoid alcohol, too, as it can contribute to depression and headaches. And cutting way back on salt to reduce water retention may combat bloating.

Behavioral changes can help. Learn to handle stress through stress reduction techniques. Take a class, learn to meditate, or listen to tapes which help you relax. Treat yourself to a prolonged bubble bath, a stint in the hot tub, or a full body massage. Developing greater time management skills also can help reduce stress. Oftentimes, more can be accomplished in less time simply by being better organized and planning ahead.

24. EXERCISE AND PREGNANCY

I am frequently asked if exercise is a good idea for a woman who is pregnant, and especially for a woman who is pretty far along. The person asking the question usually is not a pregnant woman. Rather, it's likely to be a concerned spouse, mother, father, or friend — someone who cares about the welfare of a pregnant woman who exercises. Most often, they believe she should stop exercising and they want me to verify their fears that it's too dangerous for the mother and the baby.

My response is, exercise can be a positive thing, if it's done with caution and common sense. There are many advantages associated with exercise during pregnancy. There also are dangers, of course, and such dangers must be taken into consideration. Let's take a look at the pros and cons.

Can Exercise Hurt the Baby?

Until recently, the prevailing attitude was that exercise, and vigorous exercise in particular, could damage the baby. The concern was based in sound logic. Exercise imposes considerable demand on the mother's cardiovascular system. Since the fetus also places considerable demand on the mother's cardiovascular system, it was argued that exercise could create a competition between the fetus and the mother's working muscles for blood flow and oxygen. If this occurred, there might be danger of inadequate oxygen going to the developing fetus with disastrous consequences.

There has been considerable research in this area with interesting findings. It appears as if expectant mothers make changes in their cardiovascular system which allow them to exercise safely. Additional red blood cells are produced and put into the circulation which help the mother's blood carry more oxygen. In addition, the red blood cells give up oxygen more easily, thus reducing the amount of blood that is required to circulate to a given area of the mother's body.

Despite these adaptations, common sense says don't push it, and I strongly agree. Mom shouldn't train like an athlete with a goal of increasing her fitness during pregnancy. Additional precautions are warranted as well. Exercise lying down (supine) is best avoided, because it reduces the heart's capacity to pump blood, especially during the final trimester. Exercising at higher altitudes is best avoided, too, because it makes the heart work harder and there is evidence that there may be reduced blood flow to the uterus.

Another concern is body heat. During exercise metabolic rate rises, increasing the amount of heat produced inside the body. Vigorous and prolonged exercise could raise mom's body temperature to a danger point for the fetus. This is of particular concern during the first trimester when the baby's development is dramatic. On the plus side, physiologic changes in the mother help combat this problem, but, again, don't push it.

Exercise which causes metabolic heat production and an increased body temperature will cause sweating, and sweat loss can be excessive when exercising in a warm environment. Fluid loss during pregnancy must be monitored and all lost fluid must be replaced immediately, because dehydration could endanger the fetus. Fortunately, this is easy to do. Weigh before and after exercise. Any lost weight is water from sweating, and one pint of sweat weighs one pound. A loss of two pounds would require the drinking of two pints of fluid.

What about the baby's birth weight? Research studies offer conflicting results. Some researchers suggest that if mom exercises at levels substantially above the level she exercised at prior to conception, the baby's weight will be lower. Others have found no effects of exercise on the weight of the fetus. And still others have found that the fetus is heavier in exercising moms. The overall opinion of experts appears to favor the latter findings, especially if mom is conscientious about monitoring her caloric intake and follows a healthful diet with guidance from a registered dietitian.

What about the length of pregnancy? Opponents of exercise suggest that the adrenalin released in mom during exercise could trigger premature labor. The majority of evidence, however, argues against this and suggests that exercise influences term length in a positive way. A culprit of shortened gestation appears to be standing for prolonged periods, rather than being physically active.

Can Exercise Hurt the Mom?

Available evidence suggests positive effects of exercise for mom. Studies report reduced discomfort associated with pregnancy and a reduction of symptoms such as nausea and lower back pain.

Women I know who exercise feel strongly that exercise helped reduce the length of labor and the strain. Several studies support this notion, but not all. Some studies report no relationship between level of exercise and/or fitness, and circumstances surrounding delivery.

One issue where there appears to be widespread agreement is the positive effects of exercise to combat the impact of gestational diabetes. Exercise helps to make cells more receptive to the effects of insulin. This effect would, of course, be extremely helpful in combating gestational diabetes, because insulin resistance can arise during pregnancy due to hormonal changes. But, to be safe, women with gestational diabetes should exercise under the supervision of their doctor and take extra precautions, including closely monitoring their blood glucose levels, carefully timing meals and following a diet appropriate for their condition. Whether exercise can prevent gestational diabetes is open to question and more research is needed.

A big plus for exercise is weight management. Often, dietary indiscretions during pregnancy and gaining much more weight than you should, create a lifelong struggle with bodyweight. Exercise can help keep weight gain in check, and this is often offered as the principle reason why women choose to exercise during pregnancy.

To be safe, avoid high impact exercise and stick with user friendly activities such as walking and nonweight bearing exercise such as swimming. Jarring weight bearing exercises such as jogging may increase the risk of injury to the mother. This makes sense, because pregnancy increases body weight, and when jogging, the impact of each foot strike increases dramatically with each additional pound added to the body. The pregnancy also impacts balance and mobility, which could make jogging and moving rapidly somewhat precarious.

The Bottom Line

While exercise can be a positive factor in pregnancy, it may not be helpful for everyone. It's best to check with your doctor before starting, or continuing, an exercise program, and keep your doctor well informed along the way. Monitor the situation carefully and stop immediately if any warning signs surface (pain, dizziness, shortness of breath, vaginal bleeding, etc.). Above all, add a generous dose of common sense and don't try to do too much.

25. GOT KIDS? TAKE 'EM ALONG WHEN YOU EXERCISE

Some determined parents include young offspring as part of their exercise program by taking them along in jogging strollers, bike seats, and backpacks. This practice is controversial and is viewed by many as irresponsible and dangerous. But those who indulge claim the process can be safe and the results highly rewarding for both parent and baby.

Before striking out with baby in tow, however, there is much to consider. Foremost is the degree of risk involved. In general, the younger the child, the greater the risk. A modest collision, for example, involving a swiftly moving jogging stroller and a curb could be disastrous to a newborn. How likely is such an occurrence? It's difficult to pinpoint the probability with accuracy, but there are many factors which could increase risk.

When jogging at a fairly rapid pace (6 mph or greater), or cycling at a faster pace, there is a reduced margin of error with which to operate. The margin is reduced farther with a stroller which precedes the jogger by several feet. Despite the best of intentions, the jogger may be concentrating on the act of jogging or cycling and may be lost in thought, or there may be the gradual build-up of fatigue which can impact judgement. Terrain is a factor, and otherwise harmless minor potholes, divots, cracks or rocks could derail a rapidly moving stroller or cycle, especially one that has gained momentum moving downhill.

On the other hand, we must give parents a little credit. Responsible parents are going to take every precaution before placing their baby's life on the line. Here are some common sense safety tips.

Jogging Strollers
- Take a practice jog or two (without the baby) to get used to maneuvering the stroller. Scope the terrain with focus on what the

baby will encounter. Never jog at night, even if there appears to be adequate lighting available. Using a familiar route may be boring, but it's the safest approach. Keep firmly in mind that a clear path ahead is not necessarily without hazard. Reaction time will be reduced when pushing a stroller and therefore it is important to anticipate the unexpected (a car door opening, approaching cyclists, etc.) and take conservative preemptive action. Avoid traffic and close quarters of any kind.

- A smooth running surface is a must to prevent the baby's head from bouncing about (an important consideration until the baby is at least a year old). A bicycle helmet offers added protection for the head. Large tires that are slightly deflated can ease road impact.

- Pushing the additional weight of the stroller and the baby will require greater effort to sustain your normal pace. Slow down and don't drive yourself to exhaustion.

- Purchase a suitable carrier and don't shop for price. Expect to pay in excess of $250 for a good one. Sturdy construction is important. If you require the ability to transport the carrier in a car, make certain it collapses and reassembles quickly and easily. A deep seat and seat belt are important, or the capacity to accommodate a well made car seat. The baby must fit the seat, so take the baby along when purchasing. Look into the future and make certain the stroller will accommodate the baby as it grows in size. Be sure your stroller comes equipped with a locking brake and a secure handle which sustains a sweaty grip. A safety wrist strap will prevent the stroller from getting away from you. Never leave the stroller unattended, even for a moment.

- Check the weather. Conditions suitable for jogging may not be suitable for an infant passenger. Heat and humidity are particularly brutal, especially if the baby is clothed to avoid the sun's effects. Sun block and an overhead canopy help shield from the sun's rays. Cold and windy weather also presents risk. While a lightly dressed jogger will progressively produce increasing amounts of metabolic heat, the baby's internal thermostat will remain unchanged during the jog, or possibly even drop if you are not careful, and, therefore, don't judge the baby's comfort on how you feel. A windshield or plastic bubble offer the baby added protection from the elements.

Bike Seats and Trailers

Cycling with a baby passenger is viewed as potentially more dangerous than jogging with a stroller. Some experts reject totally the idea of child bicycle seats. Bicycles are, by nature, unstable and adding a seat decreases stability even more, because the added weight can shift unpredictably, especially if the baby weighs more than 40 pounds. Other experts contend that cycling can be safe with adequate precautions.

All experts seem to agree on at least two items. First, only expert cyclists should even consider taking a baby along. And, second, if you choose to cycle, be certain the baby can hold its head up. Trunk support also is critical, and the minimal age for baby passengers is one year.

The rear-mounted seat is the most popular. Is it safer than the front-mounted seat? This is controversial and there are positives and negatives associated with either choice.

In the rear-mounted seat, there is more centrifugal force imposed on the baby if the parent needs to pedal hard up hills (especially while standing). This can whip-lash the baby's head and neck. However, most cyclist are used to bearing extra weight from the rear, and this familiarity could make the ride more stable. Rear-mounted seats can be larger, with high backs which offer greater support.

Critics of the front-mounted seat contend that while communicating with a baby seated in front may have advantages, the rider may focus too much attention on the baby if it is positioned in the line of sight, thus sacrificing concentration on the road ahead. Older babies, on the other hand, who are aware of what is going on during the ride can observe what's ahead and anticipate the need to brace or shift weight. Regardless of the choice of a front- or rear-mounted seat, many common safety tips apply. (See tips above for strollers — avoid traffic, don't cycle at night, never leave the baby and cycle unattended, make certain the seat fits the baby, dress the baby properly (and especially avoid clothing that could unravel and get caught in the spokes, etc.).

• Helmets are a must for the cyclist and the baby. The helmet should fit snugly and offer adequate padded protection. Verify the quality of helmets with an expert who is familiar with qualifications of various certification organizations (such as the Snell Memorial Foundation or the American National Standards Institute).

- Use a helmet mounted mirror to increase overall vision.
- A high-flying fluorescent warning flag will help others see you before you see them.
- Seats must have spoke guards, security belts and adequate padding.
- The seat must be properly and securely fitted to the frame. Shifting a seat to another bike can be tricky, and the safest approach is never to shift a seat to a borrowed cycle.

An alternative to the mounted seat is the bike trailer. But while many of the objections to mounted seats are removed, new hazards may arise. The baby is farther removed from the parent which reduces communication. The trailer is close to the ground and the ride can be quite rough. There is extra length to contend with which can reduce the ability to maneuver quickly in an emergency. Another consideration is cost. Trailers can cost much more than seats and go as high as $350.

Backpacks

Backpacks are probably the safest way to transport an infant, but they are not without danger and many of the common sense safety tips cited above apply. Carrying a backpack can impact balance, and a fall could be devastating. Take smaller steps, avoid rough (uncertain, slick, soggy, etc.) terrain, and avoid momentum (especially downhill) while walking. Never engage in fly fishing or other activities involving implements and accessories which can carry out of sight or get out of control. Here are some additional things to consider.

- Comfort for the parent is important, especially on long walks. Padded shoulder straps and a waist belt help support the weight of the backpack and take much of the load off the lower back. If more than one parent uses the backpack, take time to adjust straps according to size to maximize comfort and stability.
- Backpacks come in various sizes. Large backpacks are more comfortable for baby and offer greater support. But because of their size, large backpacks can be too cumbersome for many activities — traversing shopping aisles, for example, or mingling in a crowd — and they take considerable room to transport. The backpack must be

sufficiently deep to comfortably support the baby's back, trunk and head in an upright position.

- Safety straps constrain the baby if you should fall, and they keep the baby from crawling out.
- Ample padding over the frame ensures baby comfort and avoids damaging impact with the baby's head in an emergency.

The bottom line when transporting a baby during exercise, regardless of the mode employed, is to appreciate that danger exists even if all possible safety measures are taken. Anticipate the unexpected and assume a defensive posture throughout to reduce risks to a minimum.

26. EXERCISE AND ARTHRITIS

The key to using exercise as a therapy for sufferers of arthritis is to constantly work toward improving, or at least sustaining, the range of motion of the joints. Without exercise, the joints deteriorate and ultimately freeze-up, making even the slightest movement painful.

Water exercise (see next chapter) is particularly helpful because water supports the body and you weigh only a fraction of your normal weight while submerged up to the chest. This takes the pressure off tender joints, and when immersed in water, arthritic patients usually can move their joints through a greater range of motion and with less pain. Unfortunately, water exercise may not be an option for many elderly individuals.

Doing exercises while seated in a chair is conceptually similar (although not as effective) as exercising while immersed in water. The chair supports the body weight. The chair doesn't, however, support the weight of the upper body and arms. Regardless, there is much that can be accomplished while sitting. Simply take into consideration how the various joints in the body move, then try as well as possible to take those joints through their movements.

Start with the toes and work up to the head. The toes can be curled and spread apart, for example. With the lower leg supported by a stool, the ankle can be flexed and extended. Each knee can be flexed and extended while supporting the upper leg on a stool. You get the idea.

But what about aerobics?

A chair aerobics program would emphasize performing exercises for fitness rather than specifically for enhancing range of motion. Fitness movements would require lots of rapid repetitions, possibly in-time with upbeat music. You could pump your arms as if reaching to pluck apples from a tree, for example. The key would be continuous movement for several minutes. This would get the blood flowing and it could be good for the range of motion if the exercises were performed correctly. What's more, if there is a video to watch while doing it, it could be fun.

For more information on these types of programs and whether they are recommended for sufferers of arthritis, I suggest contacting the Arthritis Foundation (P.O. Box 19000, Atlanta, Georgia, 30326: phone # 1-800-633-5335) to see if they have any information. Also, ask them for information on exercise alternatives for those who cannot get in the water. I have found the people at the Foundation to be very helpful over the years, and I am confident you will find that to be the case.

A note of caution. Never push yourself to the point of intense pain. Obviously, there may be some pain in the joints because of the arthritis. But don't aggravate the situation by trying to do too much. It's a good idea to discuss your exercise plan with your doctor and ask for advice that is pertinent to your personal situation.

An important thing to keep in mind is that increased body weight makes greater demands on the joints, especially joints (like the hips and knees) which have to support the weight. As such, keeping the weight down is a worthy strategy, and getting the fat and sugar out of the diet (as I have discussed many times) is the most effective approach.

Glucosamine — A Truly Effective Supplement?

Glucosamine is emerging as a supplement that enjoys widespread acceptance among mainstream physicians for the treatment of osteoarthritis. Osteoarthritis is deterioration (from injury and/or long term wear and tear) of the articular cartilage that covers the ends of bones that come together to form joints. Articular cartilage is like teflon and acts to reduce friction, until the layer of cartilage is worn down, then bone rubs on bone, resulting in intense pain.

Glucosamine occurs naturally in the body and has been used extensively in Europe as a supplement for many years, because Europeans are much more comfortable with alternative medical therapies than we are, and they are more likely to investigate such therapies. A recent three year study reported in the British medical journal, the *Lancet*, found very positive evidence that glucosamine is effective in preserving articular cartilage in joints, and reducing pain, inflammation and disability. No side effects were recorded.

Because of the tremendous popularity of glucosamine, and positive findings from Europe, the National Institutes of Health (NIH) in the U.S. has undertaken it's own multi-year study. Since the research is funded by the government, this overcomes the profit motive dilemma — natural products cannot be patented. Results should be forthcoming in the next two years.

Chondroitin Sulfate Too?

Articular cartilage, like all other tissues in the body, is constantly being torn down and replaced, in the same way that old dollar bills are taken out of circulation and replaced with new ones. If the tearing down process can be slowed, while the building up process is accelerated, the net result would be greater articular cartilage.

Chondroitin sulfate is also naturally occurring in the body and is believed to help retard the tearing down process. When combined with the effects of glucosamine to attach to articular cartilage and build it up, these two seemed to be the perfect combination for the treatment of osteoarthritis, and the two often have been promoted as a team. Recently, however, there is doubt that chondroitin sulfate can be absorbed, and most experts now advise the use of glucosamine without chondroitin sulfate.

Feast or Famine

I have received many anecdotal reports on the effects of glucosamine. Many are positive, bordering on the miraculous, and the effects have been long lived. Others report no effect. I suspect that the deciding factor is the condition of the joints before glucosamine therapy is initiated. Since glucosamine attaches to existing cartilage to bolster its mass, it's obvious that no effects are likely to occur if you have completely worn away your articular cartilage, because there's nothing to attach to.

The Bottom Line

Glucosamine appears to be safe and effective and it's not expensive. Whether it will work for you is unknown until you try it. If you do, let your doctor know. Because there is the possibility that glucosamine may interfere with the body's ability to process blood sugar, it may be a problem for diabetics and should be avoided. There is no scientific evidence to support this, but it's best to err on the conservative side.

27. WATER EXERCISE

Vigorous aerobic exercise is hard on your joints. So, what do devoted exercisers do when their joints cry out for rest? Nowadays, they head for the water.

Water exercise exerts a very different influence on the body, because in shoulder-deep water you weigh only about 10 percent of what you weigh on land. The result is no pounding, even during high intensity exercise. Arthritis patients have known for years that water exercise pampers sore joints. Other groups — pregnant women, cardiac rehab patients, people with multiple sclerosis, and the elderly — also have used water exercise as a means to a "gentle," yet aerobically demanding, workout.

Water exercise does more than prevent injury. With the limbs virtually weightless, it's a great way to increase range of motion in joints while experiencing minimal pain. Vigorous exercise in the water challenges your heart and lungs to work harder, which increases aerobic fitness. It also can be used to increase strength. Since water pressure is much greater than air pressure, pushing or pulling your arms and legs through the water provides a significant challenge to contracting muscles. And water exercise is fun, adding variety to your exercise program.

There are a number of ways to exercise in the water.

Water Aerobics
Water aerobics classes are similar to regular aerobics classes held in a studio. The leader leads the class from the edge of the pool, demonstrating the various moves to be duplicated in the water. Pupils push and pull, leap, kick, twist and turn, and get a great workout. The risk of injury is reduced substantially compared with land aerobics, because body weight is supported by the water.

But no exercise is fool-proof. Because of the freedom of movement allowed in the water, there is the temptation to push a movement farther than you should — overstretching the knee, for example — possibly causing slight muscle tearing or joint strain. This, and other problems, can easily be avoided by being cautious, listening to the instructor and applying a little common sense.

Aqua-Walking

The resistance offered by water is much greater than air, and therefore the energy cost of walking in water will be substantially greater than walking on land at the same speed. Depth of the water is an important consideration. In waist-deep water, the upper body is above the water and does not have to overcome resistance. In shoulder-deep water you can greatly increase the energy cost of walking by actively involving the arms as would occur in cross-country skiing. Holding a pair of plastic water dumbbells or empty plastic jugs can further increase energy cost in the same way as holding a pair of Heavy Hands on land.

Using different strides will force you to work different lower body muscles, and adds variety. Forward striding can be mixed with backward and sideways strides. You can point the toes when you walk, or go heel first. Raising the knees to your chest is an option, as is kicking the leg out in front before stepping. You are limited only by your creativity.

Aqua-Running

Water depth also is an important consideration when running. Avoid water that is not at least waist deep, because the buoyancy factor is reduced.

"Shallow" water (waist to chest deep) forces the feet to push off the bottom as you run. You can change the intensity by changing stride frequency and how high you raise your knees. Another approach is to tether yourself to the side of the pool and run in place.

"Deep" water is deep enough to prevent your feet from touching bottom. Although you are virtually weightless, deep water also can provide the high intensity training most runners are looking for. While you run, a flotation vest or belt will help you keep your head above water.

It's possible to stay up without one, but you have to work much harder.

Aqua-Playtime

If you think back to summer days when you were a kid, you jumped in the water and started moving your body every which way and probably didn't stop until mom or dad dragged you out hours later. You had loads of fun, and in the process you got a lot of great exercise.

It is important when considering a water exercise program to remember that in addition to a regimented program of aerobics, walking or running, that simply moving about in the water, the way you did when you were a kid, burns calories and contributes to health. Moreover, "playing," without a specific workout in mind, can be very refreshing emotionally, especially after a long hard day.

For the Athlete

Water exercise offers a great advantage to athletes, because risk of injury during high intensity work is greatly reduced. The water stresses you, wearing you out, but it also protects you and prevents you from getting beat up. This combination allows water exercise to accommodate a number of the athlete's needs.

1. You can enhance performance by working on your speed (sprint or interval work) without risking injury.

2. You can experiment with various stride lengths and running styles, and develop strength and endurance in the water before attempting to transfer effects to land.

3. You can intersperse water workouts between regular runs for variety and to give your joints and muscles a break from the pounding.

4. You can exercise vigorously while injured.

5. You can overload with leg weights and other means to increase fitness, without increasing the impact (ground strike) force per stride.

Do's and Don'ts

When you shift your exercise from land to water, it is important to still follow universal common-sense exercise principles.

1. Always warm-up before attempting vigorous exercise. Emphasize light exercise, then stretching movements, holding each

movement for several seconds. Never bounce.

2. Gradually increase intensity over several minutes.

3. Practice good posture and running mechanics. Don't, for example, risk straining your calf muscles by running on your toes. Don't strain your back by leaning forward.

4. Beware of dehydration. Drink plenty of fluids because you can lose sweat in the pool.

The Down Side

An obvious problem with water exercise is that you must have access to a pool or some other body of water. And when you find one, you may not be able to fit the hours into your schedule. Or you may not be able to use it for walking or running, because the pool is crowded and/or reserved for lap swimming. In addition, the water temperature may not be appropriate. Water temperature should be comfortable, or about 80-85 degrees F. Warmer water may cause you to build up too much internal heat during vigorous exercise, and cooler temperatures may make you stiff.

Water exercise can be boring, especially when attached to a tether. And in deep water, since you are not responsible for your body weight, the exercise can become too comfortable. In either case, it is necessary to sustain a high level of motivation and to constantly remember to push yourself. Being comfortable is fine for the layman, but it presents problems for an athlete who needs to enhance performance. Some athletes will forego flotation devices in deep water in order to force themselves to work harder.

The unmotivated athlete will find it easy to cheat during water exercise, because the coach has no reference points by which to judge how hard he is working. The athlete may cheat himself, too, by thinking he is working harder than he really is. Unfortunately, pulse rate may not be an accurate reflection of intensity, because hydrostatic pressure (the pressure of the water "squeezing" against the body) reduces maximal heart rate.

Early fatigue can be a problem. Movements in the water may be unfamiliar, and less energy may be available. A lowered maximal heart rate due to hydrostatic pressure can reduce maximal aerobic capacity

(VO2max) by 10 percent in shallow water and by 25 percent in deep water. Through time and training in the water, however, it should be possible to reach a higher physiological stress level, resulting in a greater training effect.

When running in water, the natural tendency is to run with short choppy steps which may cause the hamstrings to shorten and lose flexibility. It is important to emphasize hamstring stretching exercises, especially immediately after water workouts.

Equipment

When a new exercise is introduced and publicized, a line of fancy equipment usually follows suit. Water exercise is no exception. Often, however, high-tech equipment is no better than everyday materials you find around the house. There is disagreement on this point, of course, and some practitioners insist that high-tech is the only way to go. Others, including those who work with highly successful professional athletes, advise that a practical low-cost approach is just as effective.

1. Specially designed plastic water dumbbells increase the resistance to your hand as you push or pull it through the water. Empty plastic bottles are another option.

2. To increase resistance in the lower body in deep water, buoyancy cuffs and fins will make leg movements more difficult. An old pair of sweatpants can do the job, too.

3. Shoes are important to cushion the feet and protect against scraping from a rough bottom. Options range from specialized footgear to old tennis shoes.

4. A number of flotation devices are available to help you stay afloat during deep-water exercise. Specialized vests and belts can be purchased, or you can opt for using a life jacket.

5. Commercially available tethers can be purchased and used in shallow water. Another option is to fashion a tether from a bicycle inner tube and nylon rope.

28. PREVENT OSTEOPOROSIS

Osteoporosis is degeneration of the bones. Women are particularly susceptible, and it has been estimated that half of women 50 years of age and older will experience broken bones due to osteoporosis. Men are not immune, but the disease tends to strike many fewer men than women, and it strikes men much later in life. Let's take a look at this degenerative process from the inside out.

The outer layer of bone is ivory-like and very hard and forms a hollow shell that contains the inner bone, called trabeculae (or spongy bone), which supports the bone's structure. Under a microscope, spongy bone is a rugged latticework that contains calcium crystals. This storehouse of calcium is important not only because it helps strengthen bones, but also because it serves as a bank deposit for calcium. A *withdrawal* of calcium is made when calcium concentration in the blood is low, and a *deposit* is made when dietary calcium is adequate. Fortunately, the bank account for calcium is huge and easily meets the body's needs in early life through young adulthood.

Later in life, the body begins borrowing more calcium from the bones than it replaces. This depletes the spongy bone of calcium crystals, weakening the latticework and reducing it to a lacy shadow of its former self. The gradual loss of strength and structure of bone is called osteoporosis. There are no symptoms along the way. It's much like the deterioration of a bridge. No problem is suspected until the bridge gives way under a load that it had accommodated easily for many years. In fact, when things get real bad, the hip joints can no longer support the bodyweight and they break, causing a fall. This scenario is probably more common than the reverse — a fall causing a break.

When a break occurs due to osteoporosis, it is much more serious than a break in a healthy bone, because the break is not clean. Far from it. The bone virtually explodes into scattered parts which cannot be reassembled. This necessitates radical surgeries such as artificial joints which often give rise to complications in older persons.

Women are much more susceptible to osteoporosis than men for three major reasons. First, women rarely meet their RDA for calcium. Men are more successful because they eat more food. Second, the bones of men are larger and more dense, providing them a greater stockpile of calcium from which to draw in old age. And third, women lose the protection of estrogen after menopause. Estrogen is important because it helps regulate calcium metabolism and bone maintenance. Testosterone does the same things in men, but the loss of testosterone is less severe and tends to be later in life.

Osteoporosis in Men

Although the risk is substantially less in men, tens of thousands of men suffer from osteoporosis, and the consequences are just as devastating. A few years ago I was walking behind an elderly man who fell. His fall was unlike any I had ever witnessed as he seemed to implode, the way a building falls in on itself when it is demolished professionally with explosives. I came to learn that his hip broke and down he went. Breaking of the bone prior to falling is typical in those who suffer from osteoporosis.

Recent research on men offered a gross profile of men who tend to be at higher risk for osteoporosis. A poor diet that is low in calcium is a big factor, as is smoking cigarettes. Lack of exercise is important, and men who are thin and who have weak muscles, especially in the legs, also tend to have increased risk. A family history of osteoporosis is important, and so is excessive use of alcohol or caffeine, and chronic use of some medications.

With regard to danger signals and knowing you are headed for trouble — unfortunately, there is little indication from your body that your bones are deteriorating. In fact, it often comes as a complete surprise when a bone breaks causing a fall. Osteoporosis is much like termite damage, in other words, and the signs don't appear until the damage is extensive. For those who have concern that they may be headed for trouble, your doctor can arrange for you to undergo a bone mineral density test. Low mineral density means you have lost calcium and may be approaching a critical stage. But not everyone who is older is in danger and in need of such a test. Consider the risk factors discussed above (smoking, poor diet, etc.) and talk it over with your doctor.

Diet

So how can diet help?

Intervention through diet and exercise is likely to be most effective early in life, during active bone growth when calcium is being deposited in large amounts. Smart money says, load up the bank and prepare for the rainy days ahead. You can do this by taking in adequate calcium. It's a good idea to get lots of calcium daily, and 1500 mg is a good target. You must also be concerned about Vitamin D, because Vitamin D is believed to help the body absorb calcium and find its way into the spongy bone.

An easy way to meet daily calcium and Vitamin D needs is through dairy products. In general, four glasses of skim milk a day can meet needs. Unfortunately, our society doesn't support the use of skim milk as much as it should. Whole milk also will meet calcium and Vitamin D needs, but it is so high in fat that it increases heart disease risk. The same is true of 2% milk, which also is very high in fat. Non-fat yogurt and non-fat cottage cheese are good dairy sources for calcium.

Getting enough calcium is possible from non-dairy products, but it is more difficult. The good news is, when you get your calcium from non-dairy and non-animal sources you may not need as much. This is demonstrated in third world countries where the diet is almost purely vegetarian and low in calcium, but osteoporosis is exceedingly rare.

Good non-dairy sources for calcium include kale, turnip greens, mustard greens, parsley, spinach, rhubarb, broccoli, figs, blackstrap molasses, kidney beans, green beans, soybeans (and soy milk), seafoods such as salmon, sardines, scallops, shrimp, and recently, calcium enriched orange juice.

Getting enough Vitamin D without drinking fortified milk is difficult. Relying on sunshine to supply Vitamin D may not be enough, especially during winter months when sunshine is weakest, and you are less likely to be outdoors. Dietary sources of Vitamin D are limited, and there are only a few healthy choices, including tuna, salmon, and cod liver oil. Less healthy choices include egg yolks and liver.

To get enough calcium many resort to supplements, and many use supplements as a safety net, ensuring an adequate daily dosage. If you decide to go with supplements, you can choose between calcium citrate and calcium carbonate. Some experts prefer the use of calcium citrate, rather than calcium carbonate, because it is more easily absorbed. Take supplements with meals to boost absorption and make sure you are getting plenty of Vitamin D.

Exercise

Exercise is critical in the prevention of osteoporosis. The saying, "if you don't use it, you'll lose it," applies to bone as well as muscle. Like muscle, bone is dynamic living tissue that needs to be challenged to be healthy, and regular exercise provides the best kind of challenge. Simply standing and moving about stresses weight bearing bones. This compressional stress stimulates growth and development, helping bones hold onto their calcium. Walking, running, skiing and other locomotor activities are highly recommended.

For upper body, non-weight bearing bones, push and pull exercises are needed. When muscles contract, they tug on bones, stressing the bones in a healthful way. Working in the garden, lifting, carrying, weight training movements, light sporting activities and any type of action requiring forceful muscular contractions are helpful.

Strive to get both types of physical activity everyday. You don't have to train like an athlete, and even very modest movements pay dividends. When you are inactive, bone loss accelerates. Severe bone and muscle loss was a major problem for early astronauts in space prior to the development of isokinetic — weightless — exercise.

Unfortunately, older persons who are at the highest risk for osteoporosis are likely to be the least active, which increases risk even further. Lack of daily physical activity reduces muscle strength which makes physical activity more difficult. This results in less activity and more debilitation. It is best to try to stop this downward spiral before it gets started.

29. TAI CHI AND YOGA

I have discovered a new form of exercise. Actually it's hundreds, if not thousands, of years old and has been gaining popularity in this country by leaps and bounds. The exercise is Tai Chi. I've been aware of this form of exercise for years, but I never took the time to check it out. Now that I have, I'm hooked, and I want to encourage others to take a look.

When the aerobics movement swept onto the American scene in the late 1960's, all other forms of exercise were pushed aside. Anything that did not drive your heart rate up and keep it there for at least twenty to thirty minutes was dismissed as useless. This included Tai Chi, yoga, and everything else that didn't cause you to huff and puff like a locomotive. But now, there's a new exercise message, which tells us that it is the process of being physically active on a daily basis that is most important to enhancing health, and that producing aerobic fitness is not essential. This has inspired us to take a new look at old exercise forms such as Tai Chi.

What's so great about Tai Chi? Claims are that it works your entire body from head to toe, strengthening muscles, bones and joints, enhancing endurance and reducing the fatigue of daily life, increasing balance and coordination, and promoting relaxation and stress reduction. And for those who believe (as the Chinese do) that energy flows through the body in channels and that blocked channels cause problems, Tai Chi movements are designed to open channels and stimulate the free flow of energy. It also is believed to be an effective means of promoting flow in the lymphatic system.

Wow! Can it really do all that? I believe it can. In my case, one outcome I am strongly touting is that my lower back feels better than it has in the fifteen years since I hurt it so badly. In fact, I gave up thinking that some day my lower back would again feel as it did before the injury. This, despite tremendous effort on my part trying to find the right kinds of rehabilitative and strengthening exercises (which always seemed ultimately to aggravate rather than heal), the right kind of mattress, the right shoes, the right chair, the right car seat, the right posture, etc.

The secret may have to do with the gentle twists and turns, flexions and extensions, inherent to Tai Chi movements. Such movements massage the joints in a therapeutic manner. Jogging, weight training, and other forms of exercise I have used over the years challenge the joints with heavy loads, which eventually can overwhelm them with micro-damage which accumulates, causing pain and deterioration. Gentle Tai Chi movements, in contrast, momentarily compress the cartilage in joints and the discs between vertebrae, then releases the pressure, creating a sort of physiologic pump within the joints. The pump is important to the health of the joint because it circulates synovial fluid which nourishes the interior of the joint. Tai Chi also has increased my flexibility, which reduces pressure on my lower back throughout the day.

There are 108 moves to the Tai Chi set (the number of moves will vary depending upon the type of Tai Chi performed), and each move is intricate and takes considerable practice to master. Learning the sequence of so many moves requires intense focus and concentration. I learned that while practicing, a stray thought would throw me off and I'd forget where I was in the set and what I was doing. The need for concentration is similar to meditation, and that's why Tai Chi is a sort of moving meditation. Once I conquered the sequence from months of work, hours daily, I now find that I don't need such mental intensity. Instead, I can put my mind into a zone that also is meditative, but in a different way.

The combination of the mental and physical aspects of this form of exercise leave your body in an unusual state that I cannot explain. After my jogging or lifting workouts, I am done in. My body demands rest and I usually fall asleep early that night from residual fatigue. Not so with Tai Chi. My sessions energize me, blessing me with more energy at the end than I had at the beginning.

I am still a beginner and have yet to get into the depths of Tai Chi. When I do, I hope I find that what I am being told is true. That as one progresses the effects become increasingly internal, enhancing the energy (or "chi") flow, creating abundant health. But already, I am aware that the base, or source, of much of the health enhancing effects of Tai Chi is the spine, and specifically proper alignment of the spine. Because my lower back feels better than it has in many years, I am encouraged.

The bottom line is that Tai Chi requires no special equipment, no fancy workout clothes, limited space and a modest time commitment. You owe it to yourself to check it out.

Yoga

Yoga is the fastest growing form of exercise in the U.S., with more than a million new practitioners each year, boosting the estimated current total to somewhere around 15 million. What's the attraction? I suspect that motivations to become involved vary greatly.

There are the short term players who get involved because yoga is "in" — it's the cool thing to do. For proof, you can put together a who's-who list of celebrities involved in yoga, ranging from glitzy Hollywood stars to sports heroes to Supreme Court justices. There are those who use yoga purely for fitness outcomes, as a means to losing weight, toning muscles, improving flexibility. Some are interested in the potential healing aspects of yoga, and come to it because they are disenchanted with western medical therapies. Some use yoga as a stress reliever. And some have deeper aspirations of exploring the mind-body connection and solidifying the union between the two.

Years ago when I was preaching the benefits of exhausting workouts, I pooh-poohed yoga as a lazy man's exercise routine. I saw it as simply laying around on a mat and assuming various goofy poses. I saw the deep breathing exercises as a rouse that falsely touted aerobic benefits from increased oxygen usage.

Now I know better. My involvement in yoga has been limited, but I found out quickly that it's not for the lazy or poorly motivated. I also quickly learned how inflexible I was and how much work my body needed, just to reach an elementary level of performance. Recently, I have begun doing modest yoga movements on a daily basis, and my body is enjoying it.

The Benefits

Exercise, in general, affords a large number of health benefits. Are there specific and unique medical benefits associated with yoga? That's not an easy question to answer.

Any time this topic is raised, the door opens to exaggeration on the one hand, versus skepticism on the other. There also is (as mentioned above) the complication of the eastern view of medicine versus the western view. In the eastern view, energy (the life force) flows through seven major energy centers of the body called chakras. When the energy flow is disrupted, disease results. Yoga is believed to promote health by enhancing the flow of energy.

Unfortunately, because high tech western medicine cannot measure such energy flow, western physicians find it hard to accept that it exists, and thus the role of yoga to promote energy flow through chakras is irrelevant when viewed from the western side. To avoid such polarizing east-versus-west arguments, it's best to restrict the scope and attempt to find a common ground.

Clearly, yoga is a first class relaxing agent. The stretches and poses and breathing techniques sweep the mind and body of the myriad of psychological stresses that crowd our everyday lives. This is important, because it is becoming more evident that psychological stress is a key contributor to many of the chronic diseases (high blood pressure, for example) that kill and disable Americans in mass. At some of the more progressive cardiac rehabilitation programs around the country, yoga is being offered as an adjunct therapy to treadmill walking.

Yoga is believed to especially stimulate the flow of fluid through the lymph system, and the greater the flow, the more efficient the system. Exercise, in general, stimulates the flow of lymphatic fluid, but certain yoga poses are believed to have a more direct stimulatory effect.

Perhaps the most publicized use of yoga as a medical tool is in the studies of Dean Ornish, M.D. Dr. Ornish was the first to demonstrate that a lifestyle that includes a vegan diet, vigorous walking, meditation and yoga can reverse atherosclerosis (clogging of the arteries). Skeptics challenge the specific contribution of yoga to the results, citing the greater importance of the vegan diet. Regardless, yoga is part of the formula for success.

Yoga is great therapy for the elderly. It reduces the incidence of falls by enhancing muscular strength and flexibility and improving balance. This, in turn, increases confidence and the willingness to be involved in everyday activities.

The Bottom Line

Yoga is great exercise. There are many different types of yoga, but the essentials are similar. Find a type that suits you and give it a try. Your body will thank you.

30. SYNERGETICS – SOMETING NEW UNDER THE SUN

There are hundreds of exercise gadgets and routines available to the American public, and new angles are introduced daily on glitzy 30-minute infomercials. Each one promises to help you lose weight, tone muscles, feel better, and be healthier. All you have to do is invest a few minutes a day performing gentle muscular actions — actions that are so much fun you will breathlessly await your next exercise session. Handsome men with bulging biceps and gorgeous women with curves in all the right places proclaim straight-faced that only a few short weeks ago they looked just like us. But now, thanks entirely to a revolutionary new exercise scheme, they were able to shed pounds of fat while adding layers of muscle, miraculously and effortlessly transforming themselves from ugly ducklings into beautiful swans.

You've heard all the hype many times and hopefully you are skeptical of bogus sales pitches that sound too good to be true. But be careful of throwing the baby out with the bath water, because there's something new on the horizon that's worth a look. I've discovered a truly unique and effective exercise routine that can make a number of beneficial claims and back them up with documentation.

The approach is called Synergetics. It's an exercise routine that treats your body as a friend, not as an enemy to be flogged and abused. Synergetics works *with* the body, creating harmonious biomechanical movements — the kind the body was originally designed to perform. This unusual exercise regimen will not only trim you and tone you, enhancing your outward appearance, it will promote inner balance and physiologic well being as well. But before I tell you more about the nitty gritty aspects of this wonderful exercise routine, you need to know something about the man who discovered it.

Taylor Hay

Taylor Hay is an original. He's one-of-a-kind and they broke the mold the day he was born in 1930. At an early age Taylor became interested in exercise and set out to build the perfect body. As a youngster, and long before the days of Arnold Swarzennegger, he lifted rusty barbells in the basement of the YMCA. He threw in some Charles Atlas dynamic tension exercises, too (see Chapter 46), and anything else he could think of that might add muscle to his frame.

He went off to college at Virginia Military Institute (VMI) in 1947 where he played football, lifted weights, performed endless bootcamp calisthenics, worked on the flying rings and parallel bars, and ran himself to exhaustion every day. Quite a regimen, and it worked. Taylor built his body into chiseled granite, a look he maintained for years after his football days were over. He looked great, but all was not well.

On the inside, things were going wrong. His joints creaked and he had chronic back and knee pain. But he persisted in his taxing exercise routine, fearing that if he didn't he'd lose his hard earned muscles. A man of strong will and determination, he continued to exercise in pain until his body forced him to stop. It had had enough.

By the time he was 50, Taylor had quit exercising, was overweight, stressed to the max with business and personal matters, and in chronic and almost unbearable pain in his back, knees and shoulders. His doctors told him he needed surgical operations to set things right, especially with his back. He was regularly undergoing treatments to have his neck stretched with pistons attached to either side of a head cage. His shoulders, knees and Achilles tendons were shot full of cortisone. Ironically, he had destroyed his body for the sake of staying in shape.

In the 1980's Taylor noticed an alarming trend among many of his former classmates at VMI. Several were debilitated by modern day chronic diseases, including heart disease, stroke, cancer, and maturity onset diabetes, their quality of life severely compromised, their prognosis uncertain. This was sobering, but nothing compared to the shock of discovering that a number of alums had died prematurely. One death in particular captured his attention, providing a chilling revelation. It was the death of a close friend and football teammate who had lived his life in much the same way Taylor had lived his. Taylor became depressed and wanted desperately to escape a similar fate. The problem is, he didn't know where to turn.

In desperation he rented a place on a deserted section of Salvo Beach, North Carolina, for a two week solitary retreat. He still had stitches from a hernia operation (caused by weight lifting), but tried to exercise anyway, thinking that that was what he needed to relieve pent up stress. He also wanted desperately to begin reclaiming his decimated body. But nothing he did worked, and everything hurt. Discouraged with life and fearful of death, he went to bed and fell into a fretful sleep.

In the middle of the night he experienced a dream. It was one of those vivid dreams that seems absolutely real. In the dream he was standing near the seashore and performing graceful, but unfamiliar motions. He awakened with full memory of the dream and began trying to mimic what he had seen in his mind's eye. He stood in front of a small mirror, joined his hands in front of his chest and moved this way and that, shifting his bodyweight, pushing and pulling with his arms. The movements didn't hurt his pain-racked body. In fact, he experienced some relief.

From that point, Taylor began working relentlessly on his exercise system which later became known as Synergetics. Amazingly, he began to reclaim his body. When it ached he did Synergetics. When he felt great he did Synergetics. Over the next several months, he lost 25 pounds of flab and brought his weight back down to the muscular proportions he enjoyed in college. Energy flowed through his body again and he was eager to take on life's challenges. So dramatic was his transformation that people he hadn't seen in years were amazed and wanted to know his secret. Immediately, he would oblige and start demonstrating Synergetics moves on the spot.

Today, Taylor Hay looks and moves like a man decades younger, and no one can believe he is in his seventies. Indeed, when I first met him several years ago, I was doubtful of his claim of being in his mid-sixties. His body has the contours and strength of a much younger man, and his face is remarkable. An integral part of the Synergetics exercise routine includes movements for the facial muscles — muscles that typically are overlooked. But since they are muscles, they require exercise to stay in shape, just like the biceps.

Taylor is married to Joanna, a woman half his age. Joanna is beautiful, talented and smart, and they make a wonderful team. Perhaps the best way to describe Taylor's transformation is to say that he and Joanna, despite the age difference, look perfectly natural together. There are no second "pop and daughter" looks on the street. Interestingly, Joanna, a former athlete, has her own story to tell about the effectiveness of using Synergetics to lose 30 pounds and reduce from a size 12 to a size 6 dress.

Synergetics Exercise

I wanted to tell the Taylor Hay story, because I know Taylor personally and I am incredibly impressed with his transformation. His story underscores the fact that it's possible to reclaim your body, regardless of its present condition, if you know what to do and commit to doing it.

Taylor destroyed his body by doing too much. I understand. I did the same thing to my body. I realize that most readers won't identify with doing too much exercise. On the contrary, most will have numerous physical and medical problems arising from doing too little. The cause doesn't matter. If your body is debilitated, it's time to get it back, and Synergetics is an approach that can help.

I tout Synergetics with enthusiasm, because it is a good fit for my 4-C's approach to exercise. Since you can do Synergetics anywhere at anytime, it's *convenient*, which contributes to *consistency*. Synergetics is *comfortable* exercise that doesn't have a rough impact component. Rather, it's composed of gentle rhythmic movements that are performed while you stand in one location. And the cost (in time and money) is minimal.

So, what exactly is Synergetics? The best description I can think of is that it is a combination of cleverly choreographed movements that resemble aspects of Tai Chi, ballet, yoga, dynamic tension, and isometrics all rolled into one 12-minute workout.

Imagine yourself standing in front of a full-length mirror, your feet shoulder-width apart, your palms touching, facing each other in front of your chest. You push your palms together, gradually increasing the tension as each palm resists the other. As you push, you move your palms to the left, rotating your upper body at the waist while sustaining

173

your gaze straight ahead. Your knees are bent slightly and you shift your weight from your right foot to your left. Now reverse directions and bring the palms to the right, shifting your weight in the opposite direction.

After several of these movements, left and right, shift the emphasis with a simple alteration. This time, interlace your fingers and pull one hand against the other. This simple change in hand position completely changes the upper body muscles involved. Do several of these movements, left and right, then shift your hands over your head, pushing for awhile, then pulling. For the next series, lower your hands to belt level.

As you can see, there are literally hundreds of different exercise combinations that can help you work nearly every muscle in your body. As you advance, you can add facial exercises to the mix, and eventually your movement patterns can become more complex and rewarding. But you start with the basics and master simple movements first.

Synergetics can be an entire exercise routine, or part of a more varied approach. In Chapter 19, I discussed cross training and its many potential components. Synergetics can be plugged in as one component among many. In my case, I do lots of different things, including light weight training, brisk walking, elliptical exercise, Tai Chi, yoga, occasional jogging, and a bit of Synergetics. I also include cutting the grass, landscaping activities, and other physically involved tasks as part of my overall exercise regimen.

New and Improved

To improve the effectiveness of the original Synergetics approach, Taylor and Joanna invented the PocketGym — a large light weight horseshoe shaped handle that is heavily padded. You hold the PocketGym in both hands and use it to push and pull while performing the various movements. The PocketGym also allows many other exercise options.

A video tape walks you through various routines, starting with the simple and gradually progressing to the complex. A compact disc is also available to talk you through the motions. Nothing is left to chance, and even poorly coordinated buffoons like me can feel like a master after just a few practice sessions.

The entire cost of the Synergetics package is quite modest — about what you would expect to pay for a meal for two at a mid-level restaurant. For more information contact:

Synergetics Health Publications, Inc.
P.O. Box 702
Frankfort, Kentucky 40602
(800) 336-1993
www.PocketGym.com

31. THE FUTURE OF EXERCISE

Do I see a great increase in the number of exercisers in the future? Hard to say, but the odds are against it. Here's why.

First, the fitness movement has been around for more than 35 years and all of us have heard the fitness message. "Get more exercise — it's good for what ails you." Exercise helps prevent such chronic diseases as heart disease, cancer, stroke, and Type II (maturity onset) diabetes. And, exercise is a key component of weight management. Second, Americans not only have heard the message, they believe it! The proof comes from a recent poll conducted by American Sports Data, Inc. of 1862 adults. Here are the surprising results.

Nearly three out of four of those polled believe that those who exercise regularly are happier and more attractive than those who don't, and 85 percent believe that exercisers will live longer. Two out of three know that exercise is an important component of a healthy lifestyle, and only 2 percent said that exercise is not important.

Was this poll conducted on a bunch of joggers — the converted? Not at all. In fact, the majority of respondents admitted being overweight and expressed the need to get more exercise. Even so, two out of three said they don't get any exercise at all, because they have no self discipline.

Obviously, having the knowledge that exercise is good does not translate into action. Why not? Most believe that exercise is boring and inconvenient, and even if it weren't, it's too time consuming to be squeezed into an already overcrowded daily schedule. The excuses are familiar. And even (as I have discussed in Part I) if there were ways to make exercise more fun and to squeeze it into a busy schedule, 25 percent of the poll's respondents would not be interested. One out of four are totally committed to the couch potato lifestyle, in other words.

The bottom line is, don't look for an upsurge in exercise participation in the near future. The sedentary lifestyle is alive and well in America and I can't see anything on the horizon to change that in a significant way. Even so, I keep trying.

PART III

BEWARE, BE SAFE

32. EXERCISE PITFALLS

Good judgement comes from experience, and experience comes from bad judgement. This old saying is especially true when it comes to exercise, where bad judgement can lead to the kind of experience you'd rather avoid — aches, pains, and moderate to severe injuries ranging from nagging shin splints to disabling stress fractures of the bone. Bad judgment also can result in wasted time and effort. Being aware of the pitfalls that plague novice and seasoned exercisers alike can prevent problems and help you maintain a comfortable and consistent program.

Here's a list of the most common exercise pitfalls to avoid. Depending upon your exercise goals and the intensity of your training, some may apply to your situation now, while others won't be important until you have considerable training under your belt. Consider those that are pertinent and alter your program accordingly. Your body will thank you.

1. Exercise as friend and foe. Exercise can improve your health in many ways. It also can be dangerous and in the extreme it can even be potentially lethal, because exercise is one of the most stressful things your body may experience, especially when performed in hostile conditions of high heat and humidity, or high altitude. If you are healthy, the body will respond to the stress of chronic exercise by making itself better able to cope with the demands imposed. It does this by upgrading many physiologic processes that contribute to enhanced performance capacity (fitness). This is why jogging a mile may at first be exhausting, but in time you can jog that mile, and do it easily.

In order for your body to make the necessary physiologic adjustments it must be healthy. An unhealthy body may not be able to make adjustments and may instead be overwhelmed by the stress. This is why it is necessary to have a physical examination by your doctor before engaging in vigorous exercise. If you are cleared for exercise, you know you can proceed safely. If, on the other hand, an unhealthy condition is uncovered (heart disease, for example), it will be necessary to address that condition before considering an exercise program. Then, the exercise should be supervised and performed in accordance with an appropriate exercise prescription.

2. Too much too soon. It's human nature to be excited about a new venture and to immerse yourself completely. Lofty goals take hold and you sprint from the starting blocks determined to remake yourself in record time. Unfortunately, this is a formula for disaster.

If you have been sedentary, there is a lack of physical stress in your life which means your body is not prepared for the kind of challenge vigorous exercise imposes. Common sense dictates that you proceed slowly, with gradual increments which allow your body to make necessary adjustments which in turn will allow you to exercise more vigorously. Without such a period of transition, the stresses may be too great too soon and may overwhelm you, leading to a breakdown.

Usually, the breakdown is orthopedic — in the muscles, bones or joints. Ironically, the cardiovascular and respiratory systems will make adjustments more rapidly than the muscles, bones and joints, and will erroneously provide feedback that your body is ready for more — more distance or a faster pace. After just a few workouts, in other words, you won't find yourself gasping for breath the way you did at first. Avoid the temptation to take this as a cue you are ready for more. Stick with a prescribed incremental program and don't allow yourself to get sucked into a "more is better" attitude. Be especially wary of the "keeping up with the Joneses" mentality. Forget about what others are doing and be concerned only with your own personal situation.

3. Increasing too fast. Even if you are a seasoned exerciser, you cannot advance more quickly than your body will allow, and you must avoid the overconfidence which can accompany being a regular exerciser. Let's assume, for example, that you have been jogging 2 miles daily and would like to bump your distance to 4 miles. As stated above, your body has become accustomed to the 2 mile distance, but is totally unprepared for 4 miles. Increase the distance gradually, a fraction of a mile per week, allowing several weeks to reach your goal.

4. Overtraining. Let's assume you have decided to progress slowly toward your goal, but that you keep adding distance and intensity to your efforts because your ultimate goal is to run a marathon (26 miles). Such demanding training is not for everyone, and may result in overtraining — doing more than your body can withstand (see Chapter 34). Your body will attempt to let you know you are doing too much in many subtle ways. You may find you are dreading your workouts, or your workouts may become exhausting, or you may be dragging yourself through the day because you are putting most of your energy into your runs. You may experience aches and pains which you can withstand, but which seem to be getting a little worse with time. If any of these apply, it's time to cut back to the point where your workouts are comfortable again and you look forward to them. Taking a few weeks off completely or exercising at a much reduced level is the way to go.

5. No pain - no gain. Athletes are taught to train in pain. The more you push yourself, the better you become. This is true, but only if you are working within the limits of your capacity. Always trying to push yourself to new limits is like playing Russian roulette, or stretching a rubber band further and further. You never know when you might reach the break point. If you are a competitive athlete, you may have no choice but to train all out as the coach demands. But for the everyday exerciser, going for the gusto can place you in harm's way.

It's also important that you understand the different kinds of pain you will encounter when training. Physiologic pain is the kind you experience when your muscles burn from sprinting as fast as you can up a steep hill. This is the kind of pain you must fight through if you are going to improve. Orthopedic pain in the bones, muscles or joints, on the other hand, often signals a problem and the need to stop and reassess. You cannot push through such pain without dire consequences which include the potential for a disabling injury.

6. Assuming that exercise must produce fitness in order to be beneficial. From your readings so far, you know better than this. Eventually, however, you may want to do more in your training, but it's nice to know you don't have to, especially when just starting out.

7. Choosing the wrong exercises. Weight bearing exercises such as walking and jogging can be too demanding on persons who are overweight or who have a history of orthopedic problems such as arthritis. This is because weight bearing exercise places considerable stress on the joints. When jogging, for example, the impact force of each stride on each foot as it encounters the jogging surface is several times the bodyweight, and most of this force is transmitted to the ankles, knees and hips. This could possibly lead to pain and swelling, and the only way to relieve the situation is to quit exercising. The alternative is exercise in which the bodyweight is supported (non-weight bearing) such as cycling or exercising in the water.

Resistance exercises which build strength by using barbells can stress joints, especially the elbows and shoulders, in a variety of ways. Persons with tennis elbow, for example, will likely aggravate the problem when performing curls and other resistance exercises for the biceps. Switching to exercise machines, particularly machines with cables which run over pulleys, can reduce joint stress and allow you to continue exercising. Using dumbbells instead of barbells also can reduce joint stress in some cases.

8. Inadequate exercise gear. Exercise gear is designed to reduce stress. Jogging and walking shoes are designed to provide support and absorb shock, and years of research and development have been invested in creating shoes with a high degree of resiliency. Such shoes are not inexpensive, but are worth the investment. Cheaper look-alike shoes may be soft and cushioned, but will not afford the qualities you need. When exercising in the heat, special clothing is necessary to allow you to remove heat from the skin to avoid overheating. In the cold, special clothing will wick moisture away from the skin helping to keep you dry and warm.

9. Surface tension. When walking or jogging, the surface you choose to exercise on is critical. User-friendly surfaces will reduce the impact shock, while harsh surfaces will increase the shock. Grass and gravel are friendly, whereas cement (sidewalks, for example) is brutal. Asphalt is better than cement, but not as good as grass. The surface also must be smooth and predictable. Avoid areas with holes, cracks or bumps such as tree roots. Also avoid snowy areas because underneath could be ice, holes or cracks. When exercising on an indoor track, the banking of the track can add stress to the joints. The shorter the track, the greater the banking. If you exercise on an indoor track make certain you don't always move in the same direction. It's best to alternate from day to day to distribute the stresses evenly on the legs.

10. Improper technique. Learn to correctly perform the exercises you choose. Walking may appear to be natural and simple, but improper technique is common and can cause problems. When increasing your pace, for example, it is natural to take longer strides. Long strides can stress the fronts of the lower legs leading to shin splints. Thus, when walking faster, shorter and more rapid strides are recommended.

11. Haste makes waste. Everyone is busy and in a hurry to accomplish as much as possible. But when it comes to exercise, haste can create more than waste. Take time to warm up and ease into your exercise. Even if you restrict yourself to walking or other mild forms of exercise, your body still needs an adjustment period. Start with a slow comfortable walk before progressing to faster speeds. If you prefer more demanding exercise, the warm-up phase takes on added importance and should be longer and more involved. Cooling down, or easing out of exercise is important too. Don't stop abruptly, but rather slow your pace progressively until you are ready to quit. Then, perform stretching exercises to promote flexibility.

12. Don't be a weekend athlete. Many people use sports as a means of getting in shape. They go out and push themselves on weekends in demanding sporting events such as basketball which can stress the body to its limits. This approach is backwards. Instead, you should get in shape first so that you can enjoy sports safely. This is especially important if you are not a regular participant and tend to leap into activities on weekends or special occasions. (See Chapter 35.)

13. Lack of respect for environmental influences. Hot and humid conditions add considerable stress to the body that increases the burden of exercise. Therefore, when exercising in the heat, don't attempt to accomplish as much as you normally do when it's cooler. Because you will sweat profusely, it is important to drink plenty of fluids before, during and after a prolonged bout of exercise. If you should venture to areas of high altitude of a mile or more, exercise will be more taxing. Again, don't expect to accomplish as much. Cold and windy conditions can cause frost bite if your skin is unprotected. Be certain to cover areas of the body that are particularly vulnerable, such as your ears, fingers and toes. (See Chapters 37 and 38.)

14. Rapid shallow breathing. Exercise increases breathing, and novice exercisers tend to breath in a rapid shallow manner because it feels natural. Unfortunately, breathing in this way is counterproductive because oxygen does not make its way to the depths of the lungs where it's needed. This increases the urge to breathe more and contributes to a sense of breathlessness. Control your breathing and consciously attempt to take deeper and longer breaths.

15. Wasting time and money on spot reduction. Most of us have problem areas that contain too much fat. In men, there are pot bellies and love handles on the sides, and in women there are flabby arms and saddlebags on the outer surface of the thighs. We'd love to get rid of this flab and in an effort to do so we perform countless calisthenic exercises or we purchase exercise gadgets that claim to get rid of flab in these spots. By doing sit-ups, for example, we believe we can reduce the waistline. Unfortunately, this is not true. There is no such thing as losing body fat in one specific area — the concept known as spot reduction. During exercise, fat is lost symmetrically from all over the body, and it's impossible to tap into the fat in the abdomen by doing abdominal exercises. Therefore, the best way to lose flab is to perform exercises that burn considerable calories per minute, and walking and jogging are best for reducing the waistline or removing flab from the arms.

16. Great expectations. Exercise can help you lose body fat, but without a healthy low-fat, low-sugar, and moderate calorie diet, little will be accomplished. Although exercise burns calories, it burns far fewer than expected. A one mile brisk walk will burn about 100 calories in an average size male, and about 80 calories in an average size female. This is helpful, but the caloric loss from exercise pales when compared with the intake of 500 or more calories from a deluxe cheeseburger.

17. Putting your finger on the pulse. Many exercise programs require that you monitor your exercise pulse. This is important if you are building fitness and you need to drive your heart rate upward to a predetermined target level. To monitor the pulse it is necessary to stop exercising briefly, put your fingers on your radial (wrist) or carotid (neck) artery, count for 15 seconds and multiply by four to get a per minute value. When taking your pulse at the neck, don't push on your fingers.

You may be pressing on a pressure point which could cause you to pass out. If you intend to monitor your pulse, practice often to be certain you are getting an accurate reading. Practice helps you find the pulse quickly which is important, because when you stop exercising to take your pulse, your pulse will decline quickly and if you don't take the reading immediately you will underestimate your exercise heart rate. This could encourage you to exercise more vigorously than you should.

18. Sleep, alcohol and smoking. Vigorous exercise takes a toll on the body and you must rest completely between workouts so that your body can recover and be ready for the next workout. This requires a good night's sleep. You also should avoid excessive alcohol and smoking which deplete the body and interfere with the recovery process.

19. Calories and protein. For those who exercise vigorously, and especially for those who desire to add muscle mass, it is important to take in sufficient calories and protein to cover everyday needs plus additional nutrients to meet the special needs created by exercise. An hour workout may create the need for 500 or more additional calories, and protein needs may increase by 50 percent or more depending upon the type of training involved.

20. Fair weather exercise. Regardless of your goals or the type of exercise you choose, nothing will be accomplished by sporadic exercise. The key to success is consistency. There may be occasions where time is limited and you can't perform all the exercise you would like. Even so, it is important to do something, no matter how limited the amount. A small amount of exercise performed daily will produce much greater results than periodic lengthy workouts.

33. EXERCISES TO AVOID

Exercise is good, but not all exercises are beneficial to all people. Younger, active people can engage successfully in almost any exercise regimen and the risk of injury is low. Older persons who have been exercising all their lives also can expect to exercise safely under most circumstances. Middle-aged and older individuals who have been sedentary for years, however, must be especially careful because some exercises can be potentially dangerous and could result in injury.

Choosing the right exercises is not always easy, because some of the most popular ones (sit-ups and toe touches, for example) are the worst. Many exercises are safer, but still carry a degree of risk depending upon a number of factors, including injury history, fitness, body composition, flexibility, technique, and age of the participant. With this in mind, choose your exercises carefully, especially if you are getting up in years and haven't exercised recently. To help you, potentially troublesome exercises are cited below, along with recommended alternatives.

Regardless of the exercises you select for your routine, apply the following principles for maximum safety.

1. Always use strict technique when exercising. Stop using an exercise when you can no longer perform it properly.

2. Employ a slow deliberate approach.

3. Never bounce. Momentum can make even a safe exercise dangerous.

4. Hold stretching exercises for at least six seconds initially, building to 30 seconds. Holding a stretched position is more effective in stretching a muscle than doing many repetitions.

5. Reject the no-pain/no-gain philosophy. Pain means something is wrong and you should stop immediately.

187

6. Stop when you are mildly fatigued in order to avoid sloppy form.

1. Lower Back/Abdominals

Many popular exercises can be stressful to the lower back. In fact, exercises we think will help us avoid a lower back problem (by stretching the lower back muscles and hamstrings, and strengthening the abdominal muscles) actually can make things worse. There are several examples.

High on the list is the standing toe touch with knees straight This is a bad exercise even if done slowly and deliberately. And if you bounce up and down, you run the risk of not only injuring your lower back, but also injuring the hamstring muscles and the back of the knees. A safer alternative is the bent-knee roll-down in which you bend forward from the waist with the knees slightly bent. Keeping the abdominal muscles tense, continue bending until you feel a stretch in your hamstring muscles. Hold that position for at least six seconds, and gradually increase the time over several weeks.

Sit-ups are popular, and many fitness tests have you perform as many sit-ups as possible in one minute. But sit-ups stress the lower back, and they don't strengthen the abdominal muscles nearly as much as people think. This is because sit-ups focus action on the hip flexors rather than the abdominals (trunk flexors). The straight-leg sit-up is particularly stressful on the lower back. Although bent leg sit-ups are somewhat less stressful on the lower back and they involve the abdominal muscles to a greater extent than the straight leg variety, they still can be a problem.

The best alternative to the sit-up is the "crunch." The starting position is identical to that of the bent leg sit-up, with the exception that the feet are unanchored and flat on the floor. Instead of rising all the way up, raise the trunk, shoulders and head a few inches and hold for several seconds, then return to a lying position and repeat. To avoid neck injury and to help ensure deliberate technique, cross your arms in front of your chest (placing your right hand on your left shoulder and vice versa) rather than holding your hands behind your head.

The double leg lift (a.k.a. leg raises) places tremendous stress on the lower back because leverage greatly increases the forces the lower back must generate to move and hold the feet aloft. Movements of this type cause your back to arch, placing the lower vertebrae and their disks and the back muscles in a vulnerable position. Scissoring the legs (raising them in an alternating fashion one at a time from a starting position with both heels slightly off the floor) also places the lower back in a dangerous position.

The raised-leg crunch is a safe alternative to leg lifts. Bend one knee keeping the foot on the floor, and raise the opposite leg. Lightly grasp the raised leg and elevate the trunk, shoulders and head toward the knee. Don't pull on the leg. Use the strength of your abdominal muscles to get the job done.

Prone (face down) back arches, or the swan stretch, jeopardize your lower back when you arch the lower back too vigorously. An alternative is the prone arm/leg raise (the floor swim). With arms extended overhead, assume a two-hand crawl stroke position while lying on the floor. Place a pillow under your abdomen to reduce stress on your lower back. Raise your right arm and left leg simultaneously four to six inches and hold for at least six seconds. Lower and repeat with the opposite sides.

The donkey kick (back/neck arch) can be dangerous. It starts with a down-on-all-fours position and entails lifting one leg as high as possible in a kicking fashion. When arching the lower back and the neck too vigorously, both areas are vulnerable to injury. The probability of injury is enhanced because of the whipping (ballistic) action of the leg, creating momentum and forcing the back arch beyond normal limits.

An alternative to the donkey kick is the rear-thigh lift. Avoid arching the neck and lower back while slowly and deliberately raising the thigh parallel to the floor. Hold for six seconds, lower and repeat with the opposite leg.

Exercises which entail twisting and pivoting can be especially dangerous. Windmills, in which you twist while bending, attempting to touch your right hand to your left foot and vice versa are extremely stressful on the disks of the lower back (lumbar vertebrae) and are best avoided. In some sports, however, twisting and pivoting movements play a major part. Driving a golf ball is a good example. Therefore, when rehabilitating from a lower back injury, performing mild twisting movements in a controlled

189

fashion pain-free, and under professional supervision, may provide a good barometer of readiness to return to the links.

2. Neck

Head rolls in which you roll your head around 360 degrees are very stressful to the upper (cervical) vertebrae. Neck stretches to the front and sides are a recommended alternative. Simply stretch the neck to the side, then the front, then the opposite side. You also can pull slightly with your hand, but keep the tension very light.

The plow, a popular yoga exercise, stretches the upper and lower back muscles. Unfortunately, because of the precarious body position, it forces the disks between the cervical vertebrae in the neck to protrude, or bulge, risking injury. The bicycle exercise also places the upper vertebral disks in danger and should be avoided as well. An excellent alternative exercise for stretching the back muscles is the fold-up stretch. While on your knees, keep your head down, forehead on the floor, and reach forward as far as possible while pressing your chest into your thighs.

3. Knees/Lower Legs

Full squats or deep knee bends can possibly damage the knee joint when squatting (lowering) with momentum, then bouncing out of the bottom position. Partial squats done slowly and under control are a safer alternative. Bend your knees and lower to the point where your thighs are parallel to the floor. Squat thrusts are a popular item in fitness tests. They also, because of the momentum, are stressful on the knee joint and should be avoided.

Jumping-Jacks (and all jumping activities, including jumping rope) entail considerable vertical forces which must be absorbed by the legs and particularly the knee joints. If you land on your toes, the Achilles tendons on your heels bear a major load which could cause a rupture in older unconditioned legs.

Many athletes engage in plyometric exercises which entail jumping down from a bench or table, then recoiling and immediately leaping upward. This obviously places tremendous stress on the knee joints and can result in injuries if technique is sloppy, or such movements are overdone. Because such training methods can be highly rewarding for young athletes, they can be included in an overall training program, but should be performed only under the supervision of a qualified professional.

4. Weight Training

Most weight training exercises are helpful and productive, assuming correct techniques are applied and appropriate resistance is used. There are some exercises, however, which, because they attempt to isolate particular muscle groups, can overstretch and overstress the joints involved. The overhead military barbell press can be an acceptable basic resistance exercise. But bear in mind that any exercise which emphasizes movements above shoulder level against resistance can strain and injure the delicate rotator cuff muscles. To make matters worse, in an attempt to concentrate more focus on the shoulder muscles, some lifters prefer to press the barbell from behind the head. While this isolates the shoulder muscles, it also stretches the shoulder joints to the limits which makes them particularly vulnerable to injury.

Many barbell exercises place the wrist joints in a vulnerable position. In the close-grip bench press, for example, the hands are only a few inches apart on the barbell which forces the wrists to bend unnaturally when lowering the weight to the chest. Forced into such a position, it is easy to strain the ligaments which support the wrist joints.

Curling a weight while the upper arm rests on an inclined bench is an excellent way to isolate the biceps muscles. It also increases the risk of overextending the elbow joint or overstretching the biceps muscle.

Cheating — using momentum or altering body position to gain an advantage and use more weight on an exercise — is a primary cause of injury. Arching the lower back when bench pressing (by lifting the buttocks off the bench), for example, places the lower back in a vulnerable position. Swinging a heavy barbell through the curling movement can injure the lower back.

Adding weight to any of the exercises discussed in the first three sections above makes a bad situation worse. Stiff-legged deadlifts, for example, are nothing more than standing toe touches while holding a barbell. If doing toe touches without weights is bad for you, you can imagine how potentially damaging performing them holding a barbell could be. The same is true for sit-ups, etc.

34. ARE YOU OVERTRAINED?

Training to improve aerobic fitness or to increase strength and muscularity requires hard work and dedication. You don't have to convince aspiring athletes of the need for extreme effort in pursuit of their goals, as they learn at an early age that the harder they work, the more they improve. They also learn quickly that those who can't cut it soon fall by the wayside. In fear, they drive themselves relentlessly into the weight room for more sets, more reps, going for the burn and beyond. They push to exhaustion in wind sprints and interval 440's, embracing pain as an essential part of the process.

But can this tried and proven road to success be taken too far? Yes, indeed. All work and no play makes Jack a dull boy. Too much work also overtrains Jack. Unfortunately, overtraining is much too common among those who exercise vigorously.

What is overtraining? It's simply an imbalance between the stimulus and the response of the organism. Too much stimulation in the form of training can overwhelm the organism, tearing it down rather than building it up. Understanding the underlying principles of training helps in the understanding of overtraining.

Training Versus Overtraining

When you train, your goal is to overload the body in some way. To overload, you must force the body to do more than it is accustomed to doing; to work harder than it wants to. To achieve increased aerobic fitness, for example, you engage in rhythmic activities such as jogging, cycling, swimming, etc. which challenge large muscle groups of the body, pushing the heart rate upward into the target zone and keeping it there for a prolonged period. In time, the body improves and eventually adjusts to the demands placed upon it. Once adjustments have been made, what you have been doing is no longer an overload, and therefore you must up the dose — running farther or faster, because if you don't, you cease overloading and progress stops. Herein lies the trap. To improve, you are taught to always push harder — the foundation of overloading.

Training (imposing an overload) stimulates improvement by assaulting the body, because when assaulted, the body is forced to make changes internally in order to better cope with similar assaults in the future. The body chooses to improve, because it finds the assaults so uncomfortable — the axiom of "no pain, no gain." The changes it makes (increased pumping capacity of the heart, increased plasma volume, increased muscle mitochondria, etc.) are called the training effect and they are manifested when the body is at rest, recovering from the assaults. It should be obvious, then, that adequate rest is as valuable as training to the overall process of improving the body's physiology. Obvious, yes. Accepted and valued, no — at least, not until recently.

Perhaps the greatest breakthrough in the training of athletes in recent years is appreciation of the need for balance between training and rest. When training is overemphasized and there is too little rest, the body cannot recover sufficiently between training doses. It's sort of like falling behind in paying your bills. At first, you are only a little behind, but eventually, if the imbalance persists, the debts mount and ultimately you are overwhelmed. Simply put, too much training and too little rest leads to overtraining. Contributing factors are lack of sufficient sleep and inadequate nutrition, both of which can retard the recuperation process.

Imbalance in the proportions of training versus rest can come from too much intensity, duration, or frequency, or all three combined. Intensity is how hard you work. Certainly, you are required to work hard in training, but not all the time. No athlete, for example, will thrive on daily high intensity interval training. Rather, they may plug in an interval training session once, or at most, twice a week. Too much volume (duration) also is a problem. This is particularly true for those who train with heavy weights, attempting to improve strength and muscularity by adding more sets and reps. And, training too frequently, especially if the intensity and duration are high, is a killer. Swimmers often train twice daily, performing long distance swims in the morning, followed by more vigorous training in the afternoon. Traditionally, swimmers are notoriously overtrained.

Symptoms of Overtraining

How much training is too much, and how much rest is needed to compensate? Hard to say. The body's ability to adjust to the demands of training is highly individualized, and what may overtrain one individual, may barely be enough stimulus for another. Each person must decide what's best for them.

To help you decide how much is too much, be aware of the symptoms of overtraining.

1. Psychological staleness: Assuming you are a highly motivated individual, perhaps the best indicator of overtraining is the loss of zeal for training. When you lose the edge and begrudge going to the gym or the track for a workout, chances are good you are overtrained. It's best to take time off and to return only when your body cries out for a workout, but not until then. Usually, when you take a layoff, you find that when you return you are likely to perform better than you have for a while — a definite indicator of overtraining, and hopefully an endorsement for increased rest along the way.

2. Decreased performance: As the body wears down, it's natural to expect a reduction in performance. Ironically, a reduction in performance often inspires athletes to work harder, attempting to reclaim former higher levels. This, of course, is the kiss of death, adding to the drain of overtraining.

3. Chronic fatigue: Overtraining drains the body to the point that everyday life is a struggle and there is chronic fatigue. Listlessness, loss of appetite, and falling asleep in the middle of the day are sure signs.

4. Loss of body weight: When the body is overwhelmed it loses muscle mass. This is a survival tactic. Muscle gobbles up energy, and the body reasons that with less muscle mass, less energy will be required, and survival will be prolonged.

5. Physiologic signs: An overtrained body cannot maximize the training effect it has achieved from months of prior training. The result is a higher heart rate and increased levels of blood lactic acid during familiar submaximal exercise. The heart rate response at rest also may be

194

elevated, especially in the morning when awakening.

6. Reduced immune capacity: Moderate training boosts immune function, but too much training combined with a lack of rest weakens the immune system. The result is increased risk of infection and succumbing to colds and the flu.

35. WEEKEND WARRIORS

As I get older, I am reminded of something many elderly individuals have told me over the years. They say, if it wasn't for looking in the mirror, or the aches and pains and various indignities visited on the physical body from the wear and tear of many decades of life, they wouldn't be aware of their age. Their thoughts on issues and their interpretation of the world is much the same at age 75 as it was when they were young adults. Sounds weird, I know, but I'm beginning to understand that statement. Through my eyes, I view the world as if I am a young person, and the greatest part of me wants to assume I am still that young person with great physical abilities. This view holds up pretty well until I have to really exert myself. Then I am reminded of my age. And, of course, others remind me, too, that there is little similarity between the me I see in my mind's eye and the me they see every day.

I say this because it has tremendous implications for weekend warriors—those who are sedentary for the most part, but who periodically engage in vigorous and often intensely competitive activities. Through their eyes, weekend warriors see themselves as young, fit, strong, impervious to injury, and confident they can still sprint to first base with the best of them, block and tackle on the football field, and slam dunk a basketball. And, indeed, many of them can. But the price for full-throttle sporadic exercise can be steep. Let me explain.

Exercise — Good Things Happen "After" You're Done

Exercise is good for you. Everyone agrees. But a closer look reveals that, actually, it is the aftermath of exercise that is good for you, and not necessarily the exercise itself. This is because, as you are now aware, exercise imposes considerable stress on the body, and the more vigorous the exercise, the greater the stress. Stress, in turn, forces the body

196

to cope as best it can, eventually making physiologic changes that will help it to cope more effectively. Such changes are called the training effect.

But when you engage sporadically in exercise, there is no opportunity to create positive changes via the training effect. Instead, when the body is exposed to random attacks of physical stress, it is never afforded the opportunity to better itself physiologically. You can probably get away with this approach when you are young. Young bodies are supple and can bounce back easily from imposed stress, even though they don't have the opportunity to develop a training effect. Older bodies, on the other hand, aren't as adaptable and they resent such an approach, eventually breaking down somewhere along the way.

Snap, Cracle and Pop

As stated earlier, the training effect involves not only fitness of the heart and lungs (ie. aerobic fitness), it also involves fitness of the muscles, tendons, ligaments, and the tender connective tissues which make up the joints. This is called orthopedic fitness.

In most athletes, orthopedic fitness lags behind aerobic fitness, unless they take specific steps to balance the two. In weekend athletes, orthopedic fitness often is woefully inadequate. This is a huge problem in sports which require short powerful bursts, such as sprinting to first base in softball, or leaping while spiking a volleyball. The stress of sprinting or leaping imposes tremendous forces on muscle and connective tissue, and the forces are even greater when connective tissue is tight and flexibility is poor.

Fitness is task specific, which means if you jog you are fit to jog. The training effect you experience from jogging impacts your body's physiology and orthopedic make-up in a very specific way. Even though you are fit for jogging, you may be totally unfit for basketball or any number of other physical activities. So, don't be fooled into believing that you can avoid the weekend warrior syndrome simply because you regularly engage in one type of exercise.

The muscles and connective tissues will make every effort to keep up with demands. But eventually, if you push too hard too often, something has to give, and that something usually involves a muscle, joint, tendon or ligament. And when it gives, it gives with a tear, or a snap, crackle and pop, followed by pain, swelling and bruising, which requires a prolonged period of rehabilitation.

Not for the Faint of Heart

There's another problem to consider which can be far more serious. Middle-aged and older bodies may be afflicted with one or more ailments that have yet to be uncovered. The perfect example is heart disease. Ninety-five percent of all heart disease is caused by atherosclerosis (clogging of the arteries). The clogging process begins early in life and progresses year by year, spurred on by a diet high in saturated fat and cholesterol, high blood pressure, cigarette smoking, psychological stress, and diabetes. Do we know this process is ongoing in our bodies? No, because there are no symptoms until the process is very advanced. Typically, symptoms such as angina pectoris (chest pain) don't occur until one or more of the coronary arteries which feed blood and oxygen to the heart muscle are clogged by nearly 80 percent, allowing only a trickle of blood to pass through.

There are no symptoms as this process progresses, because at rest, just a trickle of blood probably can meet the heart's needs. But during exercise, the heart beats faster and requires more energy, which in turn requires that more oxygen be delivered by the blood. But if more blood cannot pass through the clogged arteries, the demand for oxygen outstrips the supply and the result is chest pain. This is a warning signal the heart is in trouble. If the heart is being monitored during exercise with an electrocardiograph, electrical changes will occur in the heart that also signal the heart is in trouble.

A treadmill stress test under the supervision of a cardiologist is a good way to see if the heart is healthy, because it's difficult for the heart to hide its problems during the stress imposed by exercise. Similarly, the stress imposed by a weekend warrior playing soccer or basketball can bring out the worst in the heart. The problem is, there is not a cardiologist standing by to address the emergency. With this in mind, an occasional bout of severe exercise is like playing Russian roulette with your body. Do it once too often, and you could be asking for real trouble.

The Bottom Line

The bottom line is, being a weekend warrior is like being a kamikaze pilot. Sooner or later you are going to crash. And when you do, it's unlikely that all the king's horses and all the king's men will be able to put you back together again. Therefore, take a minute to pause and reflect. If imitating Sammy Sosa at the softball park on Sunday afternoons is important to you, spend time training during the off season to improve your aerobic and orthopedic fitness, and continue training during the week as preparation for the spotlight. But before you do, have a complete check-up with your doctor which includes a treadmill stress test to determine whether your body can withstand the demands of training. If it can, and you are given the green light by your doctor, go for it. You owe it to yourself to bring your body into line with the image you see of yourself in your mind's eye.

36. THE COMEBACK

A comeback for someone who has been highly fit in the past can present a dangerous situation; more dangerous than that encountered by the novice — one who desires to get in shape for the first time in their life. The novice knows she's out of shape and knows it will take a good while before she's able to run a 10K (a 10 kilometer — 6.2 mile) race in a respectable time. The rate of progress for the novice, regardless of intentions, also will be considerably slower than it will be for those on a comeback. It's easier to reclaim fitness on a comeback than it is for a novice to build fitness for the first time.

Those on a comeback have a misleading reference point. Because you were able to run a 10 k race in the past in good time, it is tempting to think you are able to reclaim that level of aerobic (cardio-respiratory) fitness quickly. You overestimate where you are now, in other words, and when you start training again, you overdo it. You want to assume your old workouts of running several miles at a rapid pace, and you try to get there in a hurry.

At first you may be successful in your efforts and gains may come quickly, which reinforces your efforts to do more and more. I've seen former runners coming back from a long layoff increase their aerobic fitness level by leaps and bounds over just a few weeks. Unfortunately, the fragile joints and connective tissues may lag behind in their ability to adapt to the pounding, and when fitness outstrips joint readiness, you're in for trouble.

Let me add one more negative factor to the mix. Age. The fact that you are older now than you were means your body has lost some of its resiliency. Remember the old days when you were a kid and could go out and play tackle football in a neighbor's yard for hours at a time and come back for more the next day? Try just a small dose of that now and you won't be able to move for days. The same holds true for running. A little bit takes a much larger toll than you imagine, and even just a few years of aging can make a substantial difference.

My advice is to take the approach of a novice. Start with a short distance of, say, only a half mile at a slow speed. Do this every other day (a day of rest between runs will ensure recovery by your joints between runs) for three weeks and monitor how you feel. Then add distance gradually, at the rate of a quarter mile every two or three weeks. Keep the pace slow until you can cover three miles comfortably. Use conversation as your guide — talking while you run without gasping for breath. Then, if you want, you can begin to increase the intensity of your runs by upping the pace slightly over several more weeks.

Overall, when you can again run three miles at a brisk pace, your fitness level will be high and you should be able to continue to progress (in distance and intensity) toward the kind of fitness required to run a good 10 K time again. This will require a few months to accomplish, and no doubt will entail much less progress than you'd like. But it's safe and your joints will thank you.

If a layoff is necessitated by injury, be especially careful during your comeback, because you may have done some damage to your joints that is still unresolved and which surfaces when you attempt to run again. Bear this in mind, and if you experience even the slightest twinge of pain, stop immediately. If you continue to run, the pain may subside, but usually it's because you are compensating in some way, or the pain is being masked. Compensations of any kind may address the immediate problem, but ultimately create other and possibly more severe problems down the road. When it comes to masking, perhaps it's the release of endorphins in the brain (opiate-like substances which mask pain during times of stress), or it's your self determination to keep going by consciously attempting to block out the pain. Either way, pain is a sign that something is wrong and it will only get worse as you keep pounding away on your joints. If there is pain, consult an orthopedic surgeon who specializes in sports medicine.

The Bottom Line

The bottom line is, be like the tortoise and take a long term view. A slow but steady approach will increase the odds that you will be able to run in the future. Sprinting from the starting gate like the hare probably will cut your comeback short again.

37. EXERCISE IN HOT WEATHER

Summer sunshine, high temperatures and unbearable humidity. Each can turn a modest bout of exercise into a torturous ordeal, and when combined, this fearsome threesome can be lethal. Here's why.

Humans are mammals, which means we are warm blooded. We constantly produce enough heat (through metabolism) to keep our body temperature at a sultry 98.6 degrees. We produce so much heat, in fact, our bodies are constantly locked in a struggle to lose it. If we didn't lose heat, our body temperature would rise as if we had a fever. And in just one day, our temperature could exceed 108 degrees!

Fortunately, many things contribute to our ability to dump heat from the body. When air temperature is 72 degrees, heat is transferred easily from the skin (which is usually about 93 degrees) to the cooler air. But when air temperature rises into the eighties and above, we begin to feel uncomfortable, because less heat is lost from the skin. Evaporation of sweat is another way we lose heat from the skin. But when humidity is high, evaporation is reduced and moisture stays on our skin making us feel hot and sticky.

Hot and humid weather is tough on the body, and exercise makes things worse. Exercise increases metabolism. A brisk walk can increase metabolism by four fold, which means the body must lose heat four times more rapidly in order to keep body temperature from rising. And when doing vigorous exercise, like jogging, metabolism can increase ten fold or more.

In order to help you lose heat during exercise, your body makes a number of physiological changes. Unfortunately, as you get older, your ability to make these physiological changes decreases, which means your tolerance for exercising in hot weather declines. All things being equal, older persons are much more likely to suffer heat stroke than are younger persons, and the risk rises substantially for those over sixty years of age.

Does this mean if you are eligible to join the AARP you should turn into a couch potato from May to September? Not at all. Here's some advice on how to stay safely active in hot weather.

1. Overwhelmingly, the most important thing you can do is respect the heat and beware. Use common sense and, when possible, exercise in the cooler parts of the day. The Mexican siesta is the ultimate common sense concession to the heat.

2. Don't expect to do as much in the heat as you normally do in cooler weather. Reduce your distance and speed of walking, for example, or don't work as long in the garden. Use frequent breaks and move to cooler air if you must work outside in the heat for a prolonged period.

3. After repeated exposures, your body will do a better job tolerating the heat. This is called acclimatization and it takes about two weeks. Go easy for the first week of hot weather, then gradually increase your efforts. Keeping yourself in shape year round is helpful, because those with increased physical fitness tolerate hot weather better.

4. Use comfort as your guide. If you begin to feel too hot, you are. Get out of the heat immediately.

5. Avoid sunshine. Sunshine does not heat the air, but the sun's rays will add heat to your body. That's why you can feel comfortable exercising in the shade on an 80 degree day, but can feel very uncomfortable when it's the same 80 degrees and sunny.

6. Expose your skin to the air by wearing as little as modesty will allow. Heat is lost from your skin, but only when your skin is exposed to the surrounding air.

7. Go heavy on the fluids. Drink and drink and drink some more. Consume 8 ounces of fluid just before you begin exercising. Once you start, ideally, you should consume about 8 ounces of fluid every 20 minutes. For shorter stints in the heat (an hour or two), drinking water is fine. For longer stints, a sports drink which contains modest amounts of sodium, potassium and glucose is recommended. When you finish, drink some more. Weigh yourself and if you have lost a pound, you have sweated off one pint of fluid. Two pounds is the loss of one quart (two pints), and so on. Make sure you replace all the fluid you lost (as sweat) as soon as possible.

8. Be especially wary in humid weather. High humidity can make even lower temperatures (75-80 degrees) potentially dangerous, and it can make higher temperatures (90+) intolerable. This is because evaporation of sweat is the major means by which you lose heat from the body when exercising, and high humidity means limited evaporation.

Beware ofF Dehydration

If you exercise regularly in the heat you are losing body fluids through sweat loss. At first, your body will use the fluid which surrounds the cells (the interstitial fluid) as sweat. But when sweating is extreme and the loss of interstitial fluid reaches a critical stage, another source of fluid must be found. That source is plasma from the blood, which means that severe sweating can reduce blood volume.

The potential danger of exercise in the heat is compounded by living in a climate where temperature is high, but the humidity is low, which helps sweat evaporate immediately when it appears on the skin. This can cause you to underestimate the amount of fluid you are losing. As stated above, it's possible, during vigorous exercise in the heat, to lose as much as two quarts of sweat per hour. That's 4 pounds of sweat (1 pint = 1 pound).

Acute sweat loss in one exercise session is not the only danger. Chronic sweat loss over several days can add up and impose the same danger as a huge sweat loss on one occasion. Therefore, regardless of the situation or how much sweat you think you are putting out, you must consume fluids during exercise.

You may not be able to replace all the fluids you lose during exercise and therefore the best way to be certain you have completely rehydrated is to weigh in and weigh out (before and after exercising). Weigh in the nude and record the weight. When you finish, towel excess sweat from your skin and weigh again. A loss of four pounds during exercise would be caused by the loss of four pints (or two quarts) of sweat. Drinking plenty of fluids before, during and after exercise will help keep your level of hydration reasonably stable.

Be aware that because you will satisfy your thirst before you satisfy your body's need for fluids, don't interpret a lack of thirst as not requiring more fluid intake. Sometimes it is necessary to force yourself to drink more than you would care to in order to bring your body weight back to where it should be.

I certainly would not want to discourage you from exercising, and therefore an option is to stay indoors and exercise in the coolness of air conditioning. You will still sweat and lose some fluids, but not nearly as much as you would outside.

First Aid for Heat Injury

Here's what to do to help someone who ignores the advice above and gets into trouble. First, cool the body as fast as possible by whatever means are available. Use a garden hose if you are outside. Inside, put the person in a cold shower or in cold bath water.

Second, call for professional help. If you are told to get the victim to the hospital, go to the nearest one. Call the hospital and alert them that a potential heat stroke victim is on the way. This will give them time to prepare an ice bath and other means of quickly cooling the body. Don't stop heat loss measures enroute to the hospital. Crank up the air conditioning in the vehicle, apply ice, do whatever you can to reduce body temperature.

Exercise in the Heat and Blood Pressure Medication

When medication is needed to bring the blood pressure down to a healthy level, it's important to understand that many things can exert influence on the effects of the medication, making it either more or less potent. One such factor is exercising regularly in hot weather. Here's some background.

Blood pressure is governed by three main factors and there are medications which address each factor.

1. Fluid volume — the amount of fluid (blood) in the system can determine the degree of pressure in the system. More fluid equates to more pressure. Diuretic drugs help you lose fluids from the body, and some of that fluid will be taken from the plasma in the blood.

2. The pump — the power and frequency of your heart beat determines how forcefully the blood surges through the system. Reduce the power and/or frequency and you can reduce overall blood pressure. Beta blocker drugs act on the heart muscle to slow it down.

3. The vessels — the diameter of the blood vessels determines the resistance to flow. The narrower the diameter the greater the resistance to flow and the greater the blood pressure. Vasodilator drugs act to relax the muscles in the vessel walls, expanding the diameter and reducing pressure.

Of the three types of medication, diuretics generally are the least powerful and impose the fewest unwelcome side effects. Diuretics often are the "first line of defense" in the battle against high blood pressure. They often are prescribed first, in other words, in the hopes that more powerful medications won't have to be used.

Severe sweating *and* taking diuretic drugs could possibly add up to an overdose of effects, because both act to reduce blood volume. You also could overdose on other types of blood pressure medications, because a drop in blood volume (from excessive sweating) means the substances in the blood will increase in concentration. This creates a tricky situation, and a potentially serious one, and one that must be discussed with your doctor. Be alert for any symptoms that might occur during exercise and when at rest. Also, you should be having your blood pressure taken regularly, and any change in expected values should throw up a red flag.

The bottom line is, you should be able to exercise and sweat and still benefit from taking your blood pressure medication. But you will have to be vigilant in your efforts.

Ozone and Carbon Monoxide

Sunny conditions trigger a complex series of chemical reactions (certain hydrocarbons, for example, catalyze the oxidation of nitric oxide to nitrogen dioxide) which ultimately form ozone. But conditions must be ripe for large amounts of ozone to be produced. The right combination of bright sunlight and daytime temperatures above 80 degrees F, an abundance of precursors (from automobile exhausts), and the lack of wind, causes concentrations to build.

In high concentrations, ozone causes eye irritation, coughing, chest tightness, shortness of breath, and nausea. Fortunately, although ozone is an increasingly worrisome problem, we rarely experience conditions so severe as to significantly impede a young, healthy runner.

The elderly and those with lung problems certainly are affected, however, and need to heed health warnings tied to ozone concentrations in the air. Such warnings emphasize reduced physical exertion and outdoor activity. When things get real bad, a plea is made for citizens to do less driving by using carpools and public transportation.

A temperature inversion compounds the problem. Normally, air that is closer to the earth is warm, and the air higher up is cooler. This creates air currents, because warm air naturally rises. But in an inversion, the warmer air flip-flops with the cooler air, resulting in cooler air being closer to the earth. This reduces air currents to a standstill, and pollutants accumulate.

In addition to ozone, the other major pollutant is carbon monoxide. Carbon monoxide displaces oxygen in the blood stream, because it combines with the hemoglobin of red blood cells more than 200 times faster than oxygen. Because some of the oxygen is displaced, the blood concentration of oxygen is less, and the heart has to circulate more blood to deliver the same amount of oxygen, which makes the heart work harder.

Carbon monoxide doesn't create strong overt symptoms, unless, of course, you overdose, then you turn blue from asphyxiation. Fortunately, carbon monoxide is less of a problem in the summer (unless there is a temperature inversion), because automobile engines tend to burn more efficiently than they do in the winter. But carbon monoxide pollution can still be a problem anywhere cars gather, especially when they idle at congested intersections or in mall parking lots.

Research suggests that running in traffic can increase your carbon monoxide level in the blood by many fold. This would not interfere with normal everyday activities, but it may reduce your running ability by a few percent. Experienced runners are, of course, keenly aware of a few percent reduction in performance.

Overall, when you run in hot sunny weather along roads crowded with automobiles, you should expect a decrement in performance. Some of it is caused by air pollution and some of it is caused by heat. Respect the effects of both and do yourself a favor by cutting back on your intensity (speed) and volume (mileage) of exercise.

38. EXERCISE IN COLD WEATHER

Cold weather is dangerous when too much heat is lost from the skin too quickly. Heat leaves the skin in a hurry when air temperature is low. But low temperatures are not the only concern. Wind is also an important factor, because the stronger the air current, the greater the amount of cold air that is circulated over the skin, and the greater the amount of heat that is removed.

Comfort is your best guide in cold weather. If it feels too cold to you, stay inside. Another guide is the windchill index — the impact exerted on the skin by the combined influences of air temperature and wind velocity. You will probably be reasonably comfortable (assuming you are dressed appropriately) until the index hits zero or below. This represents a wide array of combinations of temperature and wind. For example, the windchill index associated with a 30 degree temperature combined with a 25 mph wind is 0 degrees. The windchill index associated with a much lower temperature of 10 degrees but with a wind of only 5 mph is 6 degrees. As you can see, a calm very cold day can be less damaging to the skin than a warmer day with high winds. The danger zone for windchill is approximately -25 degrees F, or below, and it's best to skip your exercise in such weather.

Since windchill is critical, keep in mind when you face the wind your rate of speed adds to the effect. Running at 8 mph into a 10 mph wind, for example, results in an 18 mph windchill effect. It's a good idea to plan your route so that you go into the wind first, because you are fresh and dry. If you have been exercising for a while and are sweaty, the dampness magnifies the windchill factor. Before setting off into the wind, take time to do a thorough warmup indoors. Raising body temperature slightly, without sweating, will reduce the discomfort of stepping out into the cold and wind.

Runners dressed in shorts generally are comfortable on cold days because their metabolic rate is high. But after the run, watch out. Heat can be lost from exposed parts of the body very rapidly, and body temperature can plummet. To avoid problems, allow yourself only a few minutes to cool down after your run, then get out of the cold as quickly as you can.

Frostbite, the most common cold injury, is actually the freezing of flesh which occurs when skin temperature drops from its normal 93 degrees into the 21-28 degree range. Runners are not immune to frostbite, and peripheral areas such as the ears, fingers and toes can succumb if not protected. That's why runners in shorts also wear caps, gloves and thick socks. They also are careful to keep their feet dry, because wetness greatly increases the rate of heat loss from the skin. An additional vulnerable area for males is the penis, because nylon running shorts offer very little protection. Insulated undergarments are recommended. (More on clothing below.)

When exercising in the cold, it is important to frequently monitor how your skin feels. If you experience numbness or tingling, especially in the fingers and toes, frostbite may be on the way. Watch out for burning sensations, too, or whitening or blanching of skin on the nose and ears. The affected area also may turn red, then blue. Blisters may develop, followed by a black and blue mark.

If you suspect frostbite, get out of the cold immediately and warm the affected area as quickly as possible, preferably with towels soaked in warm (body temperature) water. Never rub the affected area. A heat lamp is not a good idea because it may burn the damaged skin. See your doctor as soon as possible.

Lung problems are unlikely while running, even on very cold days. Breathing large amounts of cold air during exercise can cause throat irritation, which has given rise to the myth that the lungs are in danger of freezing. Not so. Incoming air is warmed in the upper passages of the respiratory tract, and is within two or three percent of body temperature when it reaches the lungs.

When walking or running in the snow, use common sense. Because you can't see what's under the snow, be cautious. And always assume the terrain is slippery and act accordingly. On sunny days, sun screen may be necessary if you're going to be out for a prolonged period. Sun glasses also are a good idea.

Dressing for Exercise in Cold Weather

Your body can quickly produce sufficient heat to make you feel warm and cozy on the coldest days. With this in mind, you are overdressed if you step outside in freezing weather and you are perfectly comfortable just standing there. My advice is to dress as if it is twenty to thirty degrees warmer than it really is. On a calm day (little or no wind), for example, dress as if you were going out to exercise in a forty degree temperature, even though it is only ten degrees. In windy conditions, dress a little warmer, pretending it is only thirty degrees.

You need to avoid underdressing too. When you begin to exercise, you should feel somewhat chilly. This is because you anticipate a huge build-up of heat after running a little while. But don't go overboard. You shouldn't be shivering or chattering your teeth, and you shouldn't feel miserable. If you do, you haven't dressed warmly enough.

Underdressing can be a serious problem, and it is imperative that you protect peripheral areas, including the feet, hands and ears (and for men, the penis). Ironically, keeping the torso warm will help keep the fingers and toes warm. When the torso is cold, blood flow (which transports heat) to the periphery is reduced and redirected to the torso in an effort to warm this critical area. (The torso takes precedence over the periphery, in other words.) Keeping the head warms helps, too.

Now for the specifics. Dress in layers. It offers two advantages. First, heat is trapped between the layers which means several thin layers acts as a better insulator than one thick layer. Second, when you begin to overheat and sweat, you can remove a layer and tie it around your waist as you continue exercising. This allows air to circulate more freely over your body, evaporating the sweat. And, because you have the garment at your fingertips, you can put it back on as soon as you stop.

The layer closest to your body (the first layer) should be material that is specifically designed to draw (or wick) sweat away from the skin. Several synthetic fabrics (polypropylene, for example) have been developed for this purpose. To be effective, these fabrics must be worn next to the skin, without an intervening layer such as cotton. Never, in fact, wear cotton as the first layer, because cotton traps moisture against the skin, greatly increasing heat loss.

The second layer can be wool, down or synthetic. The third, or outer layer, should be a jacket that is both waterproof and windproof, while at the same time breathable to allow air to circulate over the torso and evaporate sweat. Gore-Tex contains this combination of characteristics and is highly recommended as the outer wear of choice.

Don't neglect your legs and head. Keep the legs warm with lycra tights, sweat pants or long johns. Always wear a hat. Layers on the head are not necessary, but because the head sweats heavily, you should select a wool or synthetic cap or hood that helps move moisture away from the skin. If it gets real cold, you may need a mask to protect your face. To protect the neck, wrap it in a terry cloth towel — not wool or synthetic turtleneck sweaters and scarfs, because this area is highly sensitive and susceptible to irritation when sweating. Finally, go with mittens instead of gloves. Mittens offer greater insulation than gloves because the fingers are together and because there is less surface area from which heat can be lost.

What about shoes? As always, shoes must provide a high degree of resiliency (shock absorption) when jogging over hard surfaces. Traction also is an important consideration, especially in very cold conditions when the ground may be frozen. Shoes should be roomy and allow an extra pair of socks. Roomy shoes also allow space for air to be trapped and warmed. Avoid tight fitting shoes — they will squeeze the feet, restricting blood flow, making the feet more vulnerable to cold injury.

The bottom line is, if you dress properly you can jog comfortably in very cold weather.

Shoveling Snow — A Deadly Chore?

Shoveling snow is tough business, and most men, especially older men, have no business subjecting themselves to this potentially life threatening activity. There are several reasons for this. First, it's high intensity work which can force health problems to the forefront. As I have stated already, bad things can be going on inside your body and you don't know it.

Take, for example, the process of atherosclerosis (clogging of the arteries), which goes unchecked and without symptoms of any kind until the process becomes quite advanced. There will be no signs until one or more of the arteries which feed the heart muscle itself is clogged by 70-80 percent, leaving only a 20 percent opening. Even then, this severe problem may go undetected. But when forcing the heart to work very hard as in shoveling, the demand for blood flow and oxygen delivery to the heart may overwhelm the ability of narrowed arteries to comply, precipitating a heart attack.

The Blood Pressure Roller Coaster

The intensity of effort involved is not the only worrisome aspect of snow shoveling. The nature of the task demands that you bend forward, thrust the shovel into deep snow, lift the load at the end of the shovel, toss the load, then return for more. When you bend and grunt while lifting a heavy load, internal forces within the chest cavity skyrocket, squeezing the interior like a vice. This is called a Valsalva maneuver, and it interferes with blood returning to the heart in the large veins which drain the upper and lower body. Since the heart can pump out only as much blood as it receives, when venous return is reduced, the amount of blood leaving the heart is reduced accordingly. This results in a sudden drop in blood pressure, possibly causing dizziness. Also, there is a reflex action in the vessels to constrict (narrow the diameter) in an attempt to increase blood pressure back to normal.

Then, when you relax between shovel loads, the blood pours through the veins back to the heart, which means the heart pumps out greater quantities. But, the heart must pump against constricted vessels which causes the blood pressure to zoom upward (increasing the risk of stroke). Thus, while shoveling snow, the blood pressure is leaping up and down, stressing the cardiovascular system.

As if this isn't bad enough, the small vessels in the skin likely will be tightly constricted when you go outside because of the cold weather. This peripheral constriction when you first go outside (before you build up metabolic heat which acts to dilate these vessels) adds insult to the scenario described above (in the Valsalva maneuver) adding even more stress to the heart. To reduce the stress of vasoconstriction, it's a good idea to warm-up thoroughly in the house before going out in the cold to do any physically demanding task.

The Paper Clip Syndrome

Beyond the risk of heart attack and stroke, snow shoveling also places the lower back at tremendous risk. The leverage involved in shoveling multiplies forces imposed on the lower back. A shovel with 10 pounds of snow on it places a much heavier load on the muscles of the lower back because of the length of the shovel handle. Thus, 10 pounds could impose 100 pounds of force. Add the twisting and turning when tossing the load, and you have the perfect prescription for lower back disaster.

This is true even for a healthy lower back, but is much more likely if your lower back is that of a typical American who is a prime candidate for what I call the "paper clip syndrome."

The stage is set when you have a belly which protrudes prominently and short hamstring muscles on the rear of the upper leg. The belly comes from overeating and poor food choices, and the short hamstrings come from sedentary living and lots of sitting. Add poor tone in the lower back muscles from chronic inactivity to the mix. These three factors cause the vertebrae in the lower back to struggle to maintain proper alignment, and often there are musculoskeletal compensations caused by an unnatural pelvic tilt. This results in a swayback, or exaggerated curve in the lower back.

With the lower back in such a pitiful state, it's easy to see how ripe it is for disaster. Indeed, something as simple as bending at the waist to pick up a paper clip from the floor can throw the back out. There is even the potential to rupture a disk simply from bending. Now, imagine the potential for disaster by bending at the waist to scoop a heavy shovel full of snow, then pivot and toss the snow aside. Ouch!

Don't get me wrong. I'm not saying that bending, lifting, and grunting while performing hard work outdoors on a cold day is necessarily bad for everyone. But if you are going to engage in such activity, you must be healthy, in good physical shape, and up to the challenge. Unfortunately, it's difficult to determine whether your body is up to the task. Assuming that you are ready for it simply because there haven't been health problems up to that point is a bad assumption. And if you have a history of health problems (such as high blood pressure, diabetes, etc.), choosing to shovel snow is nothing short of foolhardy.

If you are not regularly involved in vigorous exercise, and/or if there is even the slightest question about your health status, you have no business shoveling snow. There are plenty of youngsters out there who would love to remove snow for a modest fee. Common sense says, please take them up on it.

PART IV

STRENGTH/MUSCLE BUILDING

39. THE CHALLENGE OF BUILDING MUSCLE

Once believed to be a demeaning endeavor reserved for muscle-bound goons, lifting weights (resistance training) has become fashionable for men, women, and children of all ages. In the past, heaving barbells and dumbbells was the only choice. Today, resistance exercise machines have gone high-tech with many options and avenues to pursue. Commercial gyms abound and in most cities you can find one within easy driving distance. Equipping a home gym is an attractive alternative, and hiring a personal trainer to get you started and keep you motivated is gaining acceptance.

Weight training programs can be tailored to fit everyone's needs, regardless of age, sex, capacity, or athletic experience. This form of exercise is the exercise of the future, and there are unexpected benefits. Putting on a few pounds of muscle, for example, can increase your metabolism, making you a more effective calorie burning machine, which is helpful for weight control. Increased muscular strength makes everything you do throughout the day easier, because it demands a smaller portion of your capacity to accomplish. And scientists are beginning to realize the "fountain of youth" implications of sustaining strength into the elder years. But adding muscle to your body isn't easy, and your body will resist you mightily. Even so, if you have persistence and do the right things, you can prevail.

Muscle Building Basics

I am frequently asked about the best way to build muscle. What exercises are best? How many workouts per week? How much protein intake is required? The list goes on. An underlying theme to this litany of questions is: Why is it so doggone hard to build muscle, and why does it take so long? The answer is complex and highly individualized.

216

As a starting point, it's helpful to understand how your body feels about your efforts to gain muscle. It hates the idea. In fact, given the opportunity, your body will gladly dump as much muscle mass as it can. With this in mind, let's revisit the discussion of crash diets and how they afford the body an opportunity to lose muscle mass while clinging to body fat stores as presented in Chapter 4.

The primary and most important function of the body is survival. At the core of survival is energy. The body is always concerned about having enough energy, and that's one reason why we are so skillful at storing body fat. Stored fat is stored energy, and the more we have the more our bodies like it. In contrast, muscle is an energy drain, consuming lots of energy just to keep it alive. And, when muscles are working, the energy drain can increase ten fold, sucking in energy like a twelve cylinder engine. That's why exercise is so critical to weight management. It's also why the body hates muscle mass.

The wisdom of the body dictates that the more fat you have and the less muscle, the better equipped you are to survive. Therefore, your body will seize every opportunity to gain fat and to cast off muscle mass. All you have to do is quit using muscle for a while, and before you know it, it's gone. Break an arm and put it in a cast, for example, and several weeks later the muscles have shrunk and turned to jelly. The same thing happened to our early astronauts in the weightlessness of space. Being bed-ridden for a protracted period also will result in considerable muscle wasting.

On the other side of the coin, your body will do everything it can to prevent you from adding muscle to your body. The body is so clever, in fact, it will allow you to greatly increase your strength without adding even a little bit of muscle. Here's how.

In the early stages of a resistance training (weight lifting) program, your strength will increase dramatically, possibly even doubling if you are working hard. Even so, you won't build additional muscle mass, because your body will do everything it can to adapt to the demands of the training without having to resort to adding muscle. To do this, the connections between the nerves and the muscles are enhanced and you begin using your muscles more efficiently. The body makes changes in the existing structures, in other words, hoping such changes will be enough to get the job done.

If you continue training and continue making demands on the muscles by overloading them and forcing them to do more than they want to do, eventually, your body will give in and start building more muscle. But, again, your body will resist you every step of the way. When training, for example, your body will give you very unpleasant and painful signals when you push your muscles hard. The muscles will burn and feel as if they are being punctured with ice picks. This feeling gives rise to such sayings as "no pain-no gain" and "go for the burn."

When the pain comes on, a mind game begins. How far can you push yourself? How much pain can you endure? (Please note — I'm not talking about the kind of pain associated with injury. If you experience such pain, you must stop immediately and allow sufficient time for healing to occur. Folks with considerable training experience under their belts can quickly discern the difference between "training-pain" and pain brought on by the discomfort associated with injury.)

Your body hopes that training-pain will scare you off, forcing you to stop the exercise before you push the muscles far enough to necessitate making changes (adding muscle mass) in order to cope with the demands. This usually works. Most people who train with weights will reach a plateau in their development and continued effort merely keeps them at that level. This, even though they are convinced they are pushing themselves to the max in each workout. They're not, of course, but their body sure doesn't want them to know that.

Persistence Can Pay Off

Despite your body's efforts to thwart your attempts to gain muscle, you can succeed. But keep in mind that building muscle requires a great deal of energy and effort — energy and effort your body would prefer to invest elsewhere. And when you add muscle you create more upkeep for your body, and more resources (energy, nutrients, fluids) are required on an ongoing basis to feed your muscles and keep them strong. Your body especially hates this. Thus, only a determined and vigorous effort on your part will overcome your body's stubbornness.

But sheer effort is not enough. Your effort must be carefully controlled and intelligently applied. Simply pumping iron hours a day won't get the job done. Ironically, most who train to get bigger muscles are victims of their own efforts. They train too hard and for too long. They are overtrained, in other words. This doesn't mean you shouldn't train hard. On the contrary, intensity is the key to success. But be careful about the volume and frequency of your training. Your workouts should be limited to no more than one hour each, and you should train each body part no more than twice a week. Ask an expert to critique your training habits and if you are trying to do too much, cut back.

Another key is feeding your body properly and giving it adequate rest. Without the right nourishment and rest, your efforts at muscle building will go largely unrewarded. Here's some specific advice on diet.

Muscle is a high maintenance tissue. It requires a lot of energy — about 20 calories per pound of bodyweight per day — just to maintain it. That's 2800 calories daily for a 140 pound muscle builder. And for those trying to build muscle, even more energy is required, in the neighborhood of 25-30 calories per pound. That's about 3500-4200 calories daily for the 140 pounder who wants to get bigger. Chances are good most who aspire to get bigger are not consuming this much daily energy. And if they are, chances are they are not consuming the right foods to fuel their body.

Most strength athletes assume they need gobs of protein, and that's what they favor in their diet. To be sure, you need plenty of protein, but carbohydrates are equally important and, in fact, carbs should be the lion's share (about 70-75 percent) of your daily food intake. You should be consuming about 4.5 grams of carbs per pound of bodyweight to build muscle (at 140 pounds that's 630 grams of carbs). That's a lot, and it should be in the form of complex carbs — veggies (including starchy veggies like potatoes), legumes (lentils and various types of beans), fruits and grains. Stay away from candy, pastries and other sources of simple sugar that provide essentially no nutritional value.

As a strength athlete your protein needs are higher than the average person's, and if you are training hard, you may need twice the normal dosage. The average person requires less than 0.5 grams of protein per pound of bodyweight. When involved in intense weight training, an intake of one gram per pound may be required.

When it comes to dietary fat, a good rule of thumb is the lower the fat intake, the better. The average person should keep his fat intake to less than 20 percent of total calories. Because of the high caloric intake of strength athletes, you also can keep your percentage of fat below 20 percent, and still get plenty of fat overall. Athletes on high calorie diets need to be careful about their fat intake to be certain the vast majority of their fat intake comes from polyunsaturated and monounsaturated fats. Saturated fats (the kind found in red meats, fatty dairy products, fried foods, etc.) harm the body and clog your arteries, whether you are working out or not. Learn to read labels and shy away from foods loaded with saturated fat.

Be certain you get adequate sleep each night. Lack of sleep undermines your efforts, because the rebuilding process that occurs after a workout is done mainly when your body is completely at rest during sleep. Supplements can be helpful. Creatine is the current rage among strength athletes. There is some science backing up the use of creatine, and most athletes I've talked to are positive about its effects. But educate yourself and make an informed personal decision on such matters.

As far as other supplements are concerned, if your diet meets the criteria outlined above, you probably will be covering all your nutritional bases. But to be certain, you may want to take a good daily multiple vitamin/mineral supplement, and some extra vitamin C and E. Because you will sweat a great deal while training, be sure to keep your body hydrated. Sports drinks can be helpful in this regard. Consuming a sports drink loaded with carbs and electrolytes during and immediately after training is a good way to start the rebuilding process.

The bottom line is, work hard, work smart, fuel your body with everything it needs, and be patient. Eventually, you will reach your goal.

Drugs

The frustrations associated with adding muscle mass often give rise to desperate actions. The most desperate action is taking drugs. Serious muscle builders nowadays are tempted at every turn to take anabolic steroids, growth hormone, testosterone and other highly potent and extremely dangerous prescription medications. Such desperate acts may help create additional muscle mass, but at what price?

Think about it. Your body hates muscle mass and resists your efforts, but you outsmart it by taking drugs. Do you think your body is going to take this lying down? Of course not! One way or the other, your body will extract a price from you, and that price can be the highest price possible. Indeed, many advanced muscle builders have experienced severe medical conditions (heart attacks, liver failure, etc.), and even death, attributable to the drugs they took to build muscle. (More on this in Chapter 50.)

Pumping Up

When you flex a muscle to 60 percent or more of its maximum capacity, you squeeze off the blood vessels feeding the muscle, and they stay closed off as long as the contractions last. This makes the muscle thirsty and eager for the contractions to be over. When you stop contracting and allow the muscle to rest, blood pours into the deprived area in excess, creating the "pump." Scientists call this phenomenon reactive hyperemia.

If, in your workouts, you focus your efforts entirely on creating a pump, you may be putting your eggs in the wrong basket. You can pump the muscle with relatively light resistance which creates neither strength nor muscle mass. The muscle fibers are not overloaded sufficiently to make them grow in response to the demand.

If pumping tends not to build muscle mass and strength, why do the muscles seem to grow? While pumping during your workout, the muscles appear much larger because they are gorged with blood. Later, of course, they deflate to their normal girth. But some increases in size will occur because blood supply to the muscles increases due to increased vascularization (increased density of small blood vessels, the capillaries, which feed the muscle), and there will be increases in carbohydrate, fat and water stored in the muscle. Unfortunately, these effects can be lost very quickly when training is discontinued.

If your goal is building muscle mass, your best bet is to train for strength. If you do, the muscles will begrudgingly increase in size to help produce the increases in strength necessary to cope with the demanding workouts. During strength workouts, sometimes your muscles will pump easily, other times they won't. Don't worry about it. Go for the strength and everything else will take care of itself.

Muscle Shape and Definition

The shape of a muscle is genetically determined. This runs contrary to what you read in muscle builder books which claim you can change the shape of a muscle by performing exercises from all angles. Do your curls in a certain position to increase the peak of your biceps, for example. Hogwash. You can do your weight training exercises while standing on your head, or hanging from a trapeze and it will do nothing to change the shape of your muscles. They are as they are. All you can do is make them bigger.

Regarding defining the muscle, the key is diet. Again, the type of exercise and the combination of sets and reps will accomplish very little. Bodybuilders often are instructed to perform high reps for definition, as if the increased number of repetitions will burn off the fat overlying the muscle. Again, hogwash! When you eat right and rid the body of excess subcutaneous fat (fat just below the skin), your muscles will be revealed more clearly. They will stand our with clear definition, in other words. You may recall my discussion on the futility of spot reduction in Chapter 6.

Does Swimming Develop "Long" Muscles?

Old wive's tales suggest that swimming develops "long" muscles that are not strong, whereas sports like football develop "short" compact muscles that are powerful. This incorrect assessment comes from comparison of the physiques of swimmers versus football players. Swimmers are slender while football players are blocky in structure. Some of this may be due to heredity and preference. If I'm slender by nature I may not do well on the football field, but I may excel at swimming. As such, I choose to be a swimmer because it's natural to select things we're good at.

Training also is important. Swimmers spend long hours in the water swimming laps. This does not aid muscular development, and in fact too much swimming may interfere with building muscle. (The same is true for running, cycling, and other endurance activities which drain the body of energy.) That's not to say that swimmers do not lift weights. They do, but their purpose is to enhance strength without building large muscles which could slow them down in the water. Football players, in contrast, want to add muscle bulk and their training is designed accordingly.

The Bottom Line

Building muscle is extremely difficult, and your body will resist your efforts. But with sufficient time and tons of determination, you can pack on pounds of muscle. Just don't expect miracles, and don't resort to desperate actions. With this in mind, I have to laugh when I encourage weight training as an important component of a weight management program. Some accept the advice, but many reject the concept, afraid they will build bulging muscles overnight. There are many things in life to be afraid of, but, clearly, this isn't one of them.

40. FAST-TWITCH FRIENDS

When we arrive at our mid-fifties, some important bodily changes begin — changes that are so subtle they completely escape our attention. But ignored, these changes can have huge implications farther down the line. First and foremost, our bodies begin to weaken, and as we age, the loss of strength accelerates. If this process is allowed to proceed unchecked, we eventually get to the point where everyday activities are too challenging and we lose our independence. The source of the problem is when we begin losing our fast-twitch muscle fibers. Let me explain.

When you look at a microscopic cross-section of a muscle (the biceps muscle in your upper arm, for example), you see a mosaic blend of light and dark cells (fibers). The cells have been treated with a stain, and some of the cells take up the stain and others don't. The cells that stain are the so called slow-twitch fibers, and those that don't are fast-twitch. Slow-twitch and fast-twitch fibers lie side by side, but they have very different functions.

When your body is confronted with a physical task, it always follows a predictable pattern of response. It will try to do the task with as little effort as possible and expend as little energy as possible. It will recruit only as many muscle fibers as necessary, and it will initially recruit only the slow-twitch fibers, hoping they will get the job done. Slow-twitch fibers are easier to recruit and they require less energy when they contract. So, when you walk across the room, and perform other simple, low effort, everyday tasks, you are using only slow-twitch fibers.

Fast-twitch fibers wait in the wings, ready to be thrust into action, adding to the forces exerted by the slow-twitch fibers. When we climb a flight of stairs or lift a barbell our fast-twitch fibers offer assistance. The more demanding the task, the more the fast-twitch fibers contribute. If we avoid such task, our fast-twitch fibers become lethargic and weaken. Engaging regularly in physically demanding activities, on the other hand, keeps the fast-twitch fibers in shape.

Beyond the mid-fifties, neglecting our fast-twitch fibers has much greater implications than when we are younger. At a younger age our body is more forgiving, and even though we are sedentary, our fast-twitch fibers are preserved. Put the arm of a younger person in a cast for several weeks following a bone break, and the arm shrinks substantially. But soon after the cast is removed the arm returns to its original size and strength. The muscle cells (fast-twitch and slow-twitch) in younger individuals are still intact and ready to respond.

The response in an older person is quite different. Lack of muscular effort and neglect of the fast-twitch fibers can cause the fast-twitch fibers to break down, and literally disappear. Some of this loss is a natural part of the aging process. But most of the loss comes from inactivity later in life, especially following retirement from the work force when the performance of many mundane tasks is no longer necessary.

Taking all this into consideration, it's obvious that vigorous physical activity becomes progressively more critical the older we get. Ironically, in our society, as we get older, we become progressively less active. This leads us into a vicious downward spiral. Being less active reduces muscle mass (fast-twitch fibers) which reduces strength, which reduces our capacity to respond to physical challenges. Because of our reduced capacity, we avoid physical challenges, which causes further reductions in muscle mass (fast-twitch fibers) which in turn makes us weaker, and so it goes, until we spiral downward to the point where we can no longer perform everyday tasks (climbing stairs, etc.), and cannot care adequately for ourselves.

How long does the downward spiral take? That depends. Obviously, the more dedicated you are to being sedentary, the quicker the response. I observed this in my father. After he retired he spent most of his time in a recliner chair with a TV remote controller — the "clicker" as he called it. My mother served most of his dinners to him in his chair, and he rarely left the house. Taking care of my father was a great fitness program for my mother, but it cost my father dearly. His decline from age 65 to 75 was dramatic. He went from being a vibrant man with a spring in his step, to a man who could barely struggle out of his chair.

Eventually, years later in his eighties, he could not get out of his chair by himself. This was not due to any disease, injury, or debilitation. It was simply a lack of strength.

As lifespan in the U.S. increases, our ability to take care of ourselves and live independently becomes a more important issue. Fortunately, it doesn't take a lot of effort to stay vibrant, and there's no secret to it. Simply keep doing all the things you've been doing all your life, and particularly things which engage the fast-twitch fibers.

But unfortunately, the mindset of our society works against us, because we tend to see the elderly as needy and unable to cope with physical challenges. That's why we insist that grandma give up her two-story house—to avoid having to climb stairs. Instead, we should encourage grandma to climb the stairs more often, thus keeping her muscles in shape, and keeping her fast-twitch fibers strong and healthy.

Strength Can Mean Independence

If you ask the elderly to rank the things they value most, you will find that independence ranks right up there with friends and family, good health, and financial security. Ironically, despite a keen desire for independence, most elderly do very little to preserve the degree of muscular strength required to perform everyday tasks. And when things like walking, climbing, lifting and carrying become too difficult, independent living is no longer possible.

Initially, loss of strength is gradual with barely noticeable losses of about 20 percent from age 50 to 65. But after age 65 strength loss is accelerated and by the mid-seventies it drops to less than half what it was as a young adult. In the final stages, the vicious cycle I described develops, driving functional capacity lower and lower. Since Americans are living longer today, and most who reach their sixties are projected to make it well into their eighties and beyond, sustaining adequate strength is more critical than ever.

If you have been on a downhill spiral, is it too late to stop the momentum? Recent research says, no, it's never too late. By doing resistance exercises — any exercise which demands forceful muscular contractions — muscle strength can be reclaimed to a degree heretofore thought impossible, and in individuals ninety years of age and older.

Your bones can be strengthened too, helping you avoid osteoporosis (wasting of bones caused by loss of calcium). But you have to be diligent and put forth some effort.

One option is to join a gym or health club. Another is to hire a personal trainer. While these can be effective options, it is my experience that most older persons would rather take an approach that is less expensive, more convenient, and not too complicated. The vast majority would choose simple in-the-home exercises. Regardless of your choice, be certain to tell your doctor about your intentions. It's important to make certain you have no medical conditions that could be aggravated by exercise.

My advice is to perform common, physically demanding tasks on a daily basis. If you do, you will ensure that you can continue to do them as the years roll by.

Walk as much as you can. Getting outdoors regularly is refreshing and invigorating. For bad weather months, consider a motorized treadmill. One with a maximum speed of 5 mph is more than adequate and can be purchased for less than $500. Mall walking also is a good alternative. Most malls welcome walkers before business hours which allows you to walk unimpeded. Many malls have walking clubs that provide a good incentive to members to show up regularly and participate. Clubs also offer an opportunity for making new friends.

Climb stairs at every opportunity. If it is difficult, use your arms on the hand rails to pull you along. As your leg strength improves, depend less on your arms and eventually make it your goal to use your legs only.

Chair push-ups — Sit in a sturdy armchair with a firm seat. A typical dining room chair will do. Grip the arms tightly and push up to a standing position. Lower to a seated position, then push up again. Do this as many times as you can without exhausting yourself. Add one repetition each day to a maximum of twenty repetitions.

Add the following dumbbell exercises to make certain you are covering all the bases. Start with as little as one to five pounds on each dumbbell until it feels too light and you need to progress to a heavier weight. You can purchase inexpensive adjustable dumbbells at any sporting goods store. Exercises 1, 2, and 3 can be performed sitting upright in a sturdy chair, or standing. Perform each exercise 10 to 15 times without stopping. This is one set. Eventually, you may want to perform two or three sets of each exercise. Minimally, perform this routine at least three days a week.

1. Overhead presses — push the dumbbells overhead from the shoulders until the elbows are straight, lower and repeat. You can press both dumbbells at the same time, or alternate the right and left arms.

2. Curls — start with the elbows straight, the arms hanging at your sides. Bend the elbows (keeping the elbows at your sides) and bring the dumbbells to your chin, lower and repeat. You can curl both dumbbells at the same time, or alternate the right and left arms.

3. Lateral raises — start with the elbows slightly bent, the arms hanging at your sides. Slowly raise both arms to the sides until your arms are parallel with the floor. Hold for a moment then lower slowly and repeat. For variety, you can raise the dumbbells to the front.

4. Partial squats — stand erect and hold the dumbbells at arm's length at your sides, bend the knees and lower yourself to the level of a chair, then stand erect again. You may not need the dumbbells at first, and your bodyweight may be enough resistance.

If you are too busy on occasion to do much exercise, flex different muscle groups. Flex your biceps and hold this position for several seconds. Push your hands together in front of your chest, then attempt to pull your hands apart. Flex your abdominal muscles as if preparing to take a punch in the stomach. Flex your thighs, then rise up on your toes ballerina style. Hold these flexions, then relax and repeat.

When exercising, be certain to breathe naturally. Never hold your breath. Always employ slow and smooth movements. Never jerk or use momentum of any kind — especially when lowering a weight or returning to a starting position.

Be patient in your approach and don't attempt to accomplish too much too soon. Progress will come slowly but surely. Be comfortable when you exercise, but put forth a little effort. This type of program may be enough for you, or eventually you may want to do more. If so, the next chapters will provide everything you need to know to take the next step.

The bottom line is, don't neglect your body's muscles. If you don't use them, you'll lose them.

41. RESISTANCE TRAINING — THE BASICS

The following information is intended for the novice who is just starting out. But before taking your first workout, be sure to check with your doctor to make certain weight training is something your body can tolerate safely. Also, before starting, it's important to understand several basic concepts.

The key to successfully increasing strength is the overload principle — making a muscle do more than it normally would in everyday activities. This doesn't mean, however, that a "more is better" attitude is the best approach. On the contrary, weight training is a long-term process and caution, especially for beginners, is the way to go. What's more, the concept of overloading is relative to the individual. Lifting a five pound weight may be adequate resistance for an elderly woman who has been sedentary for years, whereas lifting 300 pounds may be required for a young male athlete.

It is important to adjust the degree of overload upward when possible to coincide with the increasing ability of the muscles to perform. A five pound weight may be adequate at the beginning, for example, but soon a heavier weight will be required if increases in strength are to continue.

Once you have achieved a satisfactory level of strength that meets your needs, you can shift to a less demanding maintenance approach. There is no need to continue overloading the muscles, and periodic exercise with the resistance you have mastered will sustain your gains.

Muscles can contract in a variety of ways.
- Concentric versus eccentric contractions — When a muscle contracts and shortens against a load, the contraction is concentric. An example is curling a barbell with the biceps from the level of the thighs to the chin. When lowering the weight to the starting

position, the same muscles contract, but this time they lengthen while contracting, acting as brakes to control the speed of lowering. This is called an eccentric contraction. Lowering a weight slowly is not only safe (reducing stress on the joints), it also exercises the muscles in an important way and both types of contractions should be included as integral parts of a weight training program.

- Isometric contractions entail contracting a muscle against an immoveable object. Tension in the muscle increases even though there is no shortening and no movement. Standing in a doorway and pushing the hands outward against the door jamb is an example. Isometric exercises can serve as a quick and effective mini-workout when there is little time or no facilities available for a weight training session. Isometrics also can be effective for rehabilitation in those with limited capacities.

- Isotonic contractions are the type used when lifting a barbell (or dumbbells). The muscles contract and move a weight through the range of motion. Many exercise machines mimic the movements of a barbell and therefore are isotonic in nature.

- Isokinetic contractions can occur only on specialized machines in which resistance is varied throughout the range of motion while the speed of movement is constant and tightly controlled by the machine. The resistance may be 100 pounds at the beginning, for example, increasing to 135 pounds mid-way, then falling off to 100 pounds again in the latter stages. Because a muscle can exert more force at certain stages of the range of motion and less in others, adjusting the resistance accordingly helps maximize the overload principle.

Training Tips

1. Warm-up thoroughly with a brisk walk or light jog, followed by a series of stretching exercises to promote flexibility. Hanging from a bar is especially effective for loosening up the shoulder joints.
2. Perform exercises through the full range of motion.
3. Always use strict form and sustain proper posture throughout every movement. Bending forward or backward to assist the working muscles is cheating and can result in injury.

4. Perform exercises slowly and without momentum.

5. Always resist gravity on downward (eccentric) movements and do not allow the weight to accelerate as it returns to the starting position.

6. Don't hold your breath. Establish a breathing rhythm which allows you to breath during the most challenging segments of each movement. Exhaling during the difficult parts and inhaling during the more relaxed (or lowering) phase is recommended.

7. Concentrate during each movement on those muscles (and those muscles only) which shorten and lift the weight to prevent unwanted assistance from other muscle groups.

8. Keep your eyes open to aid balance and control. Watch your movements in a mirror, or focus your vision on a small stationary spot at some distance at eye level and keep your eyes trained on that spot.

9. Recuperation between workouts is critical. Allow at least two days of rest between workouts, and never exercise a muscle group more than two times per week.

A Tried and Proven Basic Program

The Delorme method is an approach to weight training that works well for beginners. For each of the variety of exercises performed, establish how much weight you can lift. The amount you can lift will vary depending upon the size and strength of the muscles being exercised. Begin by lifting the weight 10 times — each "time" is called a repetition and each group of 10 repetitions is called a set. To find the right weight for each exercise requires a trial and error approach and will take some time initially. But once the starting weight for each exercise is established and recorded on a training log, the only concern thereafter will be increasing the weight when necessary to ensure an adequate overload.

Begin the process by lifting an obviously light weight 10 times. Rest a few minutes then add a small amount of weight and try it again and keep working upward until you arrive at a weight you can perform only 10 times. This is your 10 RM (repetition max) for that particular exercise.

For each exercise, three sets are performed. The amount of weight used in each set of repetitions will be based on the 10 RM. For example, if 100 pounds is your 10 RM in the bench press, the three sets will be performed at 50%, 75% and 100% of the 10 RM, or with 50, 75, and 100 pounds, respectively. The first two sets serve as a progressive warm-up, and the final set is challenging and represents the overload. Strive each day of training to perform more than 10 repetitions with 100 pounds — your 10 RM. When you can perform more than 10 repetitions, it's time to add resistance and create a new 10 RM.

Proper Technique

A well rounded weight training program will consist of movements that challenge the major muscle groups of the body. There are a number of exercises from which to choose that will challenge the legs, back, shoulders, chest, and arms. The following six exercises will be sufficient through the early stages of training. These exercises can be performed either on exercise machines which offer safety and guarantee correct movement patterns, or with a barbell (or dumbbells). Alternative exercises performed either on machines or with free weights can be substituted or can be added to expand the program later when progressing to a more advanced stage.

Bench Press — Bench presses exercise the chest (pectoral) and rear arm (triceps) muscles, with assistance from the shoulder (frontal deltoid) muscles. Lie supine (face up) on a bench, feet flat on the floor, the head, shoulders and buttocks firmly on the bench. Use an overhand grip (palms facing the rear when the arms are at the sides) that is approximately shoulder width. (Note: The wider the grip, the greater the stress on the shoulder joints.) The thumbs should be aligned with the nipples. Push the bar to arm's length, pause momentarily, then lower slowly while tensing the muscles involved and repeat. If using a machine, when lowering in each of the exercises described, prevent the moving weight stack from touching the base (weight stack).

Overhead Military Press — The overhead military press exercises the shoulder (deltoid) and rear arm (triceps) muscles. Sit erect with the back flat. An upright bench (similar to a reinforced chair) can be used to support the back. Grasp the bar with an overhand grip, the hands shoulder width apart, the elbows pointed out to the sides, the bar positioned at the base of the neck. Secure the feet flat on the floor or wedged against the rungs of the seat. Press the bar upward to arm's length, pause and lower slowly while tensing the muscles and repeat. NOTE: Resistance exercise in which the arms are extended overhead can put a great deal of stress on the rotator cuff muscles. As such, at the first twinge of pain, immediately quit doing military presses, or any other resistance exercises in which the arms are raised above shoulder level.

Rowing Motion — The rowing motion exercises the large muscles of the upper back (latissimus dorsi — the "lats"). When using a barbell, bend forward at the waist, bending the knees slightly. Grasp the barbell with an overhand grip and pull the bar to the chest. When using a "lat" machine as an alternative, sit erect, grasp the bar with a wide grip and pull down to the upper chest. An option is to pull the bar to the back of the head and touch the neck. The machine row is another option. Place the chest against the chest pad (adjusted to allow complete extension of the arms without the moving weights touching the base weight stack). Roll the shoulders forward and grasp the handles with a hammer grip (thumbs up), then straighten the shoulders and elevate the weights slightly to be used above the weight stack into the starting position. Pull the handles toward the chest, concentrating on pulling with the upper back muscles rather than the biceps (which will assist somewhat). Lower slowly and repeat.

Biceps Curl — The curl exercises the frontal arm muscles (the biceps). In the standard barbell curl, stand erect and grasp the bar with an underhand grip (palms facing forward when the arms are at the sides), hands slightly less than shoulder width apart. Curl the bar upward from the thighs to the chin, pause, lower slowly and repeat. Keep the biceps tensed when the arms are extending to reduce stress on the elbow joints. Lower until the elbows are straight and repeat. An option is the "preacher" curl. Sit erect with the chest against the rear pad of the "preacher" bench (shaped like a pulpit). Adjust seat height to allow the arm pits to hug the top of the bench with the upper arms resting comfortably on the surface. The arms should be completely extended, the elbows slightly lower than the shoulders. (Picture your arms resting over a pulpit that is turned backwards.) Curling in this position effectively isolates the biceps and prevents assistance from other, stronger, muscle groups. Be careful, however, because considerable stress will be imposed on the elbow joint and the eccentric phase (lowering the weight) must be highly controlled. It is imperative to keep the biceps muscles tensed throughout so as to control forces imposed on the elbows.

Leg Press —The leg press exercises the large thigh (quadriceps) muscles. Adjust the seat of the leg press machine to permit complete extension of the knees. Sit erect, maintaining a strict seated position with the buttocks and lower back firmly against the back of the seat while pressing. When starting, the knees should be bent to 90 degrees with the feet parallel and flat on the pedals. Grasp the handles on the sides of the chair for stability and push the pedals until the knees are straight. Do not lock the knees. Pause momentarily, tensing the muscles, then lower slowly and repeat. An option is the squat. Squats can be performed with dumbbells held at arm's length, or with a barbell across the upper back. (See description and discussion below.)

Calf Raise — Calf raises exercise the muscles of the lower leg (gastrocnemius and soleus). Calf raises can be performed sitting, or standing. Seated calf raises isolate the calves more effectively and prevent assistance from rocking back and forth. Adjust the seat to allow a 90 degree bend in the knees with the resistance pad slightly above the knees. Be certain to allow complete range of motion in the ankle joint. Place the toes and the ball of each foot on the foot pad. Push with the calf muscles raising the knees as high as possible (into a ballerina stance), tense, then lower slowly to a stretched position and repeat. An option is placing a barbell across the upper back for resistance, but balance can be a problem. The "donkey" calf raise is another option in which you bend forward from the waist, the upper body resting on the forearms which are placed on a table. A partner positions himself on your lower back and serves as resistance as you rise up on the balls of your feet. Another option is the one legged calf raise. Stand upright, one leg bent at the knee and off the floor. The opposite leg does the exercise. Holding onto a stair railing for balance, the ball of the foot on the edge of a step, rise up on the toes, then lower until the heel is slightly below the step and repeat.

Squats— Bad for the Knees?

Squats (deep knee bends with a bar held behind the neck and on the shoulders) can be very damaging to the knees when performed

234

incorrectly. The major problem is going down too rapidly into a deep squat and bouncing (recoiling) from the low position, gaining momentum for the return trip. The recoil action stretches and strains the ligaments of the knee joint, possibly causing tears. I did this to my knees, requiring an operation to pull damaged cartilage out of my left knee. Again, I must emphasize the importance of controlling the movement during the eccentric (lowering) phase of the exercise, progressing slowly while tensing the working muscles.

When the squat is performed correctly, squats strengthen the muscles and tendons surrounding the knee, and the ligaments which hold the knee joint together. This stabilizes the knee joint and helps prevent injuries. Correct form entails feet pointed forward and spaced approximately shoulder-width apart. A slow descent is used until the top of the thigh is parallel with the floor. This will be approximately half way down. From this "bottom" position, the muscles of the thighs, trunk and back cooperate to thrust the upper body upward until the knees lock. The back should be straight, the head up, the eyes focused straight ahead or slightly upward.

A weightlifting belt stabilizes the lower back while doing squats and protects it from strain. Some experts contend that wearing a belt reduces strength-building aspects of the squat on the lower back. My opinion is to err on the side of safety and go with the belt. Pull it tight, the tighter the better, and the wider the belt in the back, the greater the support it provides.

A barbell across the shoulders can be painful to the upper back and neck. A rolled towel or a pad of foam rubber under the bar can ease the strain. Commercially available plastic "holders" which hold the bar and are molded to fit the upper back are a good idea. A holder also prevents the bar from creeping down the back as you lift.

Balance can be a problem while squatting. To aid balance elevate the heels slightly, not more than an inch. Because large amounts of weight can be lifted while squatting, it is important that chest-high racks be available from which the weight can be removed easily and placed behind the neck. Injury could occur trying to lift a heavy barbell from the floor to overhead then to the back of the neck to get ready to squat.

An excellent option is use of a "Smith" machine found in most commercial gyms. The Smith machine fixes the barbell, allowing it to move only up and down a floor mounted stand. It's a much safer way to exercise, because if you get in trouble or begin losing your balance, you can lock the barbell at any level and get out from under it.

Squatting is a fantastic exercise, but it's not for everyone. My advice for the novice and older lifters is to stick with leg presses and forget about squats until you become more advanced and confident in your training. An outstanding benefit of squatting is the impact on the bones of the body. Squats apply tremendous compressional stress to the bones, causing them to take up calcium and become thicker and stronger.

42. FREE WEIGHTS VERSUS MACHINES

With the emerging popularity of resistance training and the numerous choices involved, confusion often arises concerning the best way to train. Which is best — barbells and dumbbells (free weights), or newer machines?

There are no clear answers to these questions. One type of training may suit a given individual under certain circumstances, but when circumstances change a different approach may be best. Here are some things to consider.

The Argument in Favor of Machines

- Machines have built-in safety features which reduce risk. When you can no longer push a weight, you can simply slide out from under it. With free weights, it is possible to get pinned under the weight. There is also the risk of weights falling off the end of a barbell, or a dumbbell coming apart in the middle of an exercise.
- Machines remove balance as a consideration. With free weights, the novice must learn to balance the weight while exerting force. This can be difficult and potentially dangerous when performing such movements as lifting a weight overhead, or squatting (deep knee bends while holding a weight behind the neck).
- Machines ensure correct movements within a defined scheme, which helps prevent cheating when fatigue sets in. When lifting free weights, it is possible to swing the barbell (thus creating momentum), or tilt forward or backward to remove stress from the muscles intended to do the work (the biceps, for example) and shift stress to other larger and stronger muscles (the lower back).
- Machines isolate the muscles that are exercising. This is an advantage when exercising to rehabilitate an injury or strengthen a specific

weakened body part.

- Machines can offer high-tech options (varying resistance throughout the range of motion) which tax muscles in ways that a traditional barbell cannot.
- It is a simple matter to change the resistance on a machine by inserting a pin or adjusting a dial. With free weights, plates must be hoisted to and from the bar. Machines are self contained and neat. There are no weights scattered about, creating a hazard and an eyesore.

The Argument in Favor of Free Weights

- Free weights offer extreme versatility, especially when using dumbbells. A given dumbbell exercise can be altered simply by holding the dumbbells with the palms facing forward, or facing the thighs, or facing the rear, which results in three separate versions, each working the muscles in a different way. Machines are limited by their construction, and each machine is designed to allow only one exercise. Some machines have multiple workout stations, but these are actually many individual machines combined into one large and complex unit.
- Free weights are relatively inexpensive. The expense climbs when adding benches, racks and other accessories, but the cost when compared with high-tech machines (that can run thousands of dollars each) is considerably less. Multi-station machines designed for home use are an option, but be careful when purchasing, because some lower priced machines may not offer sufficient durability for prolonged use. Such machines also may not provide smooth and true movement patterns, and may require considerable upkeep.
- Resistance training requires a high level of desire and motivation. Aspiring to lift a loaded barbell may motivate the lifter more strongly than moving a given level of resistance on a machine.
- Muscular strength is an important attribute in many sports and resistance training is an integral part of the preparation. Strength coaches believe there is greater transference of the strength derived from free weights to actual athletic competition (such as football) because of the ability to be explosive when lifting heavy barbells.

238

Machines tend to control movements and to discourage explosiveness.

- It is possible to perform barbell exercises which involve many of the major muscle groups of the body at the same time — cleaning a barbell from the floor to the chest, for example, then pressing overhead. This is an additional advantage when transferring strength effects from the gym to athletics.

The Bottom Line

Overall, there are pros and cons associated with free weights and machines. In general, machines may be preferable for the novice, because of their convenience and safety and ease of operation. Strength athletes prefer free weights to machines, because they may provide greater transferable benefits to sporting activities. Beginners may eventually include some free weight exercises as part of their routine to cover all the bases.

43. WEIGHT TRAINING FOR WOMEN

Until recently, resistance training was almost exclusively an endeavor restricted to males. There are a number of reasons for this, including the fear on the part of females that they will develop huge bulky muscles from resistance training. This fear is unfounded.

To be sure, when a woman lifts weights, eventually she will develop some additional muscle mass. But don't expect much change in the early going. The reason, as I already have explained, is you can substantially increase muscular strength and muscular endurance without appreciably changing your muscle mass. This is because much of the early gains in strength during a resistance training program are neuromuscular in nature (for either men or women). Your body learns how to take better advantage of your existing muscle mass first (when confronted with challenging weight training), then once that is maximized, your body will begin building additional muscle mass.

And when women get to an advanced stage of weight training, they will find that the potential for enhancing your muscle mass is limited compared with that of men. This is due to hormonal differences. By nature, men have more of the male sex hormone, testosterone, than women, and testosterone is a key catalyst needed to promote increased muscularity. So rest assured that women can take up weight training and not create grotesque masculine proportions. In fact, the only way women can even remotely approach a man's degree of muscularity would be through years of dedication to incredibly demanding weight training. But that would not be enough. Women need to enhance their potential for gains by taking masculinizing hormones such as anabolic steroids which mimic the effects of testosterone. Many female competitive athletes take anabolic steroids to bolster their muscle mass and enhance performance.

Other factors often influence a woman's decision not to train with weights. Traditionally, there has existed the attitude that having strong muscles is unfeminine, that women should be soft and cuddly. This attitude is changing and in many minds (male and female), firmness is replacing softness as desirable. The important thing is, women should be allowed to choose how they want to look and feel without yielding to societal expectations.

Another factor is the outdated notion that women should not engage in the kind of intense vigorous physical training inherent to training with weights, because women should not risk internal damage from intense effort which could compromise their child bearing capability. This fear is laughable. If there were any substance to it, pioneering women in the 1800's who lived the most arduous of lives never would have been able to successfully conceive or deliver healthy babies. Fortunately, we now know that women can train vigorously with weights (or by jogging or other demanding exercise regimens) well into their pregnancies without mishap. In fact, there is considerable evidence to support vigorous exercise as a way of helping expectant mothers pave the way to an easier delivery.

Can a woman become as strong as a man through weight training? The answer is, yes. If a woman trains with weights and the man does not, it is possible that the woman could become stronger, but this will take quite a while. This is because there is a long way to go to make up the gap between the sexes, as women are only about 50 percent as strong as men in the upper body. But the gap in upper body strength can indeed be overcome. I know several women who train with weights and they are quite strong — easily as strong as any average man. When it comes to lower body strength, the gap is less, and women have about 70 percent of the leg strength of men.

What kind of gains in strength can a woman expect early on in a weight training program? Research studies have shown that gains in strength among women of 25-30% are possible to achieve in as little as ten weeks of training. Such training must be vigorous and regular, however, which means dedication is required in order to assure success. But don't expect such lofty gains to continue. Gains will level out and be much slower as you get stronger.

The bottom line is, a woman can train with weights without fear of overdeveloping her muscles and looking like a muscle-bound freak. And if your goal is to be as strong as the average man, you can get there in time through dedicated effort.

The Linda Hamilton (Terminator) Look — Is it Possible?

The movie *Terminator* staring Arnold Schwarzenneger and Linda Hamilton was a big hit years ago. As the co-star, Ms. Hamilton set a precedent for leanness and muscularity for women, and since then many have aspired to look like her. Is it possible? For some, yes. For most, no.

To achieve the Hamilton look requires intense effort and strict dieting. Weight training is the key. Here are some things to consider.

As stated above, when engaging in weight training, there is a preliminary stage you must work through that will be somewhat disappointing if building muscle is your goal. You will find that you are getting much stronger initially without increasing your muscle mass. Don't be disappointed, as this is natural.

Second, in order to force your body to build new muscle, you must continually overload the muscle. You cannot simply go through the motions. Muscles will quickly adjust to the demands placed upon them, and unless you continually make new demands, they won't respond. You must push yourself and go for "the burn."

Third, you must concentrate on always using strict form, because without strict form you will unwittingly be engaging assistance from other muscles, and this will lessen the load on the muscles you want to develop. When performing the curl movement for the biceps, for example, keep your back perfectly straight and your elbows wedged in at your sides. This will force the biceps to do all the work. But if you should bend forward, or allow the elbows to leave your sides, this opens the door for assistance from the lower back muscles, the shoulders, and elsewhere.

Fourth, you must perform a large variety of exercise to be certain that all the muscles you want to show off are getting exercise. This lengthens your workouts and makes them more demanding. But if you don't do enough different exercises, the look you seek will evade you. Consider the deltoid (shoulder) muscles. To get the desired "look" you must develop the front, side and rear heads of the deltoid, and this requires at least three different exercises.

Finally, you may be doing everything right and still not achieve the look you want. You can develop increased muscle mass, but it may not show because of a layer of fat on top. By this I don't mean to infer that women are obese. Not at all. It's just that fat storage in women differs from that in men in that there is more emphasis in women on subcutaneous fat (fat stored just below the surface of the skin). Because of this tendency, women look softer and rounder than men, even though there may be considerable muscle mass "hidden" underneath. In addition, the concentrated accumulation of subcutaneous fat in women results in the condition known as cellulite on the thighs and buttocks.

In order to achieve the Linda Hamilton look (muscles etched in stone), you have to greatly reduce your overall body fatness to allow your newly developed muscles to show clearly. This entails a very strict diet (very low-fat and low-sugar intake), as well as mega-doses of exercise. If that's for you, go for it. If not, keep training and be satisfied with a bit more rounded, but firm, look.

44. THE 10-MINUTE WORKOUT

As we move through adulthood, we go through several physical stages. The first occurs in the twenties and lasts through the mid-thirties. These are our prime years when strength and physical prowess peak. Second, between 35 and 50 we start the downhill slide, losing capacity, gaining lots of body fat. Third, beyond age 50 muscle mass begins to dwindle, and additional gains in body fat are likely. Fourth, beyond age 70, muscle mass falls off the body like autumn leaves.

The loss of muscle mass in the third and fourth stages can have great impact on the body's physiology. There are more than 400 muscles in the body, and muscle mass composes 40 percent of the total body mass. Muscle is the primary determinant of metabolism — the more muscle you have the higher your metabolism and the more calories you expend each day just to keep you alive.

When you lose muscle mass your metabolism drops, which means it's easier for you to overconsume calories leading to gains in body fat. In addition, less muscle mass means less strength and stamina, which, in turn, means that each physical challenge you face, whether climbing stairs or lifting a heavy object, becomes even more challenging, demanding proportionately more of your body's resources to accomplish.

Preserving Muscle Mass

A powerful argument can be made for doing everything you can to preserve your muscle mass when you reach the mid-century mark. But why wait till then? Starting at a younger age establishes the habit, making it an integral part of your lifestyle. In addition, the more muscle mass you have, the greater your margin of error will be when you start losing it.

Unfortunately, when Americans think about working out with weights, they conjure up images of goons pumping iron for hours in the gym. Not very appealing to the average sedentary adult. For years I have preached the value of moderate physical activity and how everyone, no matter how busy they are, can fit some level of physical activity into their lifestyle. Let me add to that argument the 10-minute workout.

The 10-minute workout is exactly that. It takes only 10-minutes at most to complete, but despite its brevity it can help you preserve your muscle mass. Note, I said preserve, not build. If you want to build muscle, considerably more time and effort is required.

Preserving muscle mass requires remarkably little effort. All you have to do is regularly remind your muscles that you value their contributions by making some demands on them. There are two key items to consider. One is making the muscles do a little more than they are accustomed to doing on a regular basis. This is called overloading. And, two, overload frequently enough to let your muscles know you are serious. The 10-minute workout asks that you devote only 10-minutes a day, several times each week.

Split Routine

In order to keep the time required for each workout to a minimum, the 10-minute workout is split into two components, one for the upper body and one for the lower body, each performed on alternating days two days per week. The upper body workout entails three dumbbell exercises (already described — the curl, overhead press, and lateral raises) which challenge the muscles in the forearms, biceps, triceps (back of the upper arm), shoulders, and upper back — key areas of muscle-wasting later in life.

Here's the upper body routine. Start with very light weights that easily allow lots of repetitions (complete movements) — at least 25. But, don't try to do so many repetitions on your first outings. If you do, you will get very sore. Instead, start with just a few reps, with the goal in mind of reaching 25 eventually. The amount of weight you use will depend on you, but think in terms of 3, 5, 8, or 10-pound dumbbells initially. You may use different weights for each exercise — lightest weight on the lateral raises, for example, and more on the presses.

That's it. Simple enough. Perform each repetition under control and with strict form, never using momentum. To aid balance, sit upright in a sturdy chair while you exercise, with your back supported by the back of the chair. As you move along in your training you may want to repeat the cycle of three exercises, and you may get to the point where you can do each exercise three times in only 10-minutes, moving from one exercise to the next with little or no rest. Add weight only when the muscles tell you they can too easily perform the exercises. But, be in no hurry to get there. Take your time and be comfortable. Be sure to breathe normally, inhaling as you lower weights and exhaling as you lift them.

The lower body routine is simple as well, combining two exercises into one. Holding the dumbbells at arm's length at your side, squat by bending the knees. Squat in front of a chair and lower yourself until your bottom touches the seat of the chair, then return to a standing position. Upon standing, rise up on your toes ballerina style. Then repeat the squat. Perform one set of 25 repetitions of both movements, gradually add a second set, then a third set.

The Bottom Line

It doesn't take much to preserve muscle mass. As little as 10-minutes per day can work wonders. Give it a try. But first, check with your doctor to make sure your body can tolerate the stress of training.

45. KIDS AND BARBELLS — PROS AND CONS

There was a time when athletes were told by their coaches to avoid lifting weights. It will make you muscle-bound, slow you down, and reduce coordination. But now we know better, and there is no doubt that weight lifting aids athletic performance and reduces the likelihood of injury. Today, every successful athlete from Michael Jordan to Sammy Sosa pumps iron. This includes female athletes, too. And because young athletes, age 12 and younger, emulate the habits of their heroes, kids want to pump iron, too. I have received many questions as to whether weight training is good for kids, and if so, what's a good age to start and what precautions are necessary.

The old taboo against weight training still exists when it comes to kids, and conventional wisdom says kids and barbells don't mix. In support, some sportsmedicine authorities believe the earliest weight training should begin is after puberty, and preferably when growth in height is completed, or nearly so. They point to the stress of weight training on the muscles, bones and joints, claiming it may be too much for rapidly developing bodies. Or, worse yet, that weight training may damage the bones at the epiphyseal plates — the zones within long bonds where growth occurs. When an epiphyseal plate is damaged, the growth of the bone is arrested, and thus an arm or leg could be stunted.

Challenging the Existing Taboo

Let's take a look at these arguments against weight training for kids. Certainly, weight training imposes stress on muscles, bones and joints. Is this a bad thing? Not necessarily. In fact, we know that in order for muscles, bones and joints to grow sturdy and strong, and to stay that way, they must regularly experience stress. An example of not stressing the body adequately is observed during space travel. When our earliest astronauts returned from rather brief stints in the weightlessness of space, they were physically so weak they could barely walk. Tests revealed a substantial loss of calcium from bones, weakening the bones, and the loss of considerable muscle mass. From this we can conclude that stress can be a good thing.

But is it good for kids who are developing? Why not? A developing bone will store calcium, and this is a good thing. A developing bone that is stressed with resistance exercise may store even more calcium. The shaft of long bones (the site most often broken in athletics and in accidents) grows thicker and stronger with the stress of exercise. The earlier the stress is applied, it logically follows, the earlier the thickening process begins, and the thicker and stronger the shaft becomes.

What about epiphyseal damage? The epiphyseal plates in long bones are located near the ends of the bones, a site that is rarely damaged. In fact, the most likely way to damage an epiphyseal plate is through direct trauma — slamming into the end of the bone in an accident or with a heavy object. Weight training will stress the bone by forcing it to bear the brunt of the weight, but this should have no negative effects on the epiphyseal plate. In fact, a much stronger argument can be made that kids should not participate in vigorous sports where there is the danger of accident and injury, because the risk of epiphyseal plate damage is much more likely in football, baseball, soccer, and basketball than it is in weight training. I'm not suggesting that kids not participate in sports at a young age. (They will anyway, whether adults organize events or not.) Rather, I am suggesting that many other popular activities offer greater danger. Fortunately, regardless of the activity chosen, the risk of epiphyseal damage is extremely slight.

The Practical Side

Although kids may think they want to train with weights because their favorite athlete does, are they likely to truly buy into the process? Probably not. The downside of weight training is the long delay associated with rewards accrued, and we all know that kids want things now, not months or years from now. The younger the child the more immediate the rewards have to be in order to satisfy. Another factor is fun. Weight training is not fun. It's work, and work is not something a child wants to do. Thus, it's unlikely that a seven year-old will insist on lifting weights and sustaining a program. On the contrary, if a program is going to be sustained among young children, it will probably have to be imposed and supervised by adults.

This is exactly what I did with my two sons. More than three decades ago I examined the issues surrounding weight training for children and I concluded it would be a good thing to do. I started my oldest son at five years of age, much to the displeasure of his mother, my mother-in-law and virtually every other interested party. Their resistance, I must admit, instilled great tenacity in my stance — I was determined to prove I was right. I imposed two 20 minute workouts per week which included a few basic exercises for the upper body (mostly curls and bench presses, and never anything overhead that could strain the lower back). My oldest son didn't seem to mind, and took the workouts as part of everyday life. By eight years of age he could pump out 50 push-ups and was considerably stronger than boys his age. This was impressive because he was small for his age.

My youngest son was quite a different story. At age five he resisted and his mini workouts were quite an ordeal. Ironically, when I had decided to stop, his mother encouraged me to continue. She saw the effect exercise had on our oldest son, on his confidence and self esteem. We stuck with it and eventually, my youngest son accepted workouts as part of life. Eventually, I backed off and allowed them to continue or not as they pleased. Both continued and still work out today.

The Argument for Starting After Puberty

My youngest son is much larger than my oldest, and it didn't take long before he was nearly as strong as his older brother. This was the case until my older son hit puberty (and the onset of the masculinizing effects of testosterone). At that point, his inch-by-inch increases in muscularity and strength took off like a rocket and he left my youngest son in the dust. The eight years prior to puberty produced modest results compared with the one year following puberty. As such, it can be effectively argued that because of all the reasons cited above, it makes good common sense to wait until puberty to begin training with weights.

Another issue is safety. Young children must be closely supervised. You cannot allow young children to "play" with weights unattended. If you do, you can be certain the first thing they will do is see how much they can lift. This is especially true if there is more than one of them — they innately will want to see who is the strongest. This is a highly dangerous situation that must be avoided at all costs. In the case of my sons, we never tested the maximal strength of their muscles. On the contrary, we plotted gains in strength by seeing how much weight they could lift 10 times in various exercises, or by doing free-form exercises such as push-ups or pull-ups. In addition, without supervision, younger children will get sloppy in their form trying to lift more than they should. Again, this must be avoided.

The Bottom Line

The bottom line is, kids and barbells can mix. But there is lots to consider and very few kids who think they would like to be as strong as their favorite athletes are willing to pay the price. Moreover, most parents won't want the responsibility of overseeing a process that is tedious, no fun and cursed with long delayed rewards. As a side note, when my youngest son asked his five year-old son, my grandson, if he would like to start lifting, my grandson replied: "I'm strong enough, Dad!" To which my son, demonstrating much more wisdom than his father at his age, responded: "Fine… let me know if you change your mind."

46. DYNAMIC TENSION

Anyone old enough to remember Howdy Doody remembers seeing the Charles Atlas ad in comic books and elsewhere. In the ad the proverbial 97 pound weakling has sand kicked in his face by a bully at the beach. This embarrasses the wimp in front of his girlfriend and he decides to turn his life around by enrolling in the Charles Atlas course. In no time, muscles sprout and our weakling is transformed into a rippling stud capable of beating the daylights out of any bully. At least this is what the ad would have us believe.

The Charles Atlas course was based on a principle developed by Atlas (not his real name) called Dynamic Tension. It pits one muscle group against another. You can exercise the biceps muscle of your right arm by resisting flexion at the elbow with force from the triceps muscle of the left arm. Simply grasp hands and as you attempt to flex your right elbow, resist by pressing down with your left hand. Switch arms and repeat.

The Dynamic Tension system is technically not isometric in nature. Isometric means no movement. Pushing your hands outward as hard as you can against a door jamb is an example of strongly contracting your muscles without producing movement. Dynamic Tension is more akin to isokinetic contractions in which the degree of resistance imposed adjusts, or "accommodates" to the degree of force applied by the working muscles as they move through their range of motion.

Can you build big muscles with this method? Probably not. In his day, Charles Atlas had a pretty well developed body, but it's likely he built that body with barbells. Pitting one muscle group against another will strengthen the muscles, but much of the strength that accrues is neuromuscular in nature. This means, the recruitment of muscle cells (fibers) by nerves is enhanced and strength is increased because you are able to recruit more muscle fibers at one time than you could before commencing training. Eventually, once you have maximized the neuromuscular aspects, if you are going to get stronger the muscle fibers will have to get larger. But in order to force muscle fibers to grow you must put forth a great deal of concentrated effort. You have to overload the fibers, and make them work much harder than they'd like. You probably can't overload sufficiently to get this done with the Dynamic Tension method.

With that said, Dynamic Tension is a great way to stay in shape, especially for those who are getting up in years. As I have emphasized, as you get up in years strength declines substantially unless you take steps to prevent it, and the Dynamic Tension approach can help.

There are advantages to using the Dynamic Tension approach. You can do it anywhere. It requires no special equipment. And, an entire workout doesn't take long. To create a program, all you have to do is think creatively about how the muscles work. Resisting raising one arm in front by imposing force with the opposite arm exercises the shoulder muscles. Pressing the palms together in front of the chest and moving the palms back and forth under pressure exercises the chest muscles. Resisting the biceps muscles with the triceps and vice versa works both groups. You get the idea.

Certain movements may cause discomfort, and the best solution is to delete them from your program. Pushing and pulling overhead often is troublesome, for example. This may be due to a lack of flexibility in the upper body joints and muscles. Or, maybe there is an old injury from years ago that is bothered by certain overhead movements. The list goes on.

The bottom line is, almost any exercise is good — as long as it's not painful or dangerous. And the older you get, the more valuable your exercise program becomes.

A Reader Asks:

"I read an article about former University of Georgia running back Herschel Walker who played for the National Football League. He kept himself in outstanding physical condition by doing 3,500 sit-ups and 1500 push-ups daily. One wonders why an athlete who has been around big time football most of his life and has all kinds of exercise equipment at his disposal would do sit-ups and push-ups by the thousands. The article also said that he doesn't drink or smoke, eats one meal a day and sleeps only four hours a night. What is your opinion of such a regimen?"

My response

When you see an unorthodox training regimen like Herschel Walker's you have to wonder — is he a wonderful athlete because of what he does, or in spite of what he does? No one knows. Clearly his routine is unusual and does not conform to today's high-tech standards. What's more, if you or I tried to follow his routine (especially the one meal a day and four hours sleep part) it would probably be disastrous. But it's hard to argue with Walker's success, and his physique. At a bodyweight well in excess of 220 pounds, he is incredibly muscular and has been evaluated for percent body fat and shown to be at physiologically minimal levels of only 3 percent.

Walker was around pro football many years and had a good, if not outstanding, career. And he's been remarkably injury free, which says a lot considering he's a running back — one of the most vulnerable positions in football. I suspect a factor that contributes to his health and freedom from injury on the field is his flexibility. Walker is heavily into the martial arts, and a big part of martial arts is flexibility.

The bottom line is, Walker is a highly successful athlete. Without that success, however, I suspect his coaches would have pressed him into more "normal" training. But a smart coach knows you don't fix what ain't broke.

47. HIGH REPS CAN EASE JOINT PAIN

Lifting weights is a good thing to do, especially as you get older. It keeps your muscles strong and it strengthens your bones. You don't have to train like a Mr. America to accomplish a great deal, and it's relatively safe.

With that said, here's a warning. If you really get serious about lifting, you must be aware that lifting weights places stress not only on your muscles, but on your joints as well. Over the years, anyone who has lifted weights with intensity is likely to have a history of minor (and possibly some major) joint injuries which never completely go away. You may quit lifting for years, and the joints are pain free. But when you pick up a barbell or dumbbell and perform some of your old exercises, the pain returns with a vengeance. This presents a dilemma. Do you continue to lift in pain? Or, do you stop completely?

Some experts recommend machines rather than "free weights" (barbells and dumbbells). Unfortunately, most free weight users don't like machines, because machines do not challenge their muscles in the same way and to the same degree. The results are disappointing, in other words.

Is there a way to continue to lift free weights, but without joint pain?

I believe there is. I have lifted weights off and on since I was a youngster, and I have more than my share of joint pains, in my shoulders and elbows in particular. When I use some machines, the pain is less. On other machines the pain is at least as bad as with free weights. The pain-free machines, however, do not seem to offer the kind of challenge to my muscles I would like. As such, I have experimented with a number of free weight approaches until I came up with one that seems to work for me and may work for you.

I call it the "high-rep, pre-exhaustion" approach. It does two things. It babies the joints while challenging the muscles, and it does so without the need for heavy weights. This is a winning combination.

Let's use the barbell curl as an example. It is one of the most devastating exercises as far as the joints are concerned. In the curl, you grab the barbell with your palms facing away from your body. Standing upright and keeping your elbows at your sides, bend your elbows and flex your biceps and move the bar slowly from your thighs to your chin. Then lower slowly to the starting position and repeat. Years of heavy curls can leave you with a variety of injuries, including forehand and backhand tennis elbow and gimpy wrists.

Let's assume you can perform 10 slow and strict barbell curls with 100 pounds. If you can, you have very strong biceps. The problem is, when you do this, your wrist, elbow and shoulder joints scream in pain. The pain may be immediate and while you are exercising, or it may come on later. Either way, it's not a pleasant thing to deal with. The high-rep approach may allow you to continue to perform curls, but without pain.

Take a 25 pound barbell and perform 25 ultra-strict, slow and rhythmic repetition curls through the full range of motion. This first set of repetitions will give your biceps and your joints a good warm-up. Immediately increase the poundage to 40 pounds and do exactly the same thing. This makes two lengthy warm-up sets, and it imposes a slight degree of fatigue on your muscles. Without resting, bump the weight to 55 pounds and do 25 more reps. Finally, and again without resting, take 70 pounds and do as many ultra-strict repetitions as you can. You probably won't be able to do very many, probably less than ten. That's fine. In fact, it's the whole point. With this approach, light weights feel like heavy weights to your muscles, but they still feel light to your joints. The 70 pound barbell challenges your muscles as much as the 100 pound barbell does, but without the same stress on the joints. Pre-exhausting the muscle with high reps is the key.

This may be enough exercise for your muscles. If not, after a few months, if this works well and you are totally without pain, you can rest one minute or less and do another set or two with 70 pounds, trying for as many repetitions as possible. Always use very strict form, especially when the muscle is fatigued. Never cheat in an attempt to get an extra rep or two.

If you still have pain, even a small amount, give yourself a few months rest, then start again and increase the reps to 35 or 40 for each set and drop the weight accordingly. If you still have pain, try switching to dumbbells or machines. If pain persists, you probably shouldn't be lifting weights.

You can use the same proportions in your other exercises as well (bench presses, squats, etc.). In the first set, use 25% of the amount of weight you normally can lift ten times. If you can bench press 200 pounds 10 times, your first set would be with 50 pounds. Next, go to 40% (80 pounds), then 55% (110 pounds), then finally 70% (140 pounds).

There is a downside to this approach. Your ego will have to give up lifting heavier weights. Most of us who have progressed over the years to lifting respectable poundages in our weight lifting exercises are loath to shift to lighter weights. But if you can overcome your ego, you may be rewarded with a new lease on lifting which can be sustained well into old age.

48. BIG MUSCLES DON'T MEAN YOU ARE IN SHAPE

I grew up in Pittsburgh, Pennsylvania, and as long as I can remember I wanted to someday become a Pennsylvania State Trooper. I believed that cops were stronger than locomotives and could leap tall buildings in a single bound, and to be able to do that, I started lifting weights at age fourteen. I was a fanatic, spending hours in the gym every day, and after years of dedicated effort, I built my body to impressive proportions. I weighed 235 pounds, my waist was 32 inches, my arms were enormous, and I was as strong as I looked. (I might add that this was at a time before anabolic steroids were popular.)

But, despite my proportions, I knew I had to learn how to be an expert fighter — cops on TV were expert boxers who could fight three or four opponents at one time without breaking a sweat. I also wanted to box because it was in my family. My grandfather was quite a fighter in his day, and my dad and uncles used to tell wonderful stories about him at family gatherings. So I went to a boxing club and asked if I could train there. The man who owned the gym was in his sixties. He looked me up and down and asked what kind of shape I was in. I was insulted. Surely, he could tell by just looking at me. "I'm in great shape," I said, my arrogance showing a bit too much, I'm afraid.

He told me to change. I put on trunks and a tee-shirt and knew I looked pretty good. The old man eyed me up and down again without comment. I should have noticed the twinkle in his eye when he told one of the trainers he was going to take me outside for a little work. We went to a nearby high school track and he told me to run with him as a warm-up. I figured anything a frumpy old guy with gray hair could do, I could do better. He started running and I stayed with him. He seemed comfortable. I wasn't. I hadn't run a bit during all my weight training, and I wasn't ready for the pace he set. But I kept up until he pushed the pace harder on the second lap and I started falling behind. I pushed myself to catch up and nearly caught him when he really started cooking on the third lap and left me in the dust. I drove myself as hard as I could, desperate to avoid embarrassment. I made it through half of the third lap before I had to stop and retire to the bushes and relieve myself of my dinner. I felt like I was going to die.

The old man kept right on running. When he finally quit, he shot me a quick look and said, "Great shape, huh?" As he walked off, his parting words were, "Come back when you're ready to do some work."

He'd made his point. I looked great on the outside, but my fitness level was pretty low—far too low to take on the extreme demands of a boxing workout. I was embarrassed, but I returned the next day. It surprised the old man, but he welcomed me back. I think he liked my new (humble) attitude, but he didn't take it easy on me. On the contrary, I had to prove myself worthy of his attention and he made me work harder than I ever imagined I could. Eventually, I got myself in shape and went on to have several amateur fights and win the Diamond Belt Championship as a heavyweight. Needless to say, I was feeling pretty good about myself. I was in great shape, a big muscular fighting machine, and I was ready to become a State Trooper.

I applied and when I went for my initial interview the officer sitting across the table asked me how much I weighed. Proudly, I told him I weighed 235 pounds. He looked down at a chart, then matter-of-factly informed me that I was way overweight. He said for my height I could weigh no more than 195 pounds. I was astounded. I tried to argue that I was in shape. He sat there stonefaced. I had invested years of effort and tons of sweat building my body only to be told I had to remove 40 pounds of muscle. I thanked him for his time and walked out. On the way home, I decided to go to college and make something of myself.

Ironically, during my first year as an exercise physiologist at the University of Louisville, a muscular young man came to see me and complained that he had been trying to cut his weight in order to qualify for the Kentucky State Police. He was running 10 miles a day and starving himself and still had many pounds to go to make weight. I performed the underwater weighing test on him and found that he had only minimal body fat and that if he was going to lose more weight it would have to be muscle. I put him through a series of fitness tests and found he was in marvelous shape. Even so, he was unacceptable because of his weight. He was in the same fix I was in years before.

In protest, I wrote a letter on his behalf which chronicled my laboratory findings on him and challenged the agency to produce one officer that was as fit, as lean and as strong, as this young man. To make a long story short, the State Police reconsidered and hired him. Since then, police agencies around the country have liberalized their height/weight policies to take muscularity into account. Unfortunately, for me it was too late. But all turned out for the best, because I love what I'm doing.

49. LEAPS AND BOUNDS

Over the years I have received many questions about improving leaping ability. Some basketball players who otherwise are not all that strong are able to leap well above the rim. Others who appear to be muscular and much stronger have considerably less leaping ability. Why?

Leaping ability is largely genetically determined. Muscles are attached to bones by tendons, and the placement of tendons on the bones determines mechanical advantage. It's a matter of leverage, in other words. A small child can see-saw with a larger child by having the larger child move closer to the center. Similarly, a smaller and weaker muscle attached to a bone in an advantageous location can lift more than a larger and stronger muscle that is attached to a bone in a disadvantageous location.

The same is true for other movements. In arm wrestling, for example, leverage is a huge advantage. I have seen men with smallish upper arms and forearms who are incredibly powerful at arm wrestling. Such individuals delight in going to bars and challenging big muscle guys and putting them down in a flash. Nature was kind to some and unkind to others. It's all in how the muscles attach to the bones.

This is not to say you can't improve what nature has bestowed upon you. You can, but don't expect to progress in your leaping ability (a basic power movement) from being able to barely touch the basketball rim to slam dunking. Improvement will be small, but even a small improvement may mean the difference between getting the shot off and having it slapped back in your face.

Leaping requires power, and power is the product of strength times speed. Weight training will increase strength, and the greater your strength the greater your power. Many years ago coaches believed weight training made you muscle bound. It slowed you down and destroyed your flexibility. Actually, the opposite is true. If it weren't, Michael Jordan and every other NBA player would not engage in vigorous off season total body weight training. To verify this, just turn on the TV and look at the muscular specimens running up and down the court and compare them with the toothpick types who used to dominate the sport of basketball in the past. Today's basketball stars are heavier, stronger and quicker than ever before, and much of this has to do with weight training.

You can increase the speed of your movements up to a point, and the best way is to maximize your mechanical efficiency and coordination through "correct" (or perfect) practice. Seek advice from someone skilled in the biomechanics of movement regarding the most efficient way to leap. Next, learn how to leap from different postures and under different circumstances — while shooting jump shots or rebounding, and how to leap repeatedly without resting between leaps. Once the correct form is learned, it should be practiced over and over again in the same way you practice free throw shooting. Unfortunately, it's not as much fun as practicing shooting. It's boring and physically demanding, but it works.

Special Equipment

Many types of special exercise devices have been designed over the years for the purpose of overcoming a bad heredity. Do they work? Probably not.

There are, for example, special shoes that are designed to help increase leaping ability. These shoes are designed to increase the size and strength of the calf muscles. The sole in front of the shoe over the ball of the foot is specially designed and odd shaped. It looks as if you stepped on a plastic pancake and it stuck to the bottom of your shoe. When you flex your calf muscles as you would naturally during running or jumping, the calves must work harder to overcome the resistance of the pancake. This added resistance is supposed to strengthen the muscles. This sounds like a good idea, but I have never seen any evidence that it works. It may even interfere with trying to learn proper leaping techniques, because you wouldn't be wearing this shoe when playing the game.

The experience of having players wear weights on their ankles while practicing basketball is pertinent. The theory is that ankle weights would offer resistance to movement the way a weighted bat is swung by baseball players in the on-deck circle. But it was soon learned that when wearing ankle weights, players compensated for the extra weight by making inefficient movements. Wearing the ankle weights in practice actually taught the players to make the wrong types of moves in the game.

The bottom line is, with dedicated effort leaping ability and other power movements can improve. Don't expect miracles, but the gains you can make can be worth the effort.

50. ANABOLIC STEROIDS — THE EPIDEMIC

I frequently receive questions from parents worried that their sons are exposed to anabolic steroids and may partake. Are they dangerous? Are they addicting? What are the warning signals? In fun, I offer the following clue. Dad, if, after telling your son he can't have the car Saturday night, he picks you up over his head with just one hand and shakes you like a rag doll until the keys fall from your pocket, chances are good he's on steroids. Just kidding. But not entirely. Read on.

Symptoms

Steroids can promote unusually rapid gains in muscularity and strength. Without steroids, a gain of seven pounds of muscle mass in one year is a pretty good accomplishment. On steroids, the rate of gain can be increased several fold. But this is tricky to assess. Some young men in heavy training can make exceptional gains without steroids if they are doing everything right (highly intense training, the correct balance between training and rest, good nutrition, plenty of sleep, etc.). On steroids, the muscles often take on a puffy, bloated appearance, but again, this is tricky to assess.

Behavioral changes may be a better indicator. Look for changes in mood. Males on anabolic steroids are a combustible bunch with short fuses. The reason is, testosterone promotes aggression, and anabolic steroids are a synthetic turbo-charged version of testosterone. Add the prodigious strength and power steroids can provide, and you have a potentially volatile situation. Flash anger that is out of control is referred to as "'roid rage." In recent years, the defense offered in court for many battery and even murder charges has been temporary insanity due to 'roid rage. Other behavioral changes include exaggerated surliness and extended bouts of sullenness, withdrawal and isolation.

A replay of pubescent secondary sex characteristics can occur when the intake is excessive. These include increased acne on the skin, an unusually heavy beard, increased body hair, and odd changes in the voice (shift to a high pitch, or the other extreme). Odd physical changes are possible, including gynecomastia — breast development, and loss of hair from the head. The impact on females (yes, women and girls are involved at an alarming rate, too) is even greater and more noticeable, because females are masculinized in many ways.

Roots — The Hitler Youth

The history of anabolic steroid development may be traced back to WWII Germany and Hitler's preoccupation with building a super race. It didn't take a rocket scientist to observe that during puberty young boys begin taking on manly characteristics, including the addition of considerable muscle mass. This is due to increased testosterone production. Could taking an even greater dose of testosterone after puberty have the same effect to promote development of additional muscle mass? The answer is yes. The problem is, however, testosterone has not only anabolic properties (the capacity to promote protein build-up in the muscles), but it also has considerable androgenic effects (promotion of masculine characteristics — voice change, body hair growth, etc.)

The Hitler group wanted these muscle building effects, and the answer was anabolic steroids — drugs which emphasize the anabolic properties of testosterone, while reducing the androgenic effects. The extent to which anabolic steroids were used during the war years is open to question, but it's easy to see the implications — big, strong soldiers full of aggression. After the war, a legitimate medical use for anabolic steroids was found. Older men with limited natural testosterone production, and post-surgical patients who suffer from loss of muscle mass, could benefit.

In the 1960's anabolic steroids gained popularity among athletes when they discovered the value of weight training and further discovered that combining weights and drugs could turn a 190 pound linebacker into a stronger and faster 240 pound linebacker. The only available anabolic steroid at the time was Dianabol, a relatively (by today's standards) mild form.

In the 1970's, because of the popularity of steroids, many drug companies sought to develop and market an anabolic steroid that was superior to their competitors—the benefit of free market enterprise. More and more steroids were developed, each with a greater anabolic property and a reduced androgenic effect. Biologic results from drug usage increased in proportion to the strength of the drugs, and long time users saw themselves transformed into gargantuan creatures of mythic proportions. Eventually, steroid usage filtered down from the pros to the college level, then to high schools, and even to junior high athletes. Eventually, females got involved, too.

Backlash

When something seems too good to be true, chances are it is. And so it is with anabolic steroids. Indeed, they will promote huge muscles and great strength. They also may destroy your liver and have a detrimental effect on the heart muscle. Perhaps the most striking effect is on the blood lipids. The single most predictive indicator of heart disease risk is the ratio of the total cholesterol divided by the HDL (the good type of cholesterol). An average ratio in this country among men is 5:1 and carries an approximate fifty-fifty risk of heart disease. On steroids, the HDL is reduced dramatically, from an average of about 42 mg/dl to a lowly 5 mg/dl. This, combined with a typical athlete's diet (steak, eggs, milk, etc.) which promotes a high total cholesterol, can cause a disastrous ratio as high as 50:1! Such a ratio suggests that atherosclerosis would be accelerated, advancing the clogging process in the arteries, bringing on a heart attack decades earlier.

Fortunately, the blood lipid profile will normalize after quitting steroid usage. But the longer you are on steroids the greater the damage that is occurring to the walls of the arteries, and the greater the clogging with cholesterol. Thus, a short stint of steroid usage (say, two years), could result in the amount of arterial damage that might occur in 10, or even 20 years without steroids. Making this point to young athletes is difficult, however, because the devastating effects probably won't show up for many years. This means a heart attack may occur at age 55 rather than age 75 — a difference that is meaningless to an 18 year-old.

The health dangers involved have inspired every major governing sports body and medical organization to condemn steroids.

But this has done little if anything to curb usage, and therefore testing of athletes has been invoked. But unscrupulous interested parties have toiled to stay one step ahead of the testers, concocting biochemical strategies to "beat" the tests. Success at beating the test has inspired the belief among some experts that the use of steroids is many times greater than even the most liberal predictions. If they are right, we are in the midst of an epidemic that is growing at a frightening rate.

But, aren't anabolic steroids prescription drugs? You bet. But that offers little obstacle to an athlete seeking to procure as much as they want from the black market. Illegal steroids are regularly imported from foreign countries, especially Mexico, where regulations are less rigid. Quality control during production also is less rigid, and often foreign drugs are less pure and the composition less accurate than American drugs. Moreover, some foreign drugs are produced for animals rather than humans, making them even more dangerous. Using fake prescriptions is fashionable among athletes, and many physicians yield to pressure from patients to prescribe steroids. This is declining, however, as the number of deaths related to illegal drug usage among athletes mounts.

The Addiction

Athletes believe steroids are non-addicting. It's true. The body develops no physical dependency on these drugs. But something just as powerful takes place which can lead to an intense psychological addiction. Once the athlete has built his or her body to mammoth proportions and has achieved success, it's nearly impossible to give up the excessive muscle mass, the attention and adoration it brings. That alone is addicting, but there's more to the story.

It's common sense that if the up side of steroids is steep and the effects major, then the down side is likely to be a mirror image. When the body is on steroids, it struggles against them, because they are unnatural and the body is forced out of balance. The compensations the body makes lead to ruinous effects when steroids are discontinued. Gobs of muscle mass are lost quickly and strength plummets, forcing the athlete to return to drugs or face humiliating deterioration. Most return to drugs.

The Bottom Line

The message to young athletes is this. If you are on anabolic steroids or are considering using them, please understand they are nothing more than fool's gold. They promise much, delivering, at most, fleeting success. Ultimately, they lead to destruction, the full impact likely delayed for decades. If you doubt this, read the accounts of professional athletes who have suffered severe consequences, including death.

51. PERFORMANCE ENHANCING SUPPLEMENTS

Can you change your physique, run, cycle or swim faster and longer, or lift more weight, by taking a pill? Most athletes think they can, because the sports supplement industry is one of the fastest growing enterprises in this country. For inspiration, we have Mark McGwire admitting to taking performance enhancing substances. Bodybuilding magazines are full of ads with pictures of physique champions who claim they owe their success to this or that supplement.

Who buys this stuff? In the past, it was mostly young male wannabe athletes. More recently, the ranks have been bolstered by aging former athletes trying to stay one step ahead of father time, and by, potentially, the most lucrative market of all — the general population who prefer to believe that taking a pill will replace hours in the gym and a healthy low-fat, low-sugar diet. More women are jumping on board, and the ages of children who indulge is getting younger all the time.

Do They Work?
Hard to say. Supplements are nutrients such as vitamins, minerals and amino acids, or they are natural substances such as herbs, and agents which act on the body to promote natural functions like hormone production. Because supplements are natural in origin, they cannot be patented, and the lack of a patent discourages scientific investigation. The reason is obvious. If I am going to invest millions of dollars investigating a product, demonstrating its effectiveness and safety — Prozac, for example — I intend to recoup my investment by charging a high price when I bring it to market. The only way I can charge a high price is to protect my product with a patent. Without a patent, anyone can duplicate my product and point to my research as evidence it works, and sell it right out from under me. That's bad business.

With this in mind, it's not likely that in the near future there will be scientific proof that supplements truly work. That's not to say there is no evidence. Many manufacturers sponsor research efforts of their own or in university laboratories. Some of this research is credible, but, unfortunately, much of it is questionable. In part, this is due to poor science (lack of adequate controls, sloppy methodology, etc.). And, in part, some of the research may be slanted (biased) to please the company. The bias isn't necessarily intentional. But, as the old saying goes: "He, whose bread you eat, his song you sing."

On the other hand, the lack of scientific evidence means there isn't proof supplements don't work. This is important to consider, as well.

How then can we decide whether a supplement is worthwhile or isn't, benefiting no one but the company that produces and sells it? There's no easy answer.

Nutrients and other natural products are treated lightly by the Food and Drug Administration (FDA). This is as it should be, and manufacturers are not required to prove the efficacy or safety of their products before bringing them to market. As stated above, if manufacturers were held to the same standards as drug companies, we'd have no supplements, as the cost would be prohibitive. But on the down side, because of this open-ended policy, manufacturers can make claims that are overblown if not outrageous, and get away with it. And, you can't be sure about the quality or purity of what's in the bottle.

Here's an example of how things can go without tight controls. Several years ago, a bodybuilding friend brought me a bottle of a new supplement called Creatine. The bottle was brown (typical of vitamin bottles) with a hand-made label. On the label was typed "Creatine." That's all it said — there was no further information. He told me he paid $35 for the bottle and asked me what I thought. I examined the bottle and rifled out a number of questions. Was the white granular product inside really what it was supposed to be? If so, was it pure? Was it safe? Was it worth the price, or did someone throw this concoction together for pennies? There was no way to get answers. There was no way of knowing whether he had totally wasted his money, or worse, had purchased something that might harm him.

I spilled a little of the contents into the palm of my hand and examined it. It could be anything from salt to ground chicken bones. Or, it could be the real stuff — whatever that means. He shrugged and said he'd try it and see. Fortunately, nothing bad happened to him.

About the only thing the FDA forbids is outright health claims. You cannot claim, for example, that taking vitamin E will prevent heart disease. If you make such claims the FDA will jump on you. That's why claims are carefully worded and seem to skirt right on the edge of this boundary. With the exception of this single line of protection, we, the public, are pretty much on our own, and the best approach is — *buyer beware.*

Are we victimized by loose FDA control? Of course we are. But when Congress tried to step forward and place tighter controls on the supplement industry, there was great outcry from the public. We didn't want controls so tight that we had to go to our doctor to get a prescription for vitamin C tablets. The proposed legislation was killed quickly.

Thread of Truth

Most supplements appear at first blush to be credible. The reason is, there is a thread of scientific truth attached to the product. Take, for example, carnitine. Carnitine is a product produced in the body which helps move fatty acids into the mitochondria of cells where they are used as fuel. This suggests the more carnitine you have, the more fat you burn. A great weight loss tool, right? Maybe not. Typically, your body has all the carnitine it can use, and taking in more accomplishes nothing. Even so, when you look on the label of most weight loss supplements, carnitine is often present.

This doesn't mean that taking carnitine as a supplement is useless to everyone. If for some reason your body cannot produce enough carnitine, a supplement containing carnitine will help you burn fat. But this is not a common condition, and the vast majority of users will derive no benefit. The possibility that a supplement may help a few is a fly in the ointment which complicates the issue and explains why Joe can take a supplement and claim wonderful results. But when Joe's friends and relatives try the same thing, they experience nothing.

Another angle, of course is the placebo (sugar pill) effect. The mind has great power over the body, and if the mind tells you something will work, chances are good it will — at least for a while. Years ago I conducted research on the effects of anabolic steroids. This was at a time when it was unknown whether these powerful substances really worked to increase strength and muscle mass. The medical establishment wanted to believe they didn't, because the side effects of anabolic steroids can destroy health. My research found that, indeed, they worked. Interestingly, a placebo group involved in the study (who received nothing but sugar pills, but who believed they were on anabolic steroids) increased their strength almost as much as the group actually taking the drug. The amount of added muscle mass was much less in the placebo group, however, because this cannot be controlled by the mind. Even more interesting, however, was the fact that the placebo group reported more side effects from their sugar pills than the group on the drug. There were reports of nausea, constipation, diarrhea, acne outbreaks, voice changes, increased libido, etc.

Making an "Intelligent" Choice

The sports supplement water is muddy, to be sure, but that doesn't mean all sports supplements are bogus. Unfortunately, sorting out the good from the bad is difficult at best, and I have no magic formula. With that said, here is the philosophy I follow.

I use a two-pronged approach when judging whether or not to purchase supplements which offer the promise of doing some good. First, is the supplement harmless? In general, this is the case. Fortunately, because of the incredible liability implications of putting out a faulty product, most manufacturers in this country are careful to maintain standards that ensure their products will not be harmful. Useless, perhaps, but not harmful. The same standards may not be used in other countries, however, and the purity of the supplement may suffer.

That's not to say you should proceed without caution. On the contrary, there are many unanswered questions. A major problem with the safety of supplements is the lack of information on long term use. There also is little information on how supplements may affect a young growing body, and therefore it's best to keep supplements away from prepubescent children. Research efforts usually have been limited to college age males, and therefore little is known about the effects on women. This is important, because a woman taking supplements can be in the earliest stages of pregnancy and not know it.

Second, are the supplements expensive? Some supplements are remarkably expensive, costing several dollars a day. Often high costs are due to advertising and marketing, or to a pyramid set-up in the sales structure in which a large portion of the sales price is used as commission for those in the hierarchy of the pyramid.

If the supplements are harmless and inexpensive, you are not risking a great deal by trying them. Even so, it's best to be as informed as possible before proceeding, and teenagers should definitely be supervised. Ultimately, it boils down to an individual choice. Here are some things to consider regarding the latest supplement fads.

Creatine

Creatine has become the darling of weightlifters, even though most sports-related medical authorities advise caution and oppose use by teenagers. Unlike most supplements weightlifters take, there is some scientific evidence that creatine helps increase strength and muscular endurance and that it may help increase muscle mass. But much of the research is questioned by authorities as to the possibility of bias. Still, the majority of evidence is favorable.

The increase in muscle mass is probably due to the uptake of water. When creatine is taken up by muscles it disrupts the water balance between muscle cells and the surrounding fluid. Water is moved into the muscle cells, making them larger. This, of course, is a temporary effect and is lost when creatine is no longer taken.

A problem associated with disruption of the water balance is internal dehydration. Sweat comes from the pool of fluids which surround the cells, and creatine may reduce this pool. This means there would be less fluid available as sweat to help keep the body cool during exercise in the heat. When taking creatine it's important to emphasize the need to drink plenty of fluids. Additionally, there may be disruption of the electrolyte (sodium and potassium) balance. Many football teams have reported unusually high rates of muscle cramping among players taking creatine, and for this reason many teams have banned it.

Creatine is a natural product found primarily in meat. Because Americans are big meat eaters, our creatine status generally is quite high, and may not be boosted greatly by supplementation. Vegetarians, on the other hand, have a lower creatine status and are likely to show a much greater effect from taking this supplement.

Androstenedione

This supplement stormed into the limelight when it was revealed that Mark McGwire takes it. Boom! Overnight it was big. The name is suggestive, because it sounds like something that would belong to the anabolic steroid family. Pretty close, but androstenedione is not a hormone. It's a precursor, which means it stimulates an increase in naturally produced hormones, in this case testosterone.

Does it work? There hasn't been a lot of research, but available evidence suggests a transient rise in testosterone among users. The supposed benefit is a turbo-charged jolt which can propel the user through a workout. This raises the question: Why would highly motivated athletes need artificial stimulation to get fired up to work out? The answer is, they don't, if they are motivated. If they're not motivated, perhaps they would be better off doing something else.

Is a testosterone precursor a good thing? Probably not. Too much testosterone can be dangerous, and taking additional testosterone as a drug requires a physician's prescription and is tightly controlled by the FDA. It follows, then, that taking a substance to help you produce more testosterone is not that far removed from taking the actual hormone. At present, you can buy this stuff over the counter. But I suspect if usage becomes widespread, look for some governmental intervention which may move it to the protected list, requiring a prescription.

Pyruvate

Pyruvate is the new kid on the supplement block. It is naturally formed in the body in virtually every cell when glucose (sugar) is broken down in the process known as glycolysis. Pyruvate is derived from the consumption of carbohydrates, and along with fat, it represents the major energy source of the body. I haven't seen any evidence to support the claims that pyruvate supplements increase the loss of body fat, increase muscle mass and increase endurance.

There is some evidence that if you go on a starvation crash diet, pyruvate will help preserve muscle mass. The results of research are not terribly encouraging, however, and you still will lose lots of muscle, but not quite as much. There doesn't seem to be any other effect from pyruvate. If the only benefit appears to be in conjunction with a crash diet, and since no one should go on a crash diet, there appears to be little reason for anyone to take pyruvate.

Chromium Picolinate

Chromium is an important mineral. It works closely with the hormone insulin to help the cells take in glucose, which, in turn, increases the release of energy. When chromium is lacking, the effects of insulin are impaired, resulting in a diabetes-like condition. When chromium is combined with picolinate, it is supposed to be more easily absorbed and assimilated by the body. Advertising claims suggest that increased chromium helps muscle cells increase their uptake of amino acids. There is no support for this claim. It is also claimed that this supplement helps burn off fat. Again, there is no support.

Chromium is readily available in the diet and Americans are rarely deficient. Chromium is found in meat, cheese, cereal, dried beans, peanuts, brewer's yeast, and whole grain breads. But, if someone were deficient in chromium, a supplement would help. An inexpensive daily multiple vitamin/mineral pill probably would cover the need.

Antioxidants

Free radicals are rascals that are produced as a byproduct of oxidative metabolism (the use of oxygen by the body to produce energy). Free radicals are produced constantly, and they damage the body in many ways. Fortunately, free radicals can be neutralized by antioxidants such as vitamins C and E. Because the use of oxygen goes up dramatically during exercise, more free radicals are produced. This would seem to increase the need for antioxidants among those who train vigorously, and, indeed, many athletes take mega-doses of antioxidant vitamins.

Fortunately, when the body exercises vigorously it increases its production of natural internal antioxidants. That's not to say an external source of antioxidants is a bad idea. It probably is helpful. Research suggests daily doses of 400 I.U. (international units) of vitamin E, and 250 mg (milligrams) of vitamin C. Many health experts advocate doubling these amounts.

Other antioxidants are being examined and they include beta carotene and the mineral selenium. With the exception of vitamin E, a healthy, well rounded diet probably can come pretty close to meeting the body's need for antioxidants, and taking mega-doses of vitamins and minerals is probably going too far. What's more, overdosing can cause bad side effects, including a reduced blood coagulation time, disturbances of the gastrointestinal tract and an increase in the storage of iron which may have a damaging effect on the heart. In high doses, selenium can cause toxicity.

The Bottom Line

We are a nation of extremists. Most of us are fat and sloppy and don't intend to invest one pint of sweat in changing our physiques. The rest of us have sprinted in the opposite direction, seeking physical perfection. One thing we all have in common is our insatiable quest for the magic bullet — a pill that will transform us. With this kind of market, it's no wonder flim-flam artists flourish, offering absurd claims that challenge common sense. The pickings are ripe, because Americans are remarkably ignorant when it comes to issues concerning their own bodies. Some sports supplements may be worthwhile, most aren't, and some can be downright dangerous. Educate yourself on the issues and be cautious in your choices. And remember, if something seems to good to be true, it is. Good luck.